RENAISSANCE DRAMA

New Series **XI** ❧ 1980

Renaissance Drama

New Series XI

Tragedy

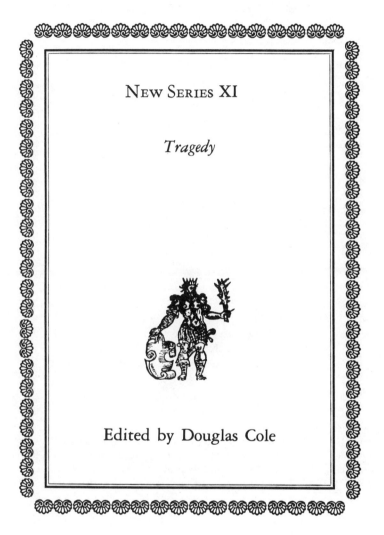

Edited by Douglas Cole

Northwestern University Press

EVANSTON 1980

Copyright © 1981 by Northwestern University Press
All rights reserved
Library of Congress Catalog Card Number 67–29872
ISBN: 0–8101–0546–2
Printed in the United States of America

THE ILLUSTRATION ON THE FRONT COVER is the Effigy by Ligier Richier for the tomb of Count René de Châlons (d. 1544). Photo credit: Bulloz, Paris. THE ILLUSTRATION ON THE BACK COVER is from the title page of the 1616 Folio of Ben Jonson's *Works*. Reproduced by courtesy of the Folger Library.

Publication of this volume was made possible by a grant from the College of Arts and Sciences, Northwestern University.

Editorial Note

R ENAISSANCE DRAMA, an annual publication, provides a forum for
scholars in various parts of the globe: wherever the drama of the
Renaissance is studied. Coverage, so far as subject matter is concerned, is
not restricted to any single national theater. The chronological limits of
the Renaissance are interpreted liberally, and space is available for essays
on precursors, as well as on the use of Renaissance themes by later writers.
Editorial policy favors articles of some scope. Essays that are exploratory in
nature, that are concerned with critical or scholarly methodology, that
raise new questions or embody fresh approaches to perennial problems are
particularly appropriate for a publication that originated from the proceedings of the Modern Language Association Conference on Research
Opportunities in Renaissance Drama.

The Editor gratefully acknowledges his debt to the members of the
Editorial Committee, and similar warm thanks are due to the editorial
assistant, Brian Ensley, and to our administrative assistant, Marjorie
Weiner. The efficient and expert help of the assistant editor, Janice
Feldstein, has been absolutely indispensable.

Guest editor for Volume XII, "Dramatic Technique," is Professor Alan
Dessen of the University of North Carolina. Correspondence, submissions,
and enquiries regarding future volumes should be addressed to Professor
Leonard Barkan, Editor, *Renaissance Drama*, English Department,
Northwestern University, Evanston, Illinois 60201.

Contents

RENAISSANCE DRAMA

New Series XI ❧ 1980

Du Monin's Revenge Tragedy Orbecc-Oronte (1585): Its Debt to Garnier and Giraldi Cinthio

ANTHONY GABLE

T HE SOMBER DECADE of the 1580s was of momentous importance for France, ushering in a new age with the end of the Valois monarchy. This same period was crucially to affect the development of serious drama. By the late 1590s a different society and a different type of tragedy had evolved, and in both cases the new directions had been firmly given by the events of the previous decade. At first sight such a claim might appear exaggerated in the field of drama: only one tragedy of the 1580s is well known, Garnier's last play *Les Juifves* (1583). Garnier was to live for several more years but write no plays. Some dramatists publishing in the decade are more celebrated in other ways—as poets, like the priest François Perrin or the lawyer Antoine Favre. Pierre Matthieu the schoolmaster left five plays from the years 1585–1589, but was to become better known as an official historian. For the rest, the writers of tragedy are obscure: Père Fronton du Duc, Pierre de Bousy, Jean de Beaubreuil (a pupil of Dorat), Jean Robelin, Jean-Edouard du Monin, and Claude Mermet, responsible for another version of the first vernacular Italian tragedy, Trissino's *Sofonisba*. In fact, there are fewer extant tragedies from the 1580s than for the previous and subsequent decades.

3

We are left with a handful of playwrights most of whom are unknown. What then of the claim for the importance of drama in the period? The claim rests on the work of two writers who stand out: one, Garnier, for his intrinsic merit and the very considerable influence he exerts on later dramatists, at least until 1615; the other, Jean-Edouard du Monin, whose strange *Orbecc-Oronte* (1585) set the precedent for the plays of the 1590s and 1600s, irregular tragedies of blood with enacted horrors. Du Monin is interesting for several reasons which have little to do with any intrinsic merit: his thematic debt to Garnier in his political and metaphysical material, his use of fictional subject matter, his preoccupation with physical violence, his prefatory and dramatic allusions to near-contemporary events. No case will be made for Du Monin as a neglected master. At best he remains a pioneering exponent of a form of French tragedy which was to die out by the 1630s, Corneille's *Clitandre* and Rotrou's *Crisante* being the last manifestations of this kind of drama. But Du Monin's incorporation of Garnier's principles and matter into a new, irregular mold is an important feature of French tragedy between 1580 and 1620, and his topical insistence on court corruption is an interesting footnote to aristocratic decadence in the period of the civil wars and immediately after.

First, however, the background to Du Monin and the new, irregular drama must briefly be examined, together with the partial eclipse of tragedy in the 1580s. The reasons for the paucity of drama are not obscure. The great hindrance to performance and publication was the political and social upheaval, with the devastating wars and the rise of the Ligue. After the abatement of hostilities in the first four years of the decade, the wars of the Ligue soon brought tension and hysteria to many parts of France. Barricades, the siege of Paris, Spanish meddling, the assassination of Guise and then of Henri III, France with two kings (Henri IV and "Charles X")—the decade was to end in chaos. Such times scarcely favored performance of tragedy. Yet civil havoc was only one of the many obstacles against the genre for years: the absence of theaters bemoaned by Montaigne, the continued dearth of patrons (noted by Du Bellay long before in the Pléiade manifesto), the hostility of Henry III and the Valois court, whether, as Brantôme tells us, owing to the well-founded superstition of Catherine de Médicis, or because there were more enticing entertainments in such times of crisis. The *ballet de cour* appealed greatly;

so too did the king's favorite troupe of Italians, I Gelosi.[1] Yet Garnier's attempts to have his tragedies performed at court were unavailing. How different from the earlier interest in vernacular tragedy—in 1556 Henri II's court at Blois had taken great pleasure in the tragic spectacle of Sophonisba in Mellin de Saint-Gellais's version. Brantôme, perhaps through national pride, preferred it to Trissino's original.[2] Charles IX had been a noted patron, whose "cher mignon" was the *Adonis* of Le Breton (unpublished until 1579). But his brother Henri III had no taste for tragedy, and was actually spared a performance of Père Fronton du Duc's *Histoire tragique de la Pucelle d'Orléans* at Pont-à-Mousson in 1580, owing to an outbreak of plague.[3] Aristocratic interest in tragedy evaporated and humanist enthusiasm waned. It is doubtful whether even college audiences of the 1580s could experience anything comparable to the thrill which Pasquier had felt seeing *Abraham sacrifiant* or *Cléopâtre captive*, and the time had long since passed when a humanist tragedy could excite both an academic and an aristocratic audience, as Jodelle's *Cléopâtre* had done in 1552/3. Those heady days of Pléiade excitement, of writers vying with Italy and confident of Valois championship, had been superseded by philistinism and war.

In the 1560s and 1570s the wars had inspired dramatists. There are few tragedies written during the period of open war which do not take civil strife as their major theme, or at least descant upon the nation's miseries. This insistence remains in the relatively few plays of the 1580s, but already there is evidence of a move away from national suffering and, instead, an exploration of private tribulations largely unconnected with national error, an emphasis on bloody family strife, whereas such topics had formerly been seen in a broader (national) perspective of collective guilt and responsibility. Du Monin presents just such a family tragedy, its

1. See Pierre de l'Estoile's *Journal pour le règne de Henri III,* ed. Louis-Raymond Lefèvre (Paris, 1943), p. 141 (for 1577); Armand Baschet, *Les Comédiens Italiens à la cour de France* (Paris, 1882), pp. 52–93.

2. *Oeuvres complètes,* ed. L. Lalanne (Paris, 1867), III, 257. Brantôme claims to have seen a performance of *Sofonisba;* no documentation exists until the Vicenza performance of 1562.

3. See the brothers Parfaict, *Histoire du théâtre françois,* 15 vols. (Paris, 1734–1749), III, 447–448.

essentials suggested by the Senecan and Italian sources. By the late 1590s, with the end of the civil wars, this movement away from national themes is complete: we find the atrocious revenges of degenerate aristocrats, no longer the inevitable desolation which expiates a people's collective guilt.

Henri III's Valois court of the 1570s and 1580s was by any standards one of the most profligate Europe had ever seen. Ample documentation exists to show how conscious Parisian society was of sordid events in aristocratic circles. L'Estoile writes in 1577 of "la cour où la paillardise est publiquement et notoirement pratiquée entre les dames, qui la tiennent pour vertu."[4] He chronicles such squalid episodes as Villequier's uxoricide: Villequier was favored by the king; his wife had tried to poison him owing to the discovery of her infidelity with Barbizi, who had already poisoned his own wife. But Villequier was pardoned—thanks to an arrangement whereby he was to act as pander for the king to debauch his wife. And all this was common knowledge. L'Estoile comments: "Ce meurtre fut trouvé cruel, comme commis en une femme grosse de deux enfants."[5] L'Estoile's reports are not confined to examples of patrician skulduggery, but these inevitably take pride of place: Vermondet's incest (1585), Mayenne's abduction of La Vauguyon's ward (1586) whom he kept "comme butin des ses hautes enterprises et conquêtes" despite the king's disapproval. And so on: a picture of barbarity which continues unabated into the early troubled years of the 1590s.

It is significant that while dramatists' prefaces of the 1570s had drawn parallels between the tragedies which follow and the events of the civil wars, those of the 1580s, such as Du Monin's, refer to near-contemporary incidents comparable to the grotesque actions of the play: "Ce suiet . . . nous pourra r'amener en souvenance quelque Histoire que notre France depuis quelques ans nous a fait voir et ouïr."[6]

Paris became the focus of the wars after 1580, and could scarcely be a thriving center for drama with Protestant guns firing at the Louvre, and the Spanish embassy's courtyard a soup kitchen. The civil disorder is

---

4. L'Estoile, pp. 151 ff.

5. *Ibid.*, pp. 151 ff. See also Brantôme, *Les Dames galantes,* ed. M. Rat (Paris, 1960), p. 8.

6. *Orbecc-Oronte: Argument* in *Le Phoenix* (Paris, 1585).

conveyed by writers of the time, and it made some strange bedfellows. In his bizarre play *La Peste de la Peste* of 1584 Du Monin has a chorus "des Ecoliers, & des Artizans" which comments on the damage done both to the artisan classes and to the cause of art:

SECOND ARTIZAN
Peu d'artistes mécaniques
Font chef d'oeuvre en nos boutiques
Comme i'ai veu du passé . . .
          TROISIEME ECOLIER
Que pensés vous etre cause
Que les arts ont fait leur pause
Dedans nos Espris François?
Et que la harpe Delphique
Mi-sourde à notre musique
Ne repond plus à nos vois?

(*La Peste de la Peste,* I)

Because printing presses were inevitably affected, far fewer books appeared, and drama suffered in particular. Only Garnier, Du Monin, and Perrin had tragedies published in Paris in the decade, whereas in the 1570s many dramatists had published there: Garnier, La Taille, Jodelle, Chantelouve, Chrestien, and Le Breton.

Against this unpromising background in the 1580s we can nonetheless distinguish two important trends in drama: on the one hand the pre-eminence of Garnier and the use of his plays as models, and on the other the emergence of writers from a younger generation who complain of stultification in the drama. These trends might seem to be contradictory, but in practice this is not the case, since the very dramatists who seek a rupture with the past are actually heavily dependent upon Garnier. Garnier's unique and dominant status is everywhere attested—a feature of the French theater until the 1620s. The *pièces liminaires* of plays well into the seventeenth century, the theory and practice of the time, the vast number of reprintings of his plays up until 1626—all bear witness to his significance. Of very major importance were the four editions of the 1580s: the 1580 edition of the plays from *Porcie* to *Antigone,* the 1582 collection with *Bradamante* added, and the 1583 (Rouen) edition of all eight plays, reproduced with amendments in 1585 (Paris). Subsequent dramatists owe a large debt to Garnier, a debt acknowledged as late as 1628 by Hardy in his *Berne des deux rimeurs de l'Hôtel de Bourgogne*. Hardy's misfortune was to publish his works too late: even his tribute to Garnier fell on deaf ears, for hardly any tragedy at all was being written by the late 1620s.

By the mid-1580s Garnier's plays had become a source book of gnomic sentences, apposite political and philosophical themes, oratorical figures, and well-developed debates: Garnier had become a sort of educational primer. His formal qualities were immediately attractive to the late-Renaissance mind, and his rhetorical excellence offered convenient stylistic models. But the substance, too, of the plays was of crucial importance, Garnier's preeminence coinciding with the activity of the neo-Stoic philosophers: Justus Lipsius produced his *De Constantia* in 1583, and Du Vair his *Philosophie morale des Stoïques* in 1585. Inasmuch as he gave currency to Senecan Stoic themes, Garnier can be considered as part of the neo-Stoic revival. His works were among the most frequently reprinted of the entire century, and they provided easy access to the ideas more systematically explored by Du Vair or Charron. But above all, for his contemporaries, Garnier's achievement was that of equaling Greek and Roman dramatists on their own ground, and thus raising humanist tragedy to a peak. This feat was recognized throughout northern Europe. Through his language and techniques Garnier had perfected a certain type of serious drama, and this very perfection rankled with some.

A number of new dramatists react to what they consider a standardization of tragic practice. Beaubreuil (*Regulus*, 1582) attacked "la règle superstitieuse des unités," mainly because he could not encompass it in his work. Du Monin (*La Peste de la Peste*, 1584, and *Orbecc-Oronte*, 1585) felt dramatists were hidebound by traditional subject matter. Another playwright to turn with hostility on the conventions of humanist drama was Jean Robelin, who published a *Thébaïde* (1584) at Pont-à-Mousson, the same center which had witnessed Fronton du Duc's tragedy of Joan of Arc. Robelin, Fronton du Duc's pupil, had doubtless seen the play, whose title (*Histoire tragique* . . . etc.) betrays a characteristic of plays by new dramatists, mingling elements of the old *moralité* and *mystère* with vernacular tragedy. In the preface to *La Thébaïde* Robelin inveighs against his predecessors' "trop grâde affectiô envers l'antiquité," and his rejection of

Greek and Senecan models is significant at this time: ". . . i'ay mieux aymé par mon industrie tel quel façôner de tout poinct ce petit poëme que de mendier l'industrie d'un plus adroit ouvrier . . ." But Robelin's play, so far from being all his own work, is highly dependent upon Garnier, and in particular Garnier's recent Greek plays. In a gloss to Act IV, Robelin's Antigone is called "vray exemplaire et miroir de piété," an inevitable reminder of Garnier's subtitle to his own *Antigone—La Piété.* In fact Robelin is typical of playwrights of the time who forsook classical sources only to use them secondhand through imitation of Garnier.

Pierre Matthieu's biblical plays and his *Clytemnestre* (1585–1589) rarely use material from ancient dramatists: they are thematically and linguistically derivative, owing much to Garnier, though exhibiting a new freedom of tone. A novelty of the 1580s is the insistence on sexual license in certain plays. Garnier's *Hippolyte* (1573) often served as a point of departure for dramatists dealing with illicit passion, but these later writers go far beyond its relatively chaste language, and the stated moralistic aims of the dramatists frequently conflict with their enthusiastic investigation of passion. Matthieu's subtitle for his *Clytemnestre* is *L'Adultère.* Egiste appeals to his paramour: "Que n'ai-je encor cent mains pour toucher le beau port De ce corps . . .?" (*Clytemnestre, I*) If Matthieu wrote this play while regent at Verceil to persuade boys of the evils of such love ("des malheureuses fins de la volupté"), then his rhetoric is ambiguous.

The new tonal freedom is inextricably linked to the new choice of subject matter, and both square ill with didactic intentions. The very title of Perrin's *Sichem ravisseur* (1589) suggests the main source of interest which the dramatist found in his subject—a subject attractive enough to tempt Pierre de Nancel in his play about the rape of Dinah (1607). Before 1580 such plays are rare. Jodelle's Cléopâtre and Didon, Garnier's Phèdre and his (married) Cléopâtre and Marc-Antoine, are by no means typical protagonists in the period 1550–1580. In Italy the lovelorn heroine was a normal figure, and had been since Trissino's Sofonisba had spoken of "Amore . . . e le dolcissime parole." Not so in France: Achille, Porcie, Alexandre, Daire, Saül, César—all die, but not for love. Indeed most dramatists are unconcerned with love as an issue. If it is a theme at all, then it is treated decorously. A negligible exception is Filleul's *Lucrece*

(1566) which in any case scrupulously avoids a confrontation of Lucretia
and Tarquin. Such an occasion would be seized upon with relish by writers
later in the century and early in the next.

There is, however, a notable early infringement of the pattern of
decorum which shunned violence: Gabriel Bounin's stark tragedy of blood
La Soltane (1561). It seems to have had little immediate impact, but it
retained a certain currency, being performed in the 1590s and used by
Fulke Greville for his somber *Mustapha* (1609). Bounin plagiarized the
Médée of his friend La Péruse (1555), a play which enjoyed frequent reprintings. He enacted the historically recent murder of Mustapha, here cut
down—onstage—at his father's command on the request of his stepmother
("cette Rose impudique"):

> SOLTAN
> Or sus donques Muets, Muets or donques sus.
> MUSTAPHA
> O meurdre . . .
> SOLTAN
> Qu'on le iette dehors . . .
>
> (*La Soltane,* V.ii)

Bounin's tale of palace butchery foreshadows the horror tragedies of the
1580s and 1590s in France. But where Bounin is dissimilar to later writers
is in his lack of emphasis on anything "impudique." Only to a very limited
extent is Bounin a precursor of the irregular dramatists.

The abandonment of national themes, and the search for new sources,
really begins with Du Monin's *Orbecc-Oronte* in 1585. Using the short story
and horror tragedy of Giambattista Giraldi Cinthio, Du Monin dramatizes
a tale of bloody revenge which eliminates the Persian ruling house. This
play resembles Bounin's *La Soltane* in its emphasis on family strife, but it
has the essential dimension of romantic love which was to become a
characteristic of tragic drama after the civil wars: Orbecche innocently
reveals to her father the incest of her mother and brother, and they are
murdered. Her mother's shade seeks vengeance and is appeased, for
Orbecche is horribly punished by her father for her clandestine marriage to
his steward. Presented with the severed head of her husband Oronte and
the bodies of her babies, she removes the daggers and stabs her father

before committing suicide. The French stage was unfamiliar with such plots. Enacted horrors and multiple revenge in the exotic setting of an Oriental palace were a far cry from the staple of humanist tragedy.

Du Monin's choice of an Italian source is noteworthy. At three important stages in the evolution of French tragedy Italy is the principal source of inspiration: for Jodelle's *Cléopâtre,* which uses Cesare de' Cesari's tragedy of 1552, for Du Monin's *Orbecc-Oronte,* and for Mairet's *Sophonisbe* (1635). The beginnings of the regular humanist tragedy, those of irregular drama, and those of classical tragedy are Italianate. Mairet was the most forthright in his debt to Italy, but throughout the entire period Italian culture had dominated Europe. Italian was the language of diplomacy, Italian fashions (especially literary fashions) were aped by France and England. As early as 1545 Jean de Tournes had written that Italian was much favored "en particulier à la Cour de notre grand Roi,"[7] and powerful Medici princesses ensured that it remained so. Courtiers spoke it; scholars even wrote in it, and Du Monin was one of these.

Du Monin's themes in his Italian verses are those of Milton in his, and of course Petrarchan love poetry was often little more than an exercise in rhetoric, a vehicle for the ingenuity of those enamored of conceits. With certain provisos, the same may be said for humanist tragedy from the time of Jodelle until the end of the sixteenth century. But increasingly in the 1580s and after, dramatists began to dispense with many of the opportunities for rhetorical brilliance, to abandon, in fact, the great set pieces such as the messenger's *récit* and elaborate stichomythic sparring, although more regular dramatists like Montchrestien continued to exploit them to the full. Du Monin by no means relinquishes occasions for display or gory narration, and his rhetoric is highly ornate. But with the new emphasis on a fictional love story and its horrific consequences he points the way toward a new dramatic conception, in which rhetoric retains its necessary part though with considerably decreased importance. Dramatists from 1585 until about 1615 prefer the enactment of sanguinary and indecorous feats, with the result that elaborate retailing of such deeds becomes otiose.

7. *Il Petrarca* (1545), preface.

Du Monin was known to most of the older bibliographers,[8] but received almost totally unfavorable mention. Niceron condemns his obscurity; Beauchamps castigates the affected language with its neologisms and compound forms, features which are also characteristic of Ronsard and Garnier, and which vitiate the work of Du Bartas. The Soleinne catalogue quotes from a *blason* sonnet and comments: "C'était un terrible poëte que ce Dumonin." In the face of such hostility it is worth noting the view of La Vallière's catalogue. It takes exception to the "versification bizarre" of *Orbecc-Oronte,* which it finds "ridiculement écrite," but notes the substance of the play which, we read, "ne manque certainement pas de cette horreur tragique si vantée dans le Théâtre des Grecs." This appraisal would have pleased Du Monin, who claims a considerable acquaintance with ancient drama in his prefaces, inserting a brief history of the Greek chorus. But his knowledge is clearly ill-digested, and some of his observations are startling, such as his notion that in Euripides' *Children of Heracles* "la mort d'un seul Euristée en fait rire plusieurs," or that in *Electra* (author unspecified, but most probably Sophocles) "chacū rit à la fin."[9] These curiously phrased references to tragedy with a happy ending are all too brief. Giraldi had expressed a preference for "tragedie de fin lieto," but not in the preface to *Orbecche.*[10] The drift of Du Monin's argument is not to champion the happy ending, but to show by the divergence of ancient practice that one cannot usefully talk of orthodoxy, or of a body of regulations. In consequence, Du Monin uses the authority of the ancients in a negative way to support his notions about contemporary tragedy. Already in a preface to *La Peste de la Peste* (1584) he had reviewed the state of French tragedy

8. See Niceron, *Mémoires* (1729–1745), XXXI, 198; Beauchamps, *Recherches sur les Théâtres de France* (Paris, 1735), III, 478–484; La Vallière, *Bibliothèque du théâtre françois* (Dresden, 1768), I, 260; Soleinne, *Bibliothèque dramatique,* ed. P. Lacroix (Paris, 1843–1844), I, 825–826; Brunet, *Manuel du libraire* (Paris, 1834), II, 147. See also Francisque Lélut, "Lettre sur Jean-Edouard du Monin, poète célèbre du XVIe siècle" (Gy, 1840); he quotes Dorat's Latin epitaph for Du Monin. More recently see P. Vulliaud, "Un Prétendant a la couronne de Ronsard," *Mercure de France,* CLXXV, 338–363; C. J. Titmus, "Jean-Edouard du Monin. A Pioneer of the Irregular Tragedy," *FS,* X (1954), 333–337.

9. *Extrait d'une apologie de l'auteur sur ses oeuvres,* in *Le Phoenix* (Paris, 1585).

10. See Philip Horne, *The Tragedies of Giambattista Cinthio Giraldi* (Oxford, 1962), pp. 36–37.

("voyant nôtre France si disiteuse en cothurne"). Tragedy is hampered by its choice of subject matter. The answer is to write philosophical tragedy on fictional subjects. Ronsard and Vauquelin were to object to such material, but Du Monin preempts the issue by lashing opponents: "C'est une lesse de Pigmees racourssis, & grammariens morfondus qui veulent rembarrer mes bouillons poëtiques dans l'étroite ecorce de ne sçai quels legislateurs de Grammaire."[11] He sees his revolutionary stance as a precedent which will silence reactionary critics, and his inelegant complacency was to find a measure of justification ten years later when dramatists began to adopt the practice.

Although unacknowledged by Du Monin, the principal source for his tragedy is Giraldi Cinthio's *Orbecche,* first performed in the author's house before Duke Ercole II of Ferrara in 1541, and published in 1543 (Venice). It was reprinted frequently throughout the century, and in 1583 it appeared with Giraldi's eight other tragedies. The story of Orbecche also occurs in Giraldi's collection of stories, the *Hecatommithi* (II, 2). Though not published until 1565, they had existed in part since 1531. Du Monin informs us that "ce suiet se lit en l'Hecatommythi, ou contes italiens," and, conveniently, Gabriel Chappuys's translation of these had appeared in 1583/4, which must have given them a certain currency. Du Monin perhaps felt he was enhancing his renown by appearing to dramatize a short story. An inspection of the text shows that he clearly knew and used Giraldi's play. The French play, however, is not the simple translation which some scholars have claimed.[12] It shows a certain ingenuity in its deliberate alterations of structure, but the major (and crucial) difference lies in the treatment of the theme of clandestine marriage. The difference of approach causes a total shift of emphasis in the moral and metaphysical dimensions of the play.

It is not known whether Giraldi's novella actually preceded his play. There is no great disparity of tone between the two, but certain differences of emphasis are worth noticing. In the novella Sulmone discovers the incest of his wife and son; in the play Orbecche as a child had innocently

---

11. *Extrait* . . .

12. Titmus, p. 334; E. Forsyth, *La Tragédie française de Jodelle à Corneille (le thème de la vengeance)* (Paris, 1962), p. 255: "la traduction assez fidèle d'une tragédie italienne."

revealed it, so that the exordial ghost seeking revenge on Orbecche is a deliberately Senecan accretion, as Philip Horne notes in his study of Giraldi.[13] Giraldi had a particular (though unfashionable) admiration for Seneca, preferring both his style and content ("assai più grave") to that of the Greek tragedies used by Trissino and his circle. Since its inception (*Sofonisba* was written in 1515), Italian vernacular tragedy had consisted mainly of broad imitations of Greek plays by friends and disciples of Trissino: Rucellai's *Rosmunda* (1525) based on Sophocles' *Antigone;* Alamanni's own *Antigone* (1533), etc. Already in 1541 Giraldi was complaining of atrophy in Italian tragedy, though he pays handsome compliments to the dramatists mentioned. Like Du Monin, who may well have appropriated some of these ideas, Giraldi calls for new themes to restore the dignity of tragedy:

> Che da nuova materia, e novi nomi
> Nasca nova Tragedia . . .
> (*Orbecche, La Tragedia a chi legge*, ll. 35–36)

by which he means fictional plots treated in a Senecan manner. Only rarely, and to commission, did he depart from this practice (*Cleopatra, Didone*).

Where the tragedy adds the Senecan revenge it subtracts the overt moralizing of Lucio, the narrator in the novella. This concerns Orbecche's lack of filial piety and her violation of Degree. Lucio's story ("pietoso e compassionevole avvenimento") seems at first to be a cautionary tale:

il quale mostrerà in che stima devono avere i figliouli i padri loro, e che i servatori dei re non deono rompere la fede a chi data l'hanno.

The reference is to Orbecche's clandestine marriage, and to her husband, Oronte, a commoner who enjoys Sulmone's favor. In the novella, but not the play, Orbecche defends her choice:

Se io faccio stima di Oronte . . . lo faccio perché egli il vale, nè mi dà noia ch'egli di basso stato si sia, perchè l'animo e le virtù sue non solo mostrano maggiore della sua sorte, ma degno figliuolo di ogni gran re.

13. Horne, pp. 51 and 53.

In the novella the couple take flight to Armenia where the king champions such a marriage, on grounds of happiness. It is a "peccato d'amore," worthy of pardon not punishment:

Nè gli (Sulmone) dee parere strano . . . ch'uomo di basso stato abbia pigliata una sua figliuola per moglie, perchè gli antichi e i moderni tempi possono dare ampia fede che vie più contente son vissute molte giovani di real sangue co' mariti da meno di loro.

In fact Lucio's moralizing is contradicted by his manner and sympathies in the story.

In the play the analysis of Degree passes from Orbecche and the king of Armenia (who is not among the dramatis personae) to Sulmone himself, in a long Senecan clemency debate (Act III, using material from *Octavia,* 440 ff.). The main defense of Orbecche's marriage and Oronte's merit comes from the counselor Malecche. The play thus brings together in the realm of rhetoric the issues of clandestine marriage and Degree. It uses the theme forensically and shifts the emphasis away from the romantic and lyrical aspects of the novella into the world of public debate, seeking choric and audience sympathy. This scene is quite the longest in the play: over six hundred lines of moral, social, and political persuasion to gain Sulmone's pardon. Never at any stage of the play is there any attempt to stress the possible magnitude of the heroine's offenses. Everything on the contrary is slanted toward the exoneration of the heroine and the condemnation of Sulmone. He is a hubristic tryant whose reasoning owes much to Seneca's Lycus and Atreus. The chorus censures him throughout, and applauds when he is brought down by Orbecche. Giraldi is here true to form. In all his plays the sympathetic nature of the heroine is set in relief. In *Altile,* a tragedy "di lieto fin" of the same period, as well as being the story which follows in the *Hecatommithi* (II. iii), clandestine marriage is presented in a comparably favorable light. In both plays the choric approval parallels that of the other storytellers in the novella:

Versarono tutti da gli occhi un fonte di lagrime. E tutte le donne spezialmente, come più tenere e più pietose, tanto di compassione ebbero alla misera . . . (ed agli) innocenti bambini, che parve loro che Sulmone altro fine non meritasse.

Such, then, is Giraldi's unhysterical attitude toward clandestine marriage and the violation of Degree. In the play the marriage is justified at great length by the normative counselor, and the chorus is sympathetic and approves Orbecche's tyrannicide. The Senecan revenge motif in Act I explains the necessity that the marriage should be discovered and punished by Sulmone, but it does not imply any condemnation of the heroine. Rather, it allows Giraldi to avoid such an implication by highlighting the Senecan themes of vengeance and fatality.

The emphasis of Du Monin's play is quite different, for the following reasons: first, social attitudes toward clandestine marriage seem to have been much more disapproving in France than in Italy. Secondly, like other dramatists of the time, and in particular Garnier, he is preoccupied with a theme born of the suffering of the civil wars: God's use of scourges. As in *Les Juifves,* the characters of *Orbecc-Oronte* exemplify certain political and theological ideas, with the result that Giraldi's straightforward Senecan tragedy is radically reorganized in its French form.

The question of social attitudes toward clandestine marriage is a problematic one, further complicated by the fact that Giraldi's play of 1541 appeared before such marriages were invalidated by the Council of Trent, which must have hardened Catholic hearts. Clandestine marriage, usually in the form of consent of the couple *per verba de presenti* ("words about the present" as opposed to betrothal), remained legally binding though it was held to be sinful. In France writers such as Rabelais[14] and Etienne Pasquier[15] are wholly opposed to such marriages. Marguerite de Navarre[16] reflects her society's disquiet, while Belleforest,[17] in his adaptation of Bandello's story of the Duchess of Malfi, inserts strong condemnation of the duchess's secret marriage to her steward. Du Monin shows his disapproval of the secret marriage of Orbecche and Oronte by removing Giraldi's sympathetic heroine from the moral center of the play. Instead of championing Orbecche's stance, he uses the double revenge to illustrate the contemporary French preoccupation with the question of God's use of scourges: *verges* or *fléaux.* There is a stronger religiopolitical strand in Du

14. Rabelais, *Le Tiers Livre* (Paris, 1552), chap. 48.
15. Pasquier, *Lettres,* III, i (not dated in Lyons edition of 1607).
16. Marguerite de Navarre, *L'Heptaméron* (Paris, 1560), XXI Nouvelle.
17. Belleforest, *Histoires Tragiques* (1565), II, xix.

Monin, involving the justification of regicide when it is actually tyran-nicide, a theme of particular relevance with the upsurge of the Ligue after 1584. Du Monin weaves his moral and metaphysical threads of crime and punishment (through *fléaux*) into his political message, all of which makes his play very different from Giraldi's, and more akin to his previous play *La Peste de la Peste* (1584). That play had included the scourge motif in its title, and there are constant references throughout the work, including a "fléau roial."

The un-Senecan theme of the "flagellum dei" (applied to Attila, ca. ninth century) had appeared in the very first neo-Latin tragedy, Mussato's *Eccerinis* of 1315, where it was linked with the tyranny of a recent Italian prince:

> Deus . . .
> dedit et tyrannos urbibus, licuit quibus
> sine ordine sine fine strictis ensibus
> saevire largo sanguine in gentes vage . . .
> Nabuchodonosor, Aegyptius Pharao, Saul . . .
>
> (ll. 328–332)[18]

The topic continues to figure in European drama, but the subject of the scourge was to have a special relevance to sixteenth-century France, and, as Gillian Jondorf shows,[19] a lively discussion existed long before Garnier's *Les Juifves* of 1583 focused on Nebuchadnezzar. Besides the political and theological examples noted by Dr. Jondorf, we find that several plays of the time, such as Jodelle's *Didon*, Rivadeau's *Aman*, and Garnier's *Cornélie* develop the topos. The instrumental nature of tryants and other wicked men, as expressed in *Cornélie*, becomes the central motif of Du Monin's play:

> Et souvent les grands dieux gardent expressément
> Les hommes scélérez pour nostre châtiment;
>
> Puis s'en estant servis, rendent avec usure
> Le guerdon de leur crime et de leur forfaiture.
>
> (*Cornélie*, III, ll. 893–896)

18. Albertino Mussato, *Eccerinis*, ed. L. Pedrin (Bologna, 1900).

19. Gillian Jondorf, *Robert Garnier and the Themes of Political Tragedy in the Sixteenth Century* (Cambridge, Eng., 1969), pp. 114–115.

In *Orbecc-Oronte* the double revenge and suicide mean that the scourges
are destroyed once they have usefully wrought punishment. This contrasts
with Seneca's revenge plays where only vague prophecies of doom warn
avengers of possible retribution: Cassandra hints darkly that Orestes will
avenge his father ("veniet et vobis furor"), Thyestes trusts in the gods to
punish Atreus ("vindices aderunt dei"). The plays themselves make scant
concession to modern and Christian expectations of adequate punishment. Garnier's *Les Juifves,* so greatly indebted to *Thyestes,* reproduces the
Senecan pattern, although enhancing the prophecy of Nabuchodonosor's
ultimate downfall with a Messianic vision. Nabuchodonosor is not, however, a wholly Senecan figure: he is a scourge: "exécrable instrument de la
rancoeur celeste" (l. 1840), an "exécuteur" of divine wrath (l. 2058).
Orbecc-Oronte has a similar tyrant-cum-scourge, whereas in Giraldi the
private punishment exacted by Sulmone is not seen in a theological light.
Giraldi's predominantly Senecan play assimilates more of the Roman
philosopher's ethical system than does Du Monin's. Indeed, *Orbecc-Oronte* is
one of the less Stoic plays of the age, a fact explained by the use of the
protagonists as scourges rather than as authentic tragic figures encounter-
ing suffering and evil.

In an original passage (and thus not adapted from the Italian) Du Monin
shows that he has two *fléaux*: Sulmon and Orbecche. Neither is sanctioned
in revenge; each is used instrumentally by God. Oronte warns Sulmon as
he is being put to death:

> . . . si de iustes yeux
> L'Eternel mire encor de la cime des cieus
> L'humain gouvernement, traitre, tu dois attendre
> Un fleau qui de tes fleaux la vêgeâce doit pendre.
> (IV, "Scene du Messager, & du Choeur")

Sulmon's role as scourge is fulfilled as he taunts Orbecche with the remains
of her husband and children ("instrumens de ma sanglante rage").
Orbecche's parallel role then becomes apparent, as she murders him.

Seen thus, Du Monin's *Orbecc-Oronte* is a simple affair, scarcely rising
above the level of a tract. But this is to ignore both the self-conscious
dramatist at work and the disastrous uncertainty of ethical focus which
blights so many French tragedies of the late sixteenth century. These

aspects of an individual dramatist and of the theater as a whole need investigation. They are in fact combined in the complex issue of the moral status of Orbecche. Since Du Monin's major problems stem from his deliberate alterations to the role of Giraldi's heroine, and since these modifications unbalance the play, they may usefully be examined at this juncture.

Logically, Du Monin's Orbecche cannot be the focus of our ethical or emotional sympathies: her clandestine marriage is presented unfavorably; her dramatic role is that of a *fléau*. In both respects Du Monin is at variance with his source. Paradoxically, he magnifies the role of Orbecche in the closing scene, introducing much new material, including a strange soliloquy ("Orbecche parlant en soi-même") which has no counterpart in Giraldi. The effect of this interpolation is temporarily to make Orbecche sympathetic and normative. Here Du Monin outdoes his source in Senecan elements, using the interior monologue to analyze moral attitudes and motivation.[20] Such psychological investigation was to become an important part of tragedy in the 1590s and beyond, but here it is dramatically disturbing. It complicates what the original simplifies. Giraldi's heroine, presented with the awful salver, acknowledges her "errors" and begs for death. When denied this, she extracts the daggers and slaughters Sulmone, to considerable choric approval. This chorus adapts Seneca's *Hercules furens* (ll. 922–924) to exonerate Orbecche and laud her justifiable, indeed desirable, tyrannicide:

> Ma non è stato mal a uccider lui;
> Ch'a Dio non s'offre vittima più grata
> D'un malvagio Tiran com'era questo.

> (V.ii)

Du Monin transfers this choric approval to Orbecche's soliloquy. The chorus which follows her suicide notes Sulmon's just deserts, but the

20. Cf. Seneca's *Agamemnon*, ll. 108–124; 226–233; *Medea*, ll. 397 ff.; 425 ff. Chantelouve's *Pharaon* (1575) has early examples of the interior monologue: Térinisse's divided loyalties are analyzed three times. Matthieu's *Guisiade* (1589) allots Henri III a "synderèse" or analysis of conscience. Such examples are rare before the 1590s.

Nurse consigns her mistress's soul to hell. Orbecche's revenge is identified with divine justice:

> Ha! Le Ciel s'y accorde, & l'Enfer s'y consent.
>
> (V)

But once more the words are Orbecche's, and she is not morally normative in the French play, whereas in Giraldi's Christian-Stoic providential scheme his heroine approaches the good life through virtue, and to that extent merits her brief "felicità mortale."

Giraldi's play makes constant reference to "Il Signore": this is potentially ambivalent, but there is in fact no confusion metaphysically, owing to Giraldi's uncomplicated ethical framework. Du Monin's play is far less clear, and here we find a characteristic of French tragedy from 1585 until the early 1630s. Du Monin's Orbecche prays to the Deity in broadly pagan terms (cf. Giraldi's chorus above).

> . . . O Dieu, grand Roi des Dieus,
> Guide ma foible main contre ce chef de crime;
> Ie crois qu'il te doit etre agreable victime.
>
> (V)

Such appeals for metaphysical approval in crime are common enough in sixteenth-century tragedy, sanction for revenge being sought of pagan powers—"Iupin," sometimes "l'infernal Iupin." Dramatists avoid the implication that a Christian God abets such deeds, and it is rare for pagan and Christian morality actually to clash in plays of the period up to *Les Juifves*. Thereafter the dualism disappears and we find a disconcerting arbitrariness. The abandonment of this dualism is already evident in Du Monin's *Orbecc-Oronte,* and it is responsible for much of the incoherence at the end of the play. Orbecche's soliloquy strains the limits of dualism with its appeals:

> O toi, qui des petis te fais le protecteur,
> De Veufves, d'Orfelins le fidelle tuteur . . .
>
> (V)

The chorus watching Orbecche's tyrannicide makes analogies with animals protecting their young, among which is the pelican, an overtly Christian image already occurring in *La Peste de la Peste* of the previous year, where its presence did not upset the propagandist fabric. In *Orbecc-Oronte* it blurs the ethical focus at a crucial moment, obliging us to reconsider our sympathies since Orbecche, as she butchers her father, enjoys the luxury of Christian symbolism. Briefly, at the play's climax, Orbecche transcends her role as *fléau* to seek sympathy and approval, which is unsettling, given that for almost five acts Du Monin has eliminated the sympathetic and essentially normative heroine of his source.

In his *Apologie* Du Monin wrote:

Ici i'enrichis le [*sic*] payenne Persique de l'histoire Chrestienne sans tant chronoligizer.

This slightly obscure claim refers not to the copious biblical allusions constantly amplifying the original's choruses, but to the whole moral direction of the new play, in which private vendettas can have no sanction and avengers are instruments of divine wrath with no call upon an audience's emotional or ethical sympathies. So austere a scheme ultimately eludes the dramatist in Du Monin as it will his successors in the 1590s. It is not simply that they all finally reject a scheme which is dramatically unpromising; the truth is that they all have a very shaky sense of moral order: uncertain of the validity of those very codes they seek to advocate, they are unable to embody a value system within their plays. None of them is able to situate a norm within his tragedy, or to present an ethical dilemma without confusion. And their dramatic structures show how they sought to hold the audience whose moral sensibilities they could not direct. These structures, involving dispersal of interest and the examination of the internal conflict of now this character now that, are ultimately derived from Garnier's "panoramic" techniques and shifts of emphasis.[21]

Du Monin, left without a moral center to his play after expunging Giraldi's Orbecche, disperses his material. His proximity to Garnier's methods is more obvious than his successors'. Garnier had frequently used

---

21. See M.-M. Mouflard, *Robert Garnier 1545–1590 L'Œuvre* (La Roche-sur-Yon, 1963), chap. 2, pp. 57–87.

balancing blocks of dramatic material: *Les Juifves* has five major figures to
engage attention without departure from the central theme. Du Monin
applies this technique to transform the Italian original. He multiplies
henchmen. He greatly expands Oronte's role, and thus justifies his new
title. Oronte replaces Giraldi's Nurse who feebly soliloquizes for 109 lines
in Act II. High on Fortune's wheel he draws us to the central theme: the
fléau which may punish his clandestine marriage:

> Toutefois un fleau sourd qui me pend sur le clos
> Me bourrelle, & me cuit du fond iusques aus os.
>
> (II)

Oronte's downfall is wrought by a villain to whom Du Monin allots the
sentiments of Giraldi's morally normative counselor, Malecche. Malecche
upholds the acceptability of revenge even if he prefers clemency:

> Il far vendetta è d'ognun proprio
> Ma il perdonar è da Signore gentile.
>
> (III.iii)

While such a view may have been part of the social codes of Imperial Rome
and Renaissance Ferrara—and indeed put into practice in Paris in 1585—
it is not part of Du Monin's moral scheme, and the idea is therefore
transfered to a villain:

> C'est un commun pouvoir de prêdre sa vêgeâce.
>
> (III)

For, as with clandestine marriage, Du Monin opposes a practice socially
widespread: and on both scores he is at variance with his source. He
eliminates Giraldi's ethical core, substitutes his topos of *fléaux*, and makes
this new issue permeate the action of all his characters. But he is unable to
organize a completely new play, sustaining the *fléau* theme throughout—
the sort of play Garnier had produced in *Les Juifves*—because he blurs his
focus in the last scenes.

It is of course no accident that Du Monin concentrates on the topos of
fléaux in 1584 and 1585: *Les Juifves* had appeared in 1583. But the notion
of scourges is not the only lead which Garnier's play gives to *Orbecc-Oronte*.

The messenger's speech conveying the murder of Oronte and his children has echoes of Garnier's verbal pathos in the Prophet's *récits,* and the situation is paralleled in the murder of Sédécie's children before his eyes. The choruses, often enormously longer than Giraldi's, develop Garnier's commonplaces, and that of Act IV concludes in an identical way to Garnier's equivalent chorus of divine justice, much more specifically than Giraldi's. Like so many dramatists of the period 1580–1620, Du Monin incorporates elements of Garnier's dramaturgy, language, and themes: the dispersed dramatic material of the later plays, the rhetorical set pieces and verbal pathos, the political and ethical ideas which dominate these depictions of power struggles, tyranny, precarious kingship, guilt, and retribution.

In fairness to Du Monin, his fellow dramatists of the 1580s should be mentioned in this connection. They are all explicitly political in their material, using themes present in Garnier since *Porcie* (1568) but which he had synthesized in *Les Juifves.* They are themes which had been part of the stock-in-trade common to thinkers and playwrights, expected by readers and audiences. But the fact remains that the greatest playwright of the age used them constantly, and he was the model for other writers. The dramatists of the 1580s deal with the nature of kingship, the collective responsibility of a nation for its tribulations, God's use of scourges, the evils of civil war—Garnier's shadow is inescapable. Antoine Favre's *Les Gordians et Maximins* (1589), one of the last plays to give eloquent voice to the horrors of civil havoc, introduces the political theme of tyranny in the context of scourges. A bad ruler is a scourge:

> S'il est traistre, sanglant, avare, sans valeur,
> Les Dieux le veulent tel, c'est pour nostre malheur,
> Ainsi de noz forfaits ils vangent l'insolence . . .
>
> (*Les Gordians et Maximins,* I)

Structurally, Favre modeled himself on Garnier's earlier Roman plays and avoids confrontation scenes. Yet the graphic details of the wars imitate Jocaste's long speech in *Antigone* (II), and the opening appeal by Favre's Iurisconsulte inevitably evokes the opening of *Les Juifves:*

> Jusqu'à quand voudrés vous, qu'un si puissât empire
> Chef d'oeuvre de vos mains, sanglante se deschire . . .?
>
> (I)

Where he is farthest from his model, and closest to Du Monin and the dramatists of the 1590s, is in his difficulty in situating a moral norm. Favre makes a disconcerting attempt to transform his tyrant into a tragic hero (Maximin désepéré") as he contemplates suicide. Like Du Monin, Favre could not end his play.

François Perrin's *Sichem ravisseur* (also 1589) echoes Garnier's crucial themes:

> Car tousjours le forfait d'un Prince abandonné
> Retombe sur le chef du peuple infortuné . . .
>
> (II)
>
> Un prince mal vivant de son peuple est suivy:
> Son peuple, s'il vit bien, fait ainsi comme luy . . .
>
> (V)

But Perrin's play shifts from political and national themes to the private revenge exacted for a crime, as Du Monin's had done, and as Pierre Matthieu's propagandist *Guisiade* (1589) does. As Matthieu writes in his *Discours,* the murder of Guise by Henri III is "une si estrange vengeance." Civil war, royal responsibility, national suffering—these themes are not ignored by Matthieu, but equally significant is the insistence on "volupté" and the King's penchant for "délices." This is the trend of drama in the late 1580s, as tragedy shifts its gaze from public issues to private concerns. Perrin and Matthieu, like Du Monin, here foreshadow the reestablished theater of the 1590s.

Jean-Edouard Du Monin's methods and his ethical disarray were to become features of the French theater a decade later, when the wars were over, the Ligue had fallen (1595), and tragedy returned to the stage in France. His preference for fictional sources which combine didacticism with horror was to find favor with many dramatists after 1595. Twenty years later, the same sort of plays were still being written. Dramatists appear obsessed with adultery, lust, incest, and revenge, topics which had scarcely been considered in the earlier period of French tragedy. The chaos of the declining Valois monarchy and the disorder of the early Bourbon dynasty provided a new climate for dramatists to reflect in their plays, not as purveyors of atrocity and depravity, but with a degree of seriousness and social concern. In the ultimate confusion of their works they reflect an age without a moral center, societies which lacked an ethical direction, and certainly received few edifying examples from their ruling classes. Dramatists after 1585 betray their insecurity and quandary in the inability to situate a moral norm within their plays. Their fundamental ambiguities both ethical and tonal, their inconsistencies and confusion, all lead to a chaotic moral vision and a theater which is aesthetically anarchic: a theater which it is all too easy to dismiss as worthless or repellent. In his own curious way Du Monin initiates this period of French drama at the close of an era of civil-war poets and dramatists. On the one hand, he resembles his immediate contemporaries in their huge debt to Garnier: in those passages where his style is not crippled by a chronic obscurity we see the rhetorical patterns which reached their climax in Garnier, the political and metaphysical preoccupations which in 1583 culminated in *Les Juifves*. On the other hand, we see the clear alternatives to the conventional methods, the new fictional source material, the psychological exploration of character coupled with a relish for visual cruelty and macabre revenge. We see the basic principles of Garnier's dramaturgy, but overlaid with horror and undermined by confusion. The characteristics of irregular French tragedy for three decades—the stream of exciting incident, the lurid details, the incoherence of the moral fabric—these are present in Du Monin. If he is more consciously organic in his structure than later writers (Nancel, Schelandre, Troterel) that is probably because of his vital proximity to Garnier.

The Iconography of Violence in
English Renaissance Tragedy

HUSTON DIEHL

I N HIS PAINTING *The Horrors of War* (1637–1638) Peter Paul Rubens depicts the psychological and physical violence of war. Wielding a bloody sword, an armed soldier terrorizes a group of fleeing civilians who fall at his feet. A woman attempts to restrain him; another throws up her arms in distress; a frightened child pleads for comfort. On the ground are the abandoned objects of peacetime existence. Capturing the turmoil and devastation of wartime, this painting has great emotional effect and, to the viewer today, seems primarily concerned with a human and very personal suffering. To its seventeenth-century creator, however, the painting was also highly allegorical. In a letter to a fellow artist, Rubens explains in detail the painting's allegorical meaning. To Rubens, each human figure represents an abstraction, each object symbolizes an idea:

The principal figure is Mars who . . . advances with his shield and his blood-stained sword, threatening the nations with great devastation and paying little

I wish to thank the State University of New York Research Foundation for a grant sponsoring research for this study.

27

heed to Venus his lady, who strives with caresses and embraces to restrain
him . . . on the ground lies a woman with a broken lute, signifying harmony,
which is incompatible with the discord of war; there is also a Mother with her
babe in her arms, denoting that fecundity, generation and charity are trampled
underfoot by war, which corrupts and destroys all things. . . . There is also, I
believe, a bundle of arrows with the cord which bound them together undone,
they when bound together, being the emblem of Concord, and I also painted,
lying beside them, the caduceus and the olive, the symbol of peace. That lugu-
brious Matron clad in black and with her veil torn, despoiled of her jewels and
every other ornament, is unhappy Europe, afflicted for so many years by rapine,
outrage, and misery. . . .

Rubens sees the human figures and objects in this painting as "both real
and symbolic." The painting is, as E. H. Gombrich suggests, an "expressive evocation of a concept"; its dramatic power and its intellectual idea
reinforce each other.[1]

Although the artist's allegorical interpretation of this painting may
seem forced to us today, its detail overelaborated, Rubens is not indulging
in the creation of his own private symbolism nor is he using an esoteric
system of signs. On the contrary, every image he depicts in his painting
and interprets in his letter—from Mars and Venus to the broken lute,
trampled figures, and bundle of arrows—is conventional, part of what
may be termed a Renaissance public symbolism.[2] This symbolism was
routinely employed by sixteenth- and seventeenth-century artists and
writers and was known, we may assume, to their audiences who were, after
all, emblem readers, imprese makers, churchgoers, pageant watchers,
masque participants. Furthermore, although we today often view allegory
and realism as mutually exclusive, the use of conventional, symbolic icons

1. *The Letters of Peter Rubens*, trans. and ed. Ruth S. Magurn (Cambridge, Mass.,
1955), no. 242, pp. 408–409, quoted by E. H. Gombrich, *Symbolic Images: Studies in the
Art of the Renaissance* (London, 1972), pp. 126–127; Gombrich, *Symbolic Images*, pp. 128–
129.

2. For examples: Mars symbolizes war in George Wither's *A Collection of Emblemes*
(London, 1635), bk. 2, no. 18; Venus symbolizes love in Thomas Combe's *The Theater of
Fine Devices* (London, 1614), p. 2; the lute symbolizes harmony in Wither's *Emblemes*, bk.
2, no. 20; the act of treading upon an object symbolizes conquest in Henry Peacham's
Minerva Britanna (London, 1612), p. 134; and the bundle of sticks symbolizes concord in
Peacham's *The Gentlemen's Exercise* (London, 1612), p. 106.

to express the idea of discord is, for Rubens, clearly not at odds with his desire to portray—in as convincing a way as possible—the violence such discord unleashes in the actual world.

That the violence depicted so realistically in Ruben's painting is identified as symbolic and conventional by the artist himself raises significant questions about the nature and function of violence in all forms of sixteenth- and seventeenth-century art. Particularly intriguing is the issue of violence in Tudor and Stuart tragedy, a form of drama where murders, dismemberments, and tortures abound, and where it is not uncommon to find such sensational violence as a heart brandished upon a sword, a severed human hand thrust into someone's unsuspecting hand, and a victim's brains seared with a burning crown. I want to consider whether such *stage* violence is allusive in the manner of Ruben's painting—that is, does a symbolism understood by Renaissance audiences extend violent acts on the stage into moral and ethical contexts?

This question is not addressed in most critical discussions of Renaissance stage violence, which focus instead on the theatrical appeal, emotional effect, and cultural basis of violence. An assumption that "the Elizabethan dramatists loved violence" underlies these discussions and usually results either in praise of this "hearty, credulous love of straightforward bloodshed, murder and mutilation" or in condemnation of a stage violence which is seen as "indiscriminate wading in blood," "purely gratuitous," and "brought in merely to make the audience shudder."[3]

---

3. Maurice Charney, "The Persuasiveness of Violence in Elizabethan Plays," *RenD*, N.S. II (1969), 65; Una Ellis-Fermor, *The Jacobean Drama* (London, 1936), p. 5; Fredson Bowers, *Elizabethan Revenge Tragedy 1587–1642* (Princeton, N.J., 1940), pp. 247 and 123. See also Louis Wright, *Middle-Class Culture in Elizabethan England* (1935; rpt. Ithaca, N.Y., 1958), p. 620, who speaks of the Elizabethans' "appetite for gore"; and Howard Baker, *Induction to Tragedy* (Baton Rouge, La., 1939), p. 202, who laments the fact that many of these tragedies are "irresponsibly sensational." One analysis of violence in Renaissance tragedy that stands apart from this critical tradition is Stephen Greenblatt's "Marlowe and Renaissance Self-Fashioning," in *Two Renaissance Mythmakers: Christopher Marlowe and Ben Jonson,* ed. Alvin Kernan (Baltimore, Md., 1977): in this stimulating essay Greenblatt considers the violence of Marlovian tragedy in terms of larger, cultural phenomena which changed the way men perceived and experienced space and time, giving them a new sense of "limitlessness" and causing them to "do violence as a means of making boundaries, effecting transformations, signalling closure," p. 46.

Whether praising or condemning the violence of the Renaissance stage, these discussions usually reject the possibility that stage violence functions symbolically, reinforces ethical concepts, or is integral to a play's thematic statement. In an article analyzing the "emotional impact" of violence in Elizabethan plays, Maurice Charney, for example, explicitly denies the existence of any significant moral dimension of stage violence, arguing instead that "There is a sense that violence is performed for its own sake and is to be judged by esthetic rather than moral criteria." Even when isolated acts of stage violence like the blinding of Gloucester in *King Lear* or the burning of Diaphanta in *The Changeling* are interpreted symbolically, such violence is usually not seen in terms of a larger, iconographic tradition, but rather as the unique and singular creation of an individual playwright.[4]

It is my hypothesis that many (but not all) of the violent elements of Renaissance English tragedy are both emotionally charged and symbolic. Stage violence may in a given context allude to existing iconographic traditions of the Renaissance, the same traditions manifested in the visual arts of that era. Such a view of violence regards the bloody instruments of murder, the grotesque limbs of dismembered bodies, and the cruel and inhuman devices of torture presented on the Tudor and Stuart stage not simply as sensational stage violence but as symbolic icons which express widely understood moral and ethical concepts. The violence, then, is not irrelevant to the drama's themes, but instead develops and advances them.

When used in an appropriate context of revenge, the bloody dagger is usually such a symbolic icon. It is, of course, a literal weapon, brandished by an impassioned avenger, stained with the blood of the murdered, and, as such, arouses intense feelings of horror and disgust in the audience. It may, however, *also* be symbolic, linking the specific act of revenge with the very concept of vengeance. In the visual arts the bloody dagger func-

---

4. Charney, "The Persuasiveness of Violence," pp. 65, 66; in an unpublished lecture, "The Logic of Elizabethan Stage Violence: Some Alarums and Excursions for Modern Critics, Editors, and Directors," delivered at The Washington Renaissance Colloquium, Alan C. Dessen makes the most comprehensive argument I know of that stage violence may be symbolic. Drawing his examples largely from the late moralities and Shakespeare, Mr. Dessen does not recognize or discuss the iconographic tradition of violence in the Renaissance.

tions this way, as a conventional icon of vengeance; it is, for example, one of the identifying attributes of personified revenge in Cesare Ripa's influential *Iconologia*. Renaissance playwrights were certainly aware of this iconographic tradition. In the morality play of *Horestes*, the vice is a character called Revenge who threatens men "with this blade," and in early tragedies like *Locrine, Jocasta, The Misfortunes of Arthur*, and *The Battle of Alcazar* personifications of revenge appear in dumb shows carrying daggers, often dripping with blood.[5] What the early tragedians isolate in dumb shows and interpret for us, later dramatists sometimes incorporate into the main action and make implicit, effectively fusing the actual instrument of revenge and the larger idea of vengeance. John Marston uses the bloody dagger in this way in *Antonio's Revenge*. His play opens with the entrance of the villain Piero who is *"smear'd in blood, a poniard in one hand, bloody"* and who associates himself with revenge: "I can scarce coop triumphing vengeance up,/ From bursting forth in braggart passion." The third act of this play recalls that opening scene when the hero Antonio enters with a bloody dagger and also associates himself with the idea of vengeance: "Look how I stroke in blood, reeking the steam / Of foaming vengeance. O, my soul's enthron'd / In the triumphant chariot of revenge." Marston uses the conventional icon of revenge in an original and highly ironic way, blurring the moral distinction between villain and hero and undercutting his hero. In later revenge tragedies like Fletcher's *The Maid's Tragedy* and Ford's *Love's Sacrifice*, bloody daggers similarly bring forward certain ideas—concerning human law, divine justice, and private revenge—in an allusive and ironic way, even as they shock and repulse the audience.[6] Indeed, the emotions these bloody daggers arouse may reinforce

5. *Iconologia* (Rome, 1603), pp. 494–495; John Pickering, *The Interlude of Vice* (*Horestes*) (1567; rpt. Oxford, 1962), ll. 793–800; *Locrine* (London, 1595), I.i.1–9, IV.iii.1573–1575; George Gascoigne, *Jocasta, Supposes and Jocasta*, ed. John Cunliffe (Boston, 1906), II.i.9–11; Thomas Hughes, *The Misfortunes of Arthur, Old English Plays*, 4th ed., ed. W. Carew Hazlitt (1874–1876; rpt. New York, 1964), p. 279; George Peele, *The Battle of Alcazar*, in *The Dramatic Works of George Peele*, ed. John Yoklavich (New Haven, Conn., 1961), II, 276–306.

6. John Marston, *Antonio's Revenge*, ed. W. Reavely Gair (Baltimore, Md., 1978), I.i, I.i.11–12, III.v.17–19; John Fletcher, *The Maid's Tragedy*, ed. Howard B. Norland (Lincoln, Nebr., 1968), V.iii.; and John Ford, *Love's Sacrifice*, in *The Works of John Ford*, ed. William Gifford and Rev. Alexander Dyce (London, 1869), V.i., V.ii.

the ideas they evoke, enabling the audience to apprehend the act of vengeance both emotionally and intellectually.

We must not assume, however, that all stage daggers are icons of revenge. The meaning of a stage dagger is established by the context in which it appears. In *Arden of Feversham,* for example, a band of murderers repeatedly stab Arden with a dagger, but this violence points to nothing beyond itself and the gruesome actual murder on which it was based. The weapon is mentioned only once, when, in the passion of the moment, Alice grabs it from her accomplices and joins in the stabbing of her husband: "What! Groans thou?—Nay, then give me the weapon!- / Take this for hind'ring Mosbie's love and mine!"[7] This domestic tragedy displays a journalistic interest in sensationalism, and the context of such violence suggests no iconographic tradition.

Context also determines the meaning of the dagger that Hieronimo carries in *The Spanish Tragedy.* In that play the hero holds a dagger and a rope while the contemplates suicide. At the moment that he rejects suicide as a solution to his predicament, Hieronimo *"flings away the dagger and halter."* His speech and action, along with the accompanying halter, connect the poniard to the act of suicide, and hence to the state of despair, a concept which the dagger and rope traditionally symbolize. In plays ranging from *The Tide Tarrieth No Man* to *The Duchess of Malfi,* as well as in many Renaissance paintings, sculpture, emblems, and poems, the dagger functions as an icon of despair, but these external examples can only support, not establish, such an interpretation of Hieronimo's dagger.[8]

In th' case of the bloody daggers in *Antonio's Revenge,* too, context establishes the presence of an iconographic allusion. Without such contextual clues as the blood, the avenging characters, and the verbal references to vengeance, Antonio's dagger could not be differentiated from Hieronimo's, nor could its symbolic meaning be recognized or understood. As E. M. Gombrich reminds us, the meaning of an image is determined by its context: "Taken in isolation and cut loose from the context in which they are embedded," visual images cannot be understood

7. *Arden of Feversham* (London, 1592), XIV. 260–262.
8. Thomas Kyd, *The Spanish Tragedy,* ed. Philip Edwards (London, 1959), III.xii. 1–20; George Wapull, *The Tide Tarrieth No Man* (London, 1576); John Webster, *The Duchess of Malfi,* ed. F. L. Lucas (London, 1958), III.ii.

to belong to an iconographic tradition.[9] Traditions external to the texts should bear on the interpretation of stage violence only when the texts support, and indeed, point to, traditional meanings through narrative action, characterization, theme, and, especially, verbal explanation.

This use of stage iconography should be viewed in the larger context of the Renaissance impulse to reduce "conceits intellectual to images sensible," an impulse which Francis Bacon praises because the resulting images "strike the memory more" than the original abstractions. Bacon is speaking here of the emblem, but the special power of the visual image to "strike the memory" is also ascribed in the Renaissance to the visual elements of drama. "The *Stage* feeds both the eare and *eye*," Owen Feltham writes in 1628, for instance, "and through this latter *sence* the Soule drinks deeper draughts. Things *acted* possesse us more, and are, too, more retainable than the *passable tones* of the *tongue*." It does not seem inappropriate, therefore, to apply Renaissance statements about the memorable effect and moral force of visual images to such violent stage images as bloody daggers. We must at least ask whether the Renaissance belief that "the powerful expedient of pictures prevented the moral lesson from evanescing or slipping away" might also inform the visual portrayal of violence on the Renaissance stage. To see stage violence, in certain contexts, as iconographic is to see it in terms of Renaissance aesthetics.[10]

The Renaissance believed, for instance, that "remarkably hideous or grotesque" images were especially memorable, and therefore were effective vehicles for the expression of moral ideas.[11] The grotesqueness of many acts of stage violence serves to make memorable certain moral ideas. When the hero of Ford's *'Tis Pity She's a Whore* enters a banquet with the heart of his sister on a dagger, the hideousness of the stage picture reinforces the conventional meanings of the heart—passion, desire, love—by startling the viewer. Earlier plays like *Tancred and Gismond*, *Cambises*, and *Claudius Tiberius Nero* also use this grotesque icon of the disembodied heart to

9. *Symbolic Images*, p. 12.

10. Bacon, *The Advancement of Learning*, ed. William Aldis Wright (1876; rpt. Oxford, 1900), II.xv.3.; Feltham, *Resolves A Second Centurie* (London, 1628), p. 65; Claude Paradin, *Symbola heroica*, quoted by Robert J. Clements, *Picta Poesis* (Rome, 1960), p. 67.

11. Frances Yates, *The Art of Memory* (Chicago, 1966), p. 92.

symbolize passion; such plays present the heart on stage and make simple, straightforward connections between the heart and the idea of passion. Gismund, for instance, speaks to and kisses the "pearced heart," seeing in it the "constancie" and "magnanimitie" of her dead lover, as well as "mine owne true love." Ford employs this same image of a detached heart, but in a more ironic way, creating a tension between the grisly, literal thing and its metaphoric significance. The very grotesqueness of the disembodied heart in his play furthers its symbolic significance, for the utter perversity of Giovanni's attempt to see the literal heart of his murdered sister as a Petrarchan conceit, to actualize the metaphor in the representational world, indicates the perversity of Giovanni's incestuous love. The compression of such ideas as passion, sexual desire, and incestuous love into a single image—the impaled heart—which can be immediately and sensually apprehended gives force to those ideas. [12] The grotesque picture of the heart on the dagger is so striking, and so offensive, that it and the idea of destructive passion which it expresses cannot be easily forgotten.

The same memorable quality, physical immediacy, and economy of expression characterize other acts of stage violence which, like the impaled heart, are also allusive. The entrance of Tamburlaine *"drawen in his chariot by* [the defeated kings] Trebizon *and* Soria *with bittes in their mouthes, reines in his left hand, in his right hand a whip, with which he scourgeth them"* creates a remarkable stage picture of man's violence against man. The picture is also a conventional one: the image of defeated kings harnessed to the chariot of a conqueror repeatedly appears in Renaissance emblem books as a symbol of fortune, for once proud and mighty men of royalty are depicted as victims of fortune, fallen, debased, and humiliated. The king-drawn chariot is also a conventional stage device. In *Liberality and Prodigality*, for example, the personification of Fortune enters riding in a chariot drawn by kings. In *Jocasta* and *The Wounds of Civil War* chariots driven by a triumphant king present symbolic stage pictures captioned by references to "such fickle chaunce in fortune doth remaine" and complaints about

---

12. John Ford, *Tis Pity She's a Whore*, ed. N. W. Bawcutt (Lincoln, Nebr., 1966), V.vi.24–29; the icon of a disembodied heart is a target of Cupid's arrows in Otto van Veen's *Amorum Emblemata* (Antwerp, 1608), p. 152, and is depicted in flames to symbolize "strong desires" in Wither's *Emblemes*, bk. 1, no. 39; Robert Wilmot, *The Tragedy of Tancred and Gismund* (1592; rpt. Oxford, 1914), V.ii.1632–1641.

being "humbled by fate" and suffering "fortunes of the world."[13] Marlowe presents this same image on the stage to attribute Tamburlaine's phenomenal rise to power to the workings of fortune. He also uses this stage picture to express ironically Tamburlaine's own vulnerability to fortune. "But forth, ye vassals," the former shepherd, now triumphant warrior, yells to the harnessed kings, "whatsoe'er it be, / Sickness or death can never conquer me" (V.ii.). That irony is reinforced when, in the concluding scene of the play, Tamburlaine once again enters in the king-drawn chariot and, afflicted with disease, dying, dismounts the chariot and urges his son to "mount my royal chariot of estate" (V.iii.178). The memorable sight of Tamburlaine ruthlessly whipping the captive kings whom he has reduced to beasts of burden thus condenses such ideas as fortune's favorite, fortune's fallen, and fortune's capriciousness into a single visual image of tremendous power.

In many other Tudor and Stuart tragedies, stage violence similarly reflects the Renaissance aesthetic aim of expressing "much in little"— *multo in parvum*. In its expression of complex ethical ideas and its allusiveness, symbolic violence achieves power and intensity on the stage. The dramatic impact of a number of stage fires, for example, derives in part from the way these fires express, in a terse and condensed manner, the danger of uncontrolled desire. Traditional associations of fire with passion and textual references to the self-destructive nature of passion underline the symbolic meaning of the stage fires in *The Tragedy of Hoffman* and *Claudius Tiberius Nero*, where burning crowns further the theme of destructive political ambition; *Women Beware Women*, where a burning treasure furthers the theme of destructive materialism; and *The Changeling*, where a

13. Christopher Marlowe, *Tamburlaine, Part II*, in *The Complete Works of Christopher Marlowe*, ed. Fredson Bowers (Cambridge, Eng., 1973), II.IV.iii. One source for this icon is Pliny who relates that the mythical Egyptian King Sesostris was said to have harnessed conquered kings for his triumphal processions. The icon of Sesostris whipping harnessed kings symbolizes the idea of fortune in such emblem books as Florentius Schoonhovius, *Emblemata* (Gouda, 1618), no. 60; Dirck Pieterzoon Pers, *Bellerophon* (Amsterdam, 1633), no. 2; and Peter Isselburg, *Emblemata Politica* (Nuremberg, 1640), no. 1; T. W. Craik discusses the king-drawn chariot in *Liberality and Prodigality*, in *The Tudor Interlude* (Leicester, 1950), p. 96; *Jocasta*, first dumb show; Thomas Lodge, *The Wounds of Civil War*, ed. Joseph W. Houppert (Lincoln, Nebr., 1969), III.iii.75–78.

burning woman furthers the theme of destructive passion. In all these instances, the immediacy and horror of the literal fire and the intense pain of the victim forcefully and economically express the nature of passion. The dramatists in these plays seem to hold to the Renaissance belief, expressed by the emblem writer Thomas Jenner, that, "because men are more led by the eye, than eare," visual images enable the viewer to "conceive of that which many words would not make so plaine unto thee."[14]

This belief in the superior power of the visual image to move and instruct underlies the Renaissance interest in rendering words—i.e., biblical verses, classical quotations, verbal metaphors, well-known proverbs—into pictures. This interest often inspires the creation of striking or unusual images of violence in the visual arts; the attempt to visualize the biblical passage, "If thy right hand make thee to offend, cut it off," (Mark 9:43) for instance, produces a picture of amputation, a knife slicing off a finger, in a Spanish emblem book.[15] It may inform, too, some of the more bizarre acts of violence performed on the Tudor and Stuart stage. The metaphor of the divided body politic is repeatedly used in *Titus Andronicus* to characterize a civilly torn Rome. Rome, we are told (in *Titus Andronicus*), is "headless"; it suffers from a "civil wound"; it is "by uproar sever'd." This metaphor of the severed body is also *visually* realized in the play's recurring acts of dismemberment which culminate in the horrifying scene where the mutilated survivors of the ruined Andronici family gather up the amputated limbs and severed heads of their dead. In a final plea for reuniting Rome, Marcus evokes this stage picture of dismemberment: "O,

---

14. Henry Chettle, *The Tragedy of Hoffman* (1631; rpt. Oxford, 1950), V.iii.2592–2598; *Claudius Tiberius Nero* (1607; rpt. Oxford, 1914), ll. 2786–2792; Thomas Middleton, *Women Beware Women,* ed. J. L. Mulryne (London, 1975), V.i.; Middleton and William Rowley, *The Changeling,* ed. N. W. Bawcutt (London, 1958), V.i. The image of fire symbolizes passion and desire, for example, in Wither's *Emblemes,* bk. 1, no. 34. For a further discussion of the burning treasure see my article, "The Thematic Juxtaposition of the Representational and the Sensational in Middleton's *Women Beware Women,*" *Studies in Iconography,* II (1976), 66–84. Jenner, *The Soules Solace* (London, 1626), sig. A₂.

15. Matthew 5:30; all citations from the Bible in this paper are from the 1560 edition of *The Geneva Bible.* Sebastian de Covarrubias Orozco, *Emblemes Morales* (Madrid, 1610), no. 24.

let me teach you how to knit . . . These broken limbs again into one body." However repulsive, dismemberment in *Titus Andronicus* seems, then, to be a thematic motif; it expresses, in an immediate, physical way the horror and impotency of a divided state. The dismembered body is, in fact, a conventional Renaissance image of the divided state. Similar images of decapitation and dismemberment suggest civil discord in other Renaissance tragedies, including *The Wounds of Civil War* where the "mangled members" of wounded bodies are both literal and metaphoric. Likewise, the picture of a shattered statue—its head, arms, and legs broken from its trunk—symbolizes the idea of political discord in a Renaissance emblem book.[16] This emblem icon and these stage pictures are both pictorial literalizations of the same verbal metaphor: the "body politic."

This technique of giving words (the "soul" of an idea) a physical reality (the "body") might also underlie the grisly banquets of human flesh so often presented in Renaissance tragedies. Although the eating of human flesh may seem to be the crudest form of theatrical sensationalism to a modern audience, Renaissance *pictures* depicting the literal consumption of human bodies frequently function as visual embodiments of well-known quotations, adages, and proverbs: the picture of a man eating a heart, for instance, embodies the saying "envy eats its heart out."[17] We should not therefore too hastily dismiss these bloody banquets as gratuitous.

The "bloudie banket" of "blood . . . Dead men's heads in dishes . . . and Dead men's bones" served to Muly Mohamet in the fourth dumb show of Peele's *Battle of Alcazar,* for example, not only foreshadows the impending slaughter of the Moor on the battlefield, but also visually embodies the metaphoric feast of death, an idea also expressed in the Presenter's words, "And warre and weapons now, and bloud and death /

16. William Shakespeare, *Titus Andronicus,* ed. J. C. Maxwell (London, 1953), I.i. 186, V.iii.87, V.iii.68, III.i.279–287, V.iii.70–72; *The Wounds of Civil War,* II.i.188, IV.ii.152, V.i.7. Nicolas Reusner, *Emblemata* (Frankfort, 1581), bk. 1, no. 13.

17. Bloody banquets occur, for example, in George Peele, *The Battle of Alcazar,* in *The Dramatic Works of George Peele,* ed. John Yoklavich (New Haven, Conn., 1961), dumb show before Act IV; Thomas Drue, *The Bloodie Banquet* (1639; rpt. Oxford, 1961), V.ii.1899–1978; *Titus Andronicus,* V.iii. A woman eating a heart personifies envy in Geoffrey Whitney, *A Choice of Emblemes* (Leiden, 1586), p. 4; a man eating a heart personifies sorrow in Combe, *Theatre of Fine Devices,* p. 8.

Wait on the counsels of this cursed king" (IV. 981–982). Likewise, "*the flesh with a skull all bloody*" which Sertorio forces his unfaithful wife to eat in *The Bloodie Banquet* literalizes—in the most gruesome way possible— the idea of sexual appetite; as the "banquet" is brought in, Sertorio reminds the audience that his wife "did from her own ardour undergoe / Adulteress baseness" with the man whose corpse she must now consume (V.ii. 1899–1900).

Even the appalling moment in *Titus Andronicus* when the mad Titus forces Tamora to eat the bodies of her sons may be more than "indiscriminate wading in blood." Like the "savage meal" of human flesh served as eternal punishment for sin in Dante's *Inferno* (Cantos 32 and 33), this banquet of human flesh served by an avenger to punish a sinful woman may be a literal realization of such biblical warnings of God's vengeance on the sinner as in Jeremiah 19:9: "I will feed them with the flesh of their sonnes and with the flesh of their daughters, and everie one shal eat the flesh of his friend." In all these instances the horror and disgust aroused by the physical consumption of human flesh extends to the larger ideas—ideas of death, sexual appetite, sinfulness—which the banquets suggest. The repugnance the audience feels at the wife's literal consumption of her dead lover's corpse in *The Bloodie Banquet,* for example, intensifies the audience's moral outrage at the sin of adultery; sexual appetite becomes linked with the horrifying image of eating human flesh.

This practice of extending the emotions aroused by physical violence to moral and ethical realms through the agency of an understood icon sometimes results in the yoking of seemingly disparate images and concepts. This yoking together of otherwise disjunctive images and concepts tends to annoy and even confound the modern reader. However objectionable the idea of adultery might seem today, it is hardly comparable to literal cannibalism; however disturbing the idea of a state divided against itself, it is hardly comparable to actual bodily dismemberment. But the Renaissance mind is fond of this very yoking of unlikely elements. By linking such widely disparate things as physical dismemberment and the concept of civil strife, the Renaissance artist can achieve both a radical condensation of meaning and a striking, memorable effect. The interest in expressing *multo in parvo* and the attempt to startle certainly inform the unlikely yoking of a violent image—a living woman bound to a dead man—with a concept—parentally arranged marriages—in a Whitney emblem. Although the difference between the taboo of binding a living person to a human corpse and the social practice of arranged marriages is extreme, Whitney forcefully and economically attacks this social convention by linking it to just such an act of violence. The intense feelings of outrage and repugnance aroused by the image of a woman bound to a corpse are extended to the idea of parentally arranged marriage.[18]

The modern reluctance to see stage violence as symbolic or ethical may be in part a failure to recognize this Renaissance practice of extending the emotions aroused by violent images to moral concepts and the yoking of otherwise disparate images and concepts which sometimes results. The shocking moment at the end of Kyd's *The Spanish Tragedy* when Hieronimo bites out his tongue, for instance, has puzzled a great many critics. The silence Hieronimo espouses before biting out his tongue seems insignificant in the light of this masochistic act, especially since Hieronimo has already revealed the secrets of his conspiracy. But a similar action—cutting out one's own tongue—is seriously presented in a Peacham emblem to celebrate the philosophical virtue of *silentium,* the horrifying act of self-mutilation embodying the contemplative ideal of self-imposed silence.[19] Hieronimo's similar act of self-mutilation, in the context of the final act of *The Spanish Tragedy,* does not, of course, serve to identify the hero with the philosophical man. But the violent act does, I think, function symbolically, expressing a conventional belief in the fundamental opposition of words and action.

Avengers are traditionally associated with silence because, unable to articulate their grievances, they forsake words and turn to violence, letting their actions speak for themselves. "Where words prevail not, violence prevails," Lorenzo remarks early in Kyd's play, and, indeed, language breaks down altogether when Hieronimo uses the polylingual play to carry out his revenge. The same opposition of words and action confronts Hamlet, too, when he must avenge his father's death. A contemplative and articulate man, Hamlet can speak only "wild and whirling words"

18. *A Choice of Emblemes,* p. 99.
19. *The Spanish Tragedy,* IV.iv. 179–194; *Minerva Britanna,* p. 156.

after he learns of his father's murder; he is distressed that he "can say nothing" to express his anger and grief, finds all language unsatisfactory ("Words, words, words"), and eventually decides to substitute violent action for ineffective speech: "For murder, though it have no tongue, will speak / With most miraculous organ." This tradition of the silent avenger is parodied in both Kyd's *Soliman and Perseda* and Marston's *Antonio's Revenge* where comic avengers make the visual gesture of silence while they draw their swords.[20]

When Hieronimo bites out his tongue, then, his violent act symbolizes his—and all revengers'—renunciation of language for the tongueless "speech" of murder, an action so final and irreversible, it expresses what words fail to articulate. Before we dismiss such violent acts as ludicrous or hopelessly sensational, we should consider whether the violent image is purposely yoked to an abstract idea, however disparate image and concept may seem to us.

Such a yoking of disparate image and concept does not occur in every act of stage violence that functions symbolically; a similarity between violent image and the idea it embodies, rather than a dissimilarity, characterizes one of the most common types of stage violence, the eschatological. Like the hellish punishments of the damned in artists' renderings of the after-life, many violent acts depicted on the Renaissance stage suggest, by means of temporal, physical horrors, the idea of eternal, spiritual suffer-ing. In these theatrical visions of the afterlife, as in paintings of hell, the horrible physical violence inflicted on tormented individuals serves as a graphic illustration of the nature and divine punishment of sin; the bodily suffering is a direct product of a misspent life, the grotesque physical torture, a reflection of the spiritual sin. When, for example, characters fall to their deaths through stage trapdoors, already associated in the theater with the mouth of hell, the eschatological image of the sinners' fall into hell is surely evoked, especially when the stage fall is accompanied by such confessions of guilt as, "My own ambition pulls me down to ruin," or " 'tis the property / Of guilty deeds to draw your wisemen downward," or "I

---

20. *Hamlet*, ed. E. Dowden (London, 1911), I.v.133, II.ii. 554, II.ii. 191, II.ii.579–580; Thomas Kyd, *Soliman and Perseda*, in *Works of Thomas Kyd*, ed. Frederick Boas (Oxford, 1901), I.iii.68–69; *Antonio's Revenge*, II.v.38.

now doe find ther's a revenging fate / That doomes bad men to be unfortunate." This practice of using physical falls to convey the idea of damnation was a well-established one on the Renaissance (and the medieval) stage. It is used in many mid-sixteenth-century moralities which end in the defeat of the central character. In these earlier plays the eschatological significance of the fall is made explicit. Moros falls down in *The Longer Thou Livest,* and the character of God's Judgment explains that God "throweth down iniquity"; Worldly Man falls down in *Enough is as Good as a Feast,* and the devil claims him and bears him off to hell.[21] In the later tragedies, however, the physical falls do not present such explicit depictions of men's literal fall to hell, but rather use the physical fall to allude to the idea of divine punishment.

When villains are mercilessly trampled to death by angry characters who remind them of hell, the horrifying act may also suggest the infernal punishment of such sinners, much as artists depict lost souls being trampled underfoot by demons of hell to express the idea of God's vengeance on the wicked. The contexts in which acts of trampling occur in *The Revenger's Tragedy* and *The White Devil* certainly support such an eschatological interpretation. While Hippolito stamps wildly on the sinful Duke in Tourneur's *The Revenger's Tragedy*, Vindice vows "to stick thy [the Duke's] soul with ulcers" so "it shall not rest," and the tormented Duke responds by crying out, "Is there a hell besides this, villains?" In a similar scene in Webster's *The White Devil*, the trampling of Flamineo is also linked with the idea of eternal damnation; as they stamp on him, Zanche tells Flamineo his destination is "most assured damnation," and Vittoria taunts him with the thought that his sins "do run before thee to fetch fire from hell, / To light thee thither."[22] In these scenes, the metaphoric

21. Middleton, *Women Beware Women*, V.ii.140; V.ii.174–175; Drue, *The Bloodie Banquet*, II.ii.680–710; W. Wager, *The Longer Thou Livest and Enough is as Good as a Feast*, ed. R. Mark Benbow (Lincoln, Nebr., 1967), 1. 1861; Wager, *Enough is as Good as a Feast*, ll. 1403–1428.

22. *The Revenger's Tragedy*, ed. F. A. Foakes (Cambridge, Mass., 1966), II.v.155–190; *The White Devil*, ed. John Russell Brown (Cambridge, Mass., 1960), V.vi.119–141; a devil tramples damned souls as they fall into hell's mouth in a painting entitled *Hell*, from the Studio of Hans Memling in Musée des Beaux-Arts, Strasbourg.

trampling of the sinful, alluded to in such biblical passages as Isaiah 10:6 ("I will give him a charge against the people of my wrath . . . to tread them under fete like the myre in the street") and Malachi 4:3 ("And ye shal treade downe the wicked: for they shal be dust under the soles of your fete in the day I shal do this, saith the Lord of hostes") is literalized, made visible, and given a physical reality onstage.

This impulse to realize on the physical stage the promise of divine punishment in eternity is not always recognized or appreciated by modern students of these plays, many of whom have difficulty reconciling literal acts of stage violence with spiritual ideas. Yet, in some of the lesser tragedies, scenes of violence actually seem to be inserted *for the sake of* their spiritual significance, even at the expense of audience credibility. The accidental self-execution by ax of D'Amville in Tourneur's *The Atheist's Tragedy* and the sudden thunderbolt slaying of Malefort in Massinger's *Unnatural Combat* are two such scenes which have annoyed contemporary readers by their apparent crudity, their less than subtle means of doing away with evil men. Nonetheless, these scenes are thematically important—the ax and the lightning bolt are both conventional icons of divine retribution and divine wrath.[23] In both these scenes, narrative plausibility is sacrificed to thematic statement. The violent deaths consequently seem intrusive, mechanical, and unmotivated.

Not all acts of stage violence which replicate traditional punishments of sinners in hell in order to express the idea of damnation are so simplistic, however. In many of Christopher Marlowe's tragedies, for example, characters meet violent deaths which suggest, through such conventional images as the boiling cauldron in *The Jew of Malta* and the dismembered body in *Doctor Faustus*, the final torture of the damned, but such infernal associations do not reduce the suffering individual to a mere moral exemplum. When, at the end of *Edward II*, the devillike figure Lightbourne murders the deposed king by ramming a "redhote" poker into Edward's intestines, this horrible act of violence replicates the conven-

---

23. *The Atheist's Tragedy*, ed. Irving Ribner (Cambridge, Mass., 1964), V.ii.240–266; *The Unnatural Combat*, in *The Plays of Philip Massinger*, ed. W. Gifford (London, 1805), I, V.ii. *Iconologia* uses the ax as an attribute of both punishment and retribution and the lightning bolt as an attribute of the Scourge of God, p. 165.

tional punishment in hell of men guilty of Edward's very sin—sodomy. Nevertheless, Marlowe does not use this familiar icon to make a simple, didactic point about the evils of sodomy, as the painter Taddeo di Bartolo does when he labels his figure of a flaccid, unemotional, and nonparticularized man, spitted from anus to mouth, a sodomite.[24] Instead, Marlowe brings into creative interplay the conventional message of the violent icon and the excruciating pain of the dying man, forcing his audience to confront the difference between the harsh, unrelenting sentence of divine justice and the pitiable suffering of a human being. It is this collision of iconographic tradition and tormented individual that makes Marlowe's question about the meaning and dignity of human life so haunting.

The haunting power of Edward's death scene cannot be adequately explained, however, if stage violence is seen solely as the commercial product of writers trying to please "the coarse taste of the popular audience . . . which demanded . . . shocking scenes of blood and violence." It is, of course, tempting to dismiss stage violence as ludicrous or gratuitous, especially when there is an accumulation of atrocities, a piling on of horrors such as Thomas Pynchon parodies in *The Crying of Lot 49* when revengers in his mock-Renaissance tragedy "proceed to maim, strangle, poison, burn, stomp, blind and otherwise have at" their victim. But to insist that these plays are nothing more than Renaissance versions of Hollywood "horror movies" or, even worse, "Road Runner cartoon[s] in blank verse" as two of Pynchon's less perceptive audience members do, is to view these plays anachronistically, without an appreciation of the nature and function of violence in other forms of Renaissance art. Before accepting T. S. Eliot's modern assumption that "there is a wantonness, an irrelevance" about the violence in Renaissance English tragedy, we need to consider whether such stage violence resembles the conventional icons of violence depicted in such works of the visual arts as Rubens's *Horrors of War* and, like them, expresses thematic ideas in a memorable, forceful,

---

24. Marlowe, *Complete Works*, II, V.v.30; the icon of the sodomite is part of the *Inferno* in the Collegiate Church, San Gimignana, Italy. For a discussion of the iconography of the boiling cauldron see G. K. Hunter, "The Theology of Marlowe's *The Jew of Malta*, JWCI, XXVII (1964), 211–240.

and economical way.[25] Such a consideration can be justified by the fact
that Renaissance men emphasized the *visual* appeal of the stage and even
viewed acting and painting as closely related activities: the ideal actor,
according to the playwright John Webster, for example, "is much affected
to painting, and tis a question whether that make him an excellent Plaier,
or his playing an exquisite painter."[26]

Like the icons of violence in Renaissance painting, many of the acts of
violence committed in these tragedies do, in fact, function as symbolic
icons, embodying abstract ideas through conventional visual images.
These images—ranging from bloody daggers, impaled hearts, and dismembered bodies to banquets of human flesh and demonic physical tortures—create striking stage pictures, rich in associative meaning, which
further the plays' central themes. Even though stage violence may seem to
modern readers to be particularly inhospitable to the expression of theme,
Renaissance critical statements stress the moral function of such violence.
George Puttenham, for one, explains that the violent ends of evil kings are
"painted out in playes and pageants to shew the mutabilitie of fortune, and
the just punishment of God in revenge of a vicious and evill life." John
Reynolds, for another, expresses his hope that "the consideration of these
bloody and mournfull Tragedies, may be their examples, strike astonish-
ment to our thoughts, and amazement to our senses, that the horror and
terrour thereof may hereafter retain and keep us within the lists of charity
toward men, and the bounds of filial and religious obedience towards
God."[27] These comments further support the thesis that Tudor and Stuart
stage violence, however bloody and gruesome, need not be gratuitous (like
Hollywood horror movies) or ludicrous (like Saturday-morning cartoons),
but rather may advance the ethical themes and develop the moral dimension of Renaissance drama.

---

25. These modern comments on Renaissance stage violence are found in Bowers,
Elizabethan Revenge Tragedy, p. 154; Pynchon, *The Crying of Lot 49* (Philadelphia, 1966),
pp. 48, 54, 53; and Eliot, *Essays on Elizabethan Drama* (New York, 1932), p. 26.

26. "An Excellent Actor," in *The Overburian Characters*, ed. W. J. Paylor (Oxford,
1936), p. 77.

27. Puttenham, *The Arte of English Poesie*, ed. Edward Arber (London, 1906), I.xv.49;
Reynolds, "Preface to the Reader," *The Triumph of Gods Revenge Against Murther* (London,
1670), sig. B$_2$.

Fate, Seneca, and Marlowe's Dido, Queen of Carthage

RICHARD A. MARTIN

ITHIN THE MARLOWE CANON, Marlowe's *Dido, Queen of Carthage,* is usually given a quiet corner of its own. Performed in 1587 by the Children of Her Majesty's Chapel, *Dido* reveals a sensitivity not present in Marlowe's popular works of grandiloquence and bombast, and it draws with untypical Marlovian dependence on a widely known literary source. It lacks the dramatic intensity of Marlowe's later works but remains unmistakably his by virtue of its poetry, "some of Marlowe's best," according to G. S. Rousseau. [1]

While praising Marlowe's talents as a poet, what little criticism the play produced has reflected a general dissatisfaction with Marlowe's handling of his material. In contrast to *Tamburlaine* and the later tragedies in which we sense the artist's controlling powers, *Dido* seems thematically undeveloped. Whereas some critics, like David M. Rogers, see in *Dido* a splendid but undeviating Renaissance portrayal of love's incompatibility with the

---

1. G. S. Rousseau, "Marlowe's *Dido* and the Rhetoric of Love," *EM,* XIX (1968), 35–49.

45

pursuit of honor,[2] others, like Douglas Cole, contend that Marlowe presents a "warm and sympathetic Dido"[3] whose passion outweighs the epic values that oppose it. Opinion thus creates ambiguity out of literary tradition.[4] Was Marlowe's attitude toward his subject more heavily influenced by Ovid or Vergil? Does Marlowe share Ovid's sense of Aeneas as a feelingless cad and adventurer, or does his "slavish schoolboy" reliance on Vergil glorify for the spectator the *pietas* that leads Aeneas to reject Dido in favor of his divine mission to found Rome? In short, by which values, epic or lyric, are we to judge the characters, and whom may we hold culpable?

Dido is admittedly not a work of major literary significance. It did not spark the kind of popular imitations that *Tamburlaine* and *Edward II* did, and it does not probe the Renaissance anxieties displayed in *The Jew of Malta* or *Doctor Faustus*. Yet because it is one of the earliest tragedies that was cast as neither a morality play nor an adaptation of Senecan classicism, *Dido* reveals less in contrast to the later works that overshadowed it and more in contrast to the earlier forms it refused to imitate. I should like to argue in the following discussion that in dramatizing the Dido story, Marlowe shaped the conflicting epic and lyric modes associated with the story into a dialectic that was incompatible with the tragic dramaturgy of his time and that demanded a broader understanding of tragic guilt. Indeed, through the conflicting epic and lyric modes Marlowe expresses a notion of tragedy far more Senecan—in its sense of uncertain fate and free will—than British imitators of Seneca thought to allow. To be sure, many pre-Marlovian adaptations of classical tragedy, like Norton and Sackville's *Gorboduc* or Pickering's *Horestes,* have their inconsistencies, but in these

2. See David M. Rogers, "Love and Honor in Marlowe's *Dido, Queen of Carthage,*" *Greyfriar,* VI (1963), 3–7.

3. Douglas Cole, *Suffering and Evil in the Plays of Christopher Marlowe* (1962; rpt. New York, 1972), p. 80 n. For similarly expressed views, see John D. Cutts, "'By Shallow Rivers': A Study of Marlowe's *Dido, Queen of Carthage,*" in *Studies in Medieval, Renaissance and American Literature: A Festschrift in Honor of Troy C. Crenshaw, et al.,* ed. Betsy Feagan Colquitt (Fort Worth, Tex., 1971), pp. 73–94.

4. Don Cameron Allen amasses the classical and medieval sources on both sides of the issue in his essay, "Marlowe's *Dido* and the Tradition," in *Essays on Shakespeare and Elizabethan Drama in Honor of Hardin Craig,* ed. Richard Hosley (Columbia, Mo., 1962), pp. 55–68.

plays we sense artistic clumsiness rather than an expression of thought and
feeling which strains our capacity to judge. Marlowe's *Dido* deserves our
attention not simply because of its poetry, which indeed gives it a unique
vitality, but because it is perhaps the earliest Elizabethan attempt to
abandon moral complacency in tragedy and portray a world that verifies
yet resists absolutes—a world that seeks to excuse in some measure the
very victims it condemns.

The epic and lyric modes through which the Dido story reaches us carry
with them their own distinct judgments of unchaste love and of love's
interference with the prince's duty. Renaissance moralists, of course,
turned more exclusively to Vergil's strict, epic judgments than to Ovid's
morally permissive ones.[5] They found proof in the *Aeneid* that even heroic
love can give slander the opportunity to subvert the prince's obligation to
the state. Thus Vergil's Fama gossips maliciously about Dido and Aeneas:

> nunc hiemem inter se luxu, quam longa, fovere
> regnorum immemores turpique cupidine captos.
> *(Aeneid,* IV. 193–194)[6]

Now they spend the winter, all its length, in wanton ease together, heedless of
their realms and enthralled by shameless passion.

In their infatuation, Dido and Aeneas ignore the affairs of state and lose
their reputations. Books I–IV of the *Aeneid*, Marlowe's source, were in fact
a *locus classicus* for the conventional Renaissance warning against this and
similar dangers of passion. Vergil's apparent fear that Eastern indulgence
would erode the Roman ideal of duty (*pietas*) provided a clearly unambiguous judgment against Didos voluptuousness. Victims of rumor, Dido and
Aeneas both lose their claims to the virtue that is indispensable to a prince,
and it is upon this point that the Renaissance commonplace judgment

---

5. Reuben A. Brower discusses the Elizabethan attitude toward Vergil's narrative in
his *Hero & Saint: Shakespeare and the Graeco-Roman Heroic Tradition* (New York, 1971), pp.
99–114.

6. *Virgil; Eclogues, Georgics, Aeneid 1–6*, trans. H. Rushton Fairclough, Loeb Classical
Library, ed. T. E. Page et al. (1916; rpt. Cambridge, Mass., 1960), I, 408–409. All
translations of Vergil are from the Fairclough Edition.

rested. Thus, from Vergil's point of view, Aeneas's final rejection of Dido in favor of his *pietas*—his divine mission to found Rome—saves him from dishonor, while Dido's uncontrollable passions destroy her honor utterly. Giraldi Cinthio reveals such an interpretation of the Dido story in the introduction to his *Didone* (1541): "Ove Enea reppresenta uno prudentissime [*sic*] heroe, Giove la parte superiore dell' anima humana, Mercurio la discorsive e ragionevole, e Didone la parte inferiore e sensuale."[7]

But Vergil's final judgment of Dido is not itself absolute. Vergil ends Book IV of the *Aeneid* with the narrative insight that Dido's death was neither fated nor deserved:

> . . . nec fato, merita nec morte peribat,
> Sed misera ante diem subitoque accensa furore.
>
> (*Aeneid*, IV. 696–697)

. . . neither in the course of fate did she perish, nor by a death she had earned, but hapless before her day, and fired by sudden madness . . .

Thus we learn that while the gods did not intend Dido's death when they meddled in her *affairs de coeur*, neither did Dido's tacit defiance of the Roman destiny she unwittingly served make her culpable. The reader who would blame Dido's tragedy on divine interference is told he cannot (*nec fato*), and the moralist who would hold Dido fully accountable for her own undoing finds no support in Vergil's special exculpating knowledge (*merita nec*). Whether that knowledge reveals any divine attitude in the epic or is simply Vergilian pathos, it most certainly captures the reader's sense of injustice about Dido's suffering. Indeed, the pathos of Dido's suffering is the basis for the anti-heroic tradition associated with the story. The same four books of the *Aeneid* that provided a stern judgment against passion also became a *point d'appui* for both the Ovidian notion that Aeneas loved falsely and the medieval notion that, as a false lover, Aeneas also played false at Troy, leading the Greek forces to Priam's palace in accordance with

7. In "Marlowe's *Dido* and the Tradition," Don Cameron Allen quotes Cinthio.

a secret treaty he had made with Ulysses and Diomede.[8] According to this anti-heroic view, put forth in the *Heroides* and later developed by Chaucer and other medieval love poets, Dido was a true lover scorned and Aeneas a feelingless cad and adventurer, "wery of his craft withinne a throwe" (*Legend of Dido*, l. 1286). In these terms, "Fate" became nothing more than Aeneas's excuse for treating others dishonorably. By deserting Dido, Aeneas bore entirely the guilt of her death.

In his dramatized *Dido*, with its Olympian gods and lyric expositions, Marlowe captures both the cosmology of Vergil's epic and the passion of Ovid's love poetry. But by confounding the Vergilian and Ovidian modes as he so often does, Marlowe confuses the question of fate and culpability and thus blurs orthodox judgments. At the beginning of Act III, scene iv, when a storm forces Dido and Aeneas to take shelter in a cave, the dramatic dialogue calls our attention to the story's epic framework and reminds us that the lovers are not entirely in control of their own destinies. The scene is from Vergil (*Aeneid*, IV. 160–172), but the mythological reference is more typically Ovidian (*Metamorphoses*, IV. 169–189):

> DIDO
> Tell me, dear love, how found you out this cave?
> AENEAS
> By chance, sweet Queen, as Mars and Venus met.
> DIDO
> Why, that was in a net, where we are loose;
> And yet I am not free—O would I were!
>
> (III.iv.2–5)[9]

---

8. John Lydgate portrays Aeneas as a traitor in his *Troybook* (IV. 6388–6392). Lydgate continues the medieval notion that Antenor and "fals Enee" actually conveyed the Greek forces into Troy. Lydgate and other medieval writers are listed as possible sources for Marlowe by Ethel Seaton in "Marlowe's Light Reading," in *Elizabethan and Jacobean Studies Presented to Frank Percy Wilson*, ed. Herbert Davis and Helen Gardner (Oxford, 1959), pp. 17–33.

9. All quotations from *Dido, Queen of Carthage* are taken from the Revels Edition, ed. H. J. Oliver (London, 1968).

Here the language of freedom and chance, set ironically against the story of
Mars and Venus trapped in Vulcan's net, clashes with the spectator's larger
awareness that both Aeneas and Dido are victims of Venus's divine schem-
ing, and that they are not merely "adulterers surfeited with sin," as Iarbas
later asserts (IV.i.20). Although Iarbas utters dramatically in Act IV,
scene i, the judgment Vergil makes against Dido at the corresponding
point in the narrative (*conjugium vocat, hoc praetexit nomine culpam*), that
judgment loses the rhetorical respectability Vergil gives it in the epic.
Indeed, in Marlowe's cave scene, the language suggests that we may only
judge Aeneas and Dido *after* we judge the divine world that so apparently
victimizes them.

By reminding the spectator of Dido's helplessness at the hands of the
epic gods, and thus implying uncertainty about her share of guilt (*culpam*)
in her own undoing, Marlowe not only violates the tone of Vergil's work,
but also distinguishes *Dido* from the English tragedies of the 1560s and
1570s. Those tragedies, modeled in part on William Baldwin's *A Mirror
for Magistrates*,[10] regarded tragic action as exemplary, a lesson in erring
behavior intended to bring the spectator to some clearly formulated understanding of the failure of characters and their values. Such an attitude
toward tragic action prevailed when early English exposure to Seneca's
works brought native thinking into conflict with the classical notion that
tragic responsibility was not always easily distributed between fate and free
will. Early translators of Seneca resisted choric expressions of the Graeco-
Roman imponderability of suffering's causes. In his preface to *Troades*
(1559), Jasper Heywood apologizes for adding his own moralizing chorus
to clarify a work he otherwise found "imperfite";[11] for Heywood the
dramatic statement was incomplete unless the question of guilt was
answered and those culpable were shown to have been punished justly.
Alexander Neville tenders an apology similar to Heywood's in his preface

10. Willard Farnham discusses the derivation of Elizabethan dramatic judgments from
both public and private theaters in *The Medieval Heritage of Elizabethan Tragedy* (Berkeley,
Calif., 1936), pp. 340–420.

11. *Seneca: His tenne Tragedies*, ed. Thomas Newton (1581; rpt. New York, 1927), II,
3–5.

to *Oedipus* (1563). Neville drops or changes choric comment in *Oedipus* to reestablish a story originally depicted in terms of curses and oracles as the portrayal of a man's "misguyded lyfe" and of "Gods vengeaunce for sinne." [12] Nothing was more contrary to Neville's dramatic intention than the Senecan impulse to excuse Oedipus by blaming the misfortunes of Thebes on the curse on the house of Cadmus:

> Non tu tantis causa periclis,
> non hinc Labdacidas petunt
> fata, sed veteres deum
> irae secuntur. [13]

Not thou the cause of our great perils, not on thy account do the fates assail the house of Labdacus; nay, 'tis the ancient wrath of the gods that follows us.

Seneca's chorus, composed of *dramatis personae* who constantly remind themselves of the injustices of fate, becomes in Neville's hands an authorial interpreter who sees the action more exclusively in terms of individual responsibility. In Neville's version of the lines quoted above, the chorus offers Oedipus's plight as an example of the misfortunes that men of high rank must endure, and Oedipus himself as a man possibly guilty of the charges against him:

> See, See, the myserable State, of Princes carefull lyfe.
> What raging storms? What bloudy broyles? What toyle?
> What endlesse stryfe
> Doe they endure? (O God) what plagues? what griefe do
> they sustayne? . . .
>
> Let Oedipus example bee of this unto you all,
> A Mirrour meete, A Patern playne, of Princes careful thrall,
> . . . subject to such a Cryme
> Whereat my tongue amased stayes. [14]

---

12. *Ibid.*, I, 189–191.

13. *Oedipus*, ll. 709–712, in *Seneca's Tragedies*, trans. Frank Justus Miller, Loeb Classical Library Series, ed. T. E. Page et al. (1917; rpt. Cambridge, Mass., 1968), I, 488–489.

14. See *Seneca: His tenne Tragedies*, I, 215–216.

In Neville, no appeal to our sense of a malignant universe extenuates the circumstances of Oedipus's "Cryme." If fortune deals more harshly with princes than with beggars, it is only by increasing in magnitude the sin they are capable of committing.

Neville's sense of the Senecan chorus as authorial interpreter rather than as *dramatis personae* was shared by the Inns of Court playwrights who suited their original efforts to the tastes created by Senecan themes. Thus, as British Senecanism moved into the theater, the Inns of Court playwrights merged classical form with the kind of explicit judgments native tradition seemed to demand.

Yet the playwrights did not completely lose perspective of their heroes as victims; they were simply unable to syncretize the classical notion of fate with the Christian universe they knew and portrayed. Senecan fatalism influenced all four of the extant "mirror" tragedies produced in the Inns of Court, but in all four cases the playwrights exploited the Senecan convention of the curse without the Senecan habit of using it to mitigate judgment against the central character. While the chorus at the end of Act III of *Gorboduc* recalls that an ancient curse still applies to the legendary British offspring of Troy, it regards the king's behavior as no less damnable. A far more typical use of fate, however, appears in a companion "mirror" tragedy, *Gismond of Salerne* (1568). In *Gismond,* playwright Robert Wilmot and his collaborators attempt to demonstrate, as the numerous choric comments make clear, the ruinous qualities of unchaste love.[15] In this case, Gismond, forbidden by her father to remarry after her husband's death, takes a lover, Guishard, stains her reputation, and is murdered by her vengeful father. But the measure of blame the chorus levels against Gismond conflicts with spectator acceptance of Cupid as presenter of the play, a presenter who offers Gismond's fall as an example of love's godlike destructive power. Cupid promises to "inflame the fair Gismond" so that through love she will "feel much woe." Then, asserts Cupid, skeptics will have to admit to his omnipotence:

---

15. See *Early English Classical Tragedies,* ed. John W. Cunliffe (Oxford, 1912), pp. 314–326. Cunliffe assigns each of the five acts of *Gismond* to "Rod. Staf.," Henry Noel, "G. Al.," Christopher Hatton, and "R. W[ilmot]."

> We must relent and yeld; for now we knowe,
> Loue rules the world, Loue onely is the Lorde. [16]

Thus, the prologue character asks the spectator to believe that the dramatic world is subject to the will of Cupid, an agent of fate. But the chorus
nevertheless insists on its own authority and on the free but infected will of
Christian man. The chorus of Act III argues that while Cupid is so
powerful that even the gods cannot resist him, he nevertheless "assaultes
not but the idle hart," and mortals may overcome him simply by resisting
"his first assaulte." Fate, we are told, is only powerful in pre-Christian
terms and has no control over a virtuous Christian will:

> Furies must aid, when men will cease to know
> their Goddes: and Hell shall send reuēging paine
> to those, whome Shame frō sinne can not restraine. [17]

It may of course be argued that Wilmot's judgment against love is
merely the kind of cant typical of his age, and that therefore the chorus
does not influence the spectator's attitude toward the dramatic world.
Certainly Wilmot's chorus assesses the action of *Gismond* no more accurately than it assesses the action of Shakespeare's *Antony and Cleopatra*.
Wilmot shows the lovers, Gismond and Guishard, as noble and virtuous
creatures, aware of the dangers of passion and acting less in defiance of
choric morality than of Tancred's motiveless and apparently neurotic
injunction against Gismond's remarriage. But the authority we grant to
the chorus by convention outweighs any moral uncertainties the dramatic
action seeks to express. Although Tancred's behavior would seem to make
him culpable to some degree (and indeed does so in Wilmot's source, the
Decameron), [18] the chorus of Act II supports his position and consistently
places on Gismond the full responsibility for her own tragedy. *Gismond*,
like the other "mirror" plays, considers fate only to leave it incidental and
at odds with Christian morality. As much as the dramatic world seemingly
confounds any simplified judgment by raising the issue of fate, it is still a

16. *Ibid.*, p. 169.
17. *Ibid.*, p. 191.
18. Specifically in Fiammetta's tale; fourth day, first tale.

world of absolutes—of clear, unambiguous choices and clear, unambiguous failure.

Marlowe's dramatic intention in *Dido* is obscured partly because of conflicting traditions behind the Dido story, but partly because of the absence of a clear moral frame. Unlike "mirror" tragedies, *Dido* does not make any explicit judgments through the authoritative voice of a chorus. In dramatizing the Dido story, Marlowe seems to have rejected completely both the British Senecan reliance on choric interpretation of action and the popular theater's use of Inductions, prologues, and personified virtues and vices, all, like the chorus, revealing to the spectator the moral character of the action. In fact the dramatic world of *Dido*, with its pastoral setting and its *dei ex machinae*, does not resemble so much the world of other contemporary Elizabethan tragedies as the world of John Lyly's court comedies. There, in the absence of authorial interpretation, characters continually refine their responses to a complex reality, while gods and goddesses resolve on an ideal level what mortals find hopelessly incompatible in human terms. In short, our assumptions about dramatic judgments in Elizabethan tragedy may not apply at all to Marlowe's *Dido*, a play cast not in the form of prevailing modes of tragedy, with their fixed moral boundaries, but in the manner of exploratory comedy, where paradox destroys absolutism.

While the moral boundaries of Marlowe's *Dido* appear movable in the absence of a chorus, traditional values nevertheless speak the loudest. The audience of *Dido* is everywhere aware of the story's Vergilian origins and attitudes. The notion that love is subversive to honor forms a basic topos, expressed in Aeneas's discomfort at the "courtly ease" of Carthage and again in Achates' warning against love:

> This is no life for men-at-arms to live,
> Where dalliance doth consume a soldier's strength,
> And wanton motions of alluring eyes
> Effeminate our minds inur'd to war.
>
> (IV.iii.33–36)

The warning summarizes the epic position against sensual indulgence, and the action indeed adheres to the Renaissance idea of Vergil's point of view, revealing Aeneas's world as one of men "inur'd to warre," and depicting

Dido's world as one of sumptuousness and repose. In an even more emphatic use of his source, Marlowe calls our attention directly to epic tradition
in Aeneas's recount of the Sack of Troy (II.i., 121–288), an expository
monologue that translates in part directly from Books II and III of the
Aeneid. The story of the fall of Troy creates a miniature epic within the
dramatic world and, through narration, gives heroic values a shape and
substance they otherwise do not find in physical action. Moreover, the
narrative is an exercise in blank-verse style, repeating the earlier attempt
by Henry Howard, Earl of Surrey, to render into English the very same
passage from Vergil. Surrey's invention of blank verse to capture the sound
and rhythm of Roman epic poetry associates the meter's tradition at its
inception with Aeneas's narrative, and Marlowe, by relying on 180 lines of
solid narration to "dramatize" heroic action, displays his greater talents in
vividly recreating the grandeur of epic verse. Where Surrey's lines are loose
and uneven, Marlowe's are compressed and expressive. A moment in time
contains the making of legend as Neoptolemus leaps from the Trojan
horse:

> Then he unlock'd the horse, and suddenly
> From out his entrails Neoptolemus,
> Setting his spear upon the ground, leapt forth,
> And after him a thousand Grecians more,
> In whose stern faces shin'd the quenchless fire,
> That after burnt the pride of Asia.
>
> (II.i. 182–187)

Marlowe's virtuoso retelling of Vergil establishes the heroic mode as a
verbal power within the play. Through this mode the traditional judgments speak, investing themselves with the authority of the epic myth of
immutable destiny that everywhere determines Dido's world. Achates' warning against the passions is thus endorsed by the play's stylistic self-aware-
ness; the heroic poetry in Aeneas's monologue calls our attention to the
epic tradition behind Dido's tragedy, a tradition that gives that tragedy its
values and its determinants.

   More than style, of course, the presence of the gods as *dramatis personae*
emphasizes for the spectator the world of Roman destiny that Dido and
Aeneas inhabit. Here Marlowe comes his closest to providing the play

with a moral framework, some explicit indication that fate rather than individual will is the mover of human events and tragedy. And nothing could be more explicit than Jupiter's offer in Act I, scene I, to abrogate to Ganymede the power to "Control proud fate, and cut the thread of time," in exchange for his affection. The spectator is reminded by this marvelous opening scene that the Jupiter-Ganymede affair was the *casus belli* of the Trojan War and, therefore, that Jupiter's love of Ganymede contains the nucleus of Aeneas's wandering and of Dido's misery. Thus, to the extent that fate in the shape of divine interference makes its intentions known in the play, the spectator may feel certain that Achates' judgment works in accord with the will of the gods, hastening Aeneas's departure from Carthage in search of the city destined to rule the world.

But the play's moral boundaries appear somewhat larger than Achates understands them to be, for his judgment against love also clashes with an Olympian precedent in the opening scene in which Jupiter's interests lie not with epic destiny but with "wanton motions" and "dalliance." Indeed, Marlowe's rhetorical movements in the opening scene establish literary decorum only to violate it. Although the scene depicts the Venus-Jupiter encounter that occurs in Vergil, at I.223–404, it does not introduce the epic world of the play according to the Vergilian pattern. Ganymede's presence alters the significance of the encounter, and Jupiter's role as prime mover and controller of destiny is supplanted by his Ovidian role as philanderer:

> From Juno's bird I'll pluck her spotted pride,
> To make thee fans wherewith to cool thy face;
> And Venus' Swans shall shed their silver down,
> To sweeten out the slumbers of thy bed.
>
> (I.i.34–37)

This is not Vergil's Jupiter but Ovid's, and the language of persuasion in the passage, later to become more quotable in Marlowe's love lyric, "The Passionate Shepherd to His Love," finds its source in the *Metamorphoses*, in Polyphemus's pleas to Galatea.[19] Jupiter ironically establishes the Ovidian

---

19. Although the Galathea-Polyphemus myth is the *locus* for poetry of this type, the specific reference in this passage is to Book II of the *Metamorphoses*, where Ovid describes Saturnia's bird as a peacock:

mode as its own verbal power within the play, a power of sensual indulgence. When Dido explores her feelings for Aeneas, we detect the same
dominating power of the senses:

> I'll make me bracelets of his golden hair;
> His glistering eyes shall be my looking-glass,
> His lips an altar, where I'll offer up
> As many kisses as the sea hath sands.
>
> (III.i.84–87)

The Ovidian sensuality Dido expresses occupies a conflicting position in
Marlowe's epic world. As Achates suggests, that sensuality threatens
Roman destiny by opposing the prospect of conquest with the prospect of
love and the pleasures of abundance; but the play also emphasizes that
Roman destiny began with "wanton motions," with Jupiter's love of
Ganymede. Thus, as dramatically presented, the pleasures of the senses
precede any cosmic determinism in the epic world of the play, and the
implicit judgment that the Ovidian sensuality of the *Heroides* levels
against epic heroes, charging them with false love and dishonor, gains a
value it does not have in Vergil. If Dido misreads her universe by believing
that individual will, not fate, is behind Aeneas's actions, her accusations
nevertheless capture as part of the play's essence the rhetorical force of
Ovidian anti-heroism:

> Wherein have I offended Jupiter
> That he should take Aeneas from mine arms?
> O no, the Gods weigh not what lovers do:
> It is Aeneas calls Aeneas hence.
>
> (V.i.129–132)

> habili Saturnia curru
> ingreditur liquidum pavonibus aethera pictis. . . .
>
> (ll. 531–532)

The most frequently cited work on Marlowe's use of Ovid is Boleslaus Knutowski's *Das
Dido-Drama von Marlowe und Nash* (Breslau, 1905). Knutowski's source work is in his last
chapter, pp. 61–73.

Here Dido eloquently raises the question of injustice in gods and men. Jupiter, she avers, would not move against a sincere and innocent passion; only man could harbor such treachery. This is the judgment we associate with Ovid's *Heroides,* a judgment heard through the inconsolable cry of the forsaken maiden and the complaint to a faithless lover. Thus, Ovid's Dido to Aeneas:

> quo fugis? obstat hiemps. hiemis mihi gratia prosit!
> adspice, ut eversas concitet Eurus aquas!
> quod tibi malueram, sine me debere procellis;
> iustior est animo ventus et unda tuo.[20]

Whither are you flying? The tempest rises to stay you. Let the tempest be my grace! Look you, how Eurus tosses the rolling waters! What I had preferred to owe to you, let me owe to the stormy blasts; wind and wave are juster than your heart.

In Marlowe, Vergil's charges against Dido—her lust and faithlessness to the memory of Sychaeus—do not gain the rhetorical impact that Ovid's charges against Aeneas gain. Moreover, Marlowe's Dido draws our sympathies with the Ovidian spirit of her suffering. If the senses are to have any value in the play, and the Jupiter-Ganymede scene implies they must, then we cannot judge honor solely in terms of epic norms, but must hold Aeneas culpable to some degree for failing to act upon his emotions. Within the epic context of the play, with its emphasis on human subservience to the will of the gods, Marlowe does not completely deny the possibility that guilt may exist independently of divine law, that those who further the cause of destiny may nevertheless be judged and censured. In these terms, the price of Aeneas's honor is not an "effeminating" passion that would controvert destiny, but that part of his humanity for which the spectator may hold him to account.

The Aeneas of epic tradition is, of course, a creature of destiny, for he exists in Vergil only to fulfill the designs of the gods, not to exercise free will. And indeed nowhere does Marlowe indicate that his play will com-

---

20. *Heroides,* VII. 41–44, in *Ovid: Heroides and Amores,* trans. Grant Showerman, Leob Classical Library, ed. T. E. Page et al. (1914; rpt. New York, 1931), pp. 86–87.

pletely overturn its Vergilian source to demonstrate the triumphs and failures of the will. Nevertheless, the Aeneas Marlowe does portray is not incontrovertibly Vergil's, and the demand to subordinate the self to divine prophecy clashes in Marlowe's play with an un-Vergilian impulse toward emotional frankness. The heroic achievement portrayed in Aeneas's recount of the Sack of Troy in Act II, scene i, lines 121 through 288, is pursued at the expense of humanity, and the narrative sequence reveals an Aeneas who reacts with uncharacteristic sensitivity to his own imaginative recreation of the horrors of war. Dido prompts the retelling by raising the question of the medieval notion of Antenor's treachery, a notion in which honor is blurred by betrayal. Aeneas clarifies the concept of honor by insisting on the classical version of the story and, in his "invocation," prepares his audience for tales of bloodshed:

> Then speak, Aeneas, with Achilles' tongue,
> And, Dido, and you Carthaginian peers,
> Hear me, but yet with Myrmidons' harsh ears,
> Daily inur'd to broils and massacres,
> Lest you be mov'd too much with my sad tale.
> (II.i.121–125)

Aeneas's desire to speak through Achilles is explained in his reference to the Myrmidons, Achilles' followers. The violence and brutality of his story are such that they require a speaker as insensitive to bloodshed as his listeners. Achilles, who slew Hector and bore Troy an unrelenting malice, qualifies as such a speaker, whereas Aeneas, who breaks his narration off twice under the strain of emotion, does not. Indeed, the audience, listening with Dido's ears, begins to share Dido's feelings of shock and revulsion at the world of epic conquest. The promise of heroic achievement merely gives way to sadistic absurdity. The image of Hecuba "swung . . . howling in the empty air" is emblematic of a universe where heroes are mindless savages and women mere victims of their savagery.

Dido's reaction to the brutality of conquest reveals a sensitivity compatible with her role as an Ovidian lover. But Aeneas's emotional responses to whatever reminds him of Troy, be it Priam's statue (II.i.15–36) or his own recount of the sack, alter his stature as an epic hero. Aeneas assumes a very passive role in the play, and whether heeding the will of the gods or, like Hamlet's actor, moved by the pathos of his own "conceit," he proves susceptible to the pressures of poetic persuasion. He is particularly suscep- tible to the language of Ovidian sensuality, a language through which the play perpetually seeks to escape from the epic mode, and he weighs the claims of love equally against those of the Fates. The renewed sense of destiny with which Aeneas prematurely orders the Trojan fleet launched in search of Rome (IV.iii.16–30) immediately gives way to thoughts of sensual indulgence and the poetically paradoxical assumption that Dido and Aeneas may fulfill Roman destiny together:

> Aboard, aboard, since Fates do bid aboard,
> And slice the sea with sable-colour'd ships,
> On whom the nimble winds may all day wait
> And follow them, as footmen, through the deep!
> Yet Dido casts her eyes, like anchors, out,
> To stay my fleet from loosing forth the bay.
> "Come back, come back!" I hear her cry afar,
> "And let me link thy body to my lips,
> That, tied together by the striving tongues,
> We may as one sail into Italy."
>
> (IV.iii.21–30)

As the heroic mode exerts its verbal power, the dramatic world swells with epic excitement. But for Aeneas, whose emotions place him beyond the epic confines of his universe, the imperatives of destiny are not heard alone, and the lyric mode acknowledges once again the claims of love. If Giraldi Cinthio holds Dido's sensuality to be inferior to man's god- inspired parts, Marlowe asks us in passages like this to give that sensuality equal value. The beliefs implicit in either mode, epic or lyric, simultan- eously prevail. While Achates' judgment against passion upholds the heroic context of the play, it is insufficient to deny the nobility of the senses; honor attained through heroic achievement does not displace honor lost in love.

But if the pursuit of love is no less noble than the pursuit of honor, it is still not the means by which man exercises his individual freedom. There is no freedom from fate in abandoning oneself to the senses. Marlowe establishes this notion early in the opening scene where, with the appear- ance of Venus, he reasserts the literary decorum he violated with the

Jupiter-Ganymede affair. Venus gives the play its Vergilian context by denying Jupiter's lyricism and, ironically, her own attributes as the goddess of love. Whereas Vergil's passive Venus pleads with a Jupiter already concerned with the shape of human affairs (I.288 ff.), Marlowe's Venus assumes a more reproachful tone, interrupting Jupiter's dalliance in order to bring his attention to the pressing matter of Aeneas's fate. Angry and resentful at Juno's attempts to destroy Aeneas, Venus is herself a picture of epic wrath. Her language draws on epic rhetoric as she describes Aeneas's voyage as another fall of Troy:

> Poor Troy must now be sack'd upon the sea,
> And Neptune's waves be envious men of war;
> Epeus' horse, to Aetna's hill transform'd,
> Prepared stands to wrack their wooden walls,
> And Aeolus, like Agamemnon, sounds
> The surges, his fierce soldiers, to the spoil.
>
> (I.i.64–69)

In Venus's epic introduction to the action, Jupiter's love of Ganymede loses its pastoral value and becomes an indulgent retreat from an urgent call to the active world. The language of the opening scene thus refuses to affirm the values of passion and sensuality it initiates. The heroic mode awakens the spectator both to the Vergilian context of the action and to a subversiveness inherent in Ovidian sentiments.

Just as Jupiter's lyricism dissolves under the pressures of Venus's epic rhetoric, so does Aeneas's assertion of free will lose its value against the claims of destiny. Marlowe once again violates the Vergilian context of his play by allowing Aeneas to act (temporarily) against the course of fate. Vergil's Aeneas, when reproached by Dido for his planned departure from Carthage, argues that destiny and not free will leads him to Italy (IV.331–361) and, without waiting longer, departs. Marlowe's Aeneas, after making several excuses, again finds value in sensuality and remains in Carthage. In his choice of love, however, Aeneas reveals the subversiveness of the senses to the active world. He envisions in the new Carthage not a fortress of warriors and kings but a Lotus-eaters' paradise, heavy with the lethargy of pleasure:

> The sun from Egypt shall rich odours bring
> Wherewith his burning beams, like labouring bees
> That load their thighs with Hybla's honey's spoils,
> Shall here unburden their exhaled sweets
> And plant our pleasant suburbs with her fumes.
>
> (V.i. 11–15)

This hypnotic lyricism, which earlier lulled Ascanius to sleep in violation of his Vergilian character, promises to work the same transformation on Aeneas. Aeneas's lyricism is of course short-lived, for Mercury interrupts his vision of the new Carthage to remind him of divine prophesy. But for several lines the action strays from its epic source. Marlowe's Aeneas, never quite the heroic equal of Vergil's, finally exercises a freedom of choice, and the world that seems determined by fate threatens to be remade by an overmastering rhetorical power. With Mercury's appearance, as with Venus's in the first scene, the play reestablishes its epic norm. The gods move against passion, and, in spite of its rhetorical departures into the language of love, the dramatic world insists on the heroic tradition of its Vergilian source. Within that tradition, human endeavor is subject to the will of the gods and not to the will of man.

Marlowe's emphasis on fate rather than individual willfulness as the source of human unhappiness in *Dido* presents a radical change from the attitudes expressed in the Inns of Court tragedies. In a world where tragic heroes and heroines are victims of the gods, Dido's defiance of divine will cannot be judged in the same terms as Gismond's deviation from choric morality. Absolute values diminish in Marlowe's play, and in the end the spectator is asked to weigh the pursuit of honor against the guilt of forsworn love. Aeneas manifests this guilt as he reluctantly resumes the heroic role assigned him. His departure from Carthage, related by Anna, is reminiscent of Ulysses sailing by the Island of the Sirens, torn between desire and fear to listen:

> Then gan he wag his hand, which, yet held up,
> Made me suppose he would have heard me speak;
> Then gan they drive into the ocean,
> Which when I view'd, I cried, "Aeneas, stay;
> Dido, fair Dido wills Aeneas stay!" . . .

They gan to move him to redress my ruth,
And stay a while to hear what I could say;
But he, clapp'd under hatches, sail'd away.

(V.i.229–240)

This is not Chaucer's Aeneas, "wery of his craft withinne a throwe," nor is it Vergil's, who acts decisively, like a hero, *vaginaque eript ensem | fulmineum strictoque ferit retinaculo ferro* (IV.579–580). The spectator's final view of Aeneas, through Anna, is one of a man still tormented by his place in the heroic universe and by the suffering he, as a hero, inflicts upon Dido. In fulfilling the epic expectations of his character, Marlowe's Aeneas remains painfully aware of the culpability of his behavior. Having transgressed "against all laws of love" (IV.iii.48), he hides his emotions below board where Dido cannot exercise the power of her words or her will. Dido, however, stands true to her Ovidian nature and, in her suffering, turns from lyricism to bacchic frenzy:

I'll frame me wings of wax like Icarus,
And o'er his ships will soar unto the sun
That they may melt and I fall in his arms;
Or else I'll make a prayer unto the waves
That I may swim to him, like Triton's niece;
O Anna, fetch Arion's harp,
That I may tice a dolphin to the shore
And ride upon his back unto my love!

(V.i.243–250)

The passionate intensity of the play's last scene, with its triple suicide, is as much a descent into Senecan sensationalism as a demonstration of the unreadability of the moral world. If a meddling universe inspires Dido's passion, an indifferent universe presides over her self-destruction; the gods do not acknowledge Dido's suffering and death, and they do not indicate whether her end is fated or deserved. Indeed, in Anna and Iarbas's suicides, another noticeable departure from Vergil, Marlowe suggests that passion carries its own destructive power, independent of the concerns of the gods. Anna and Iarbas, who are more victims of their own willfulness than of any divine interference, mirror Dido's *accensa furore* in their hurried suicides and demonstrate the very dangers of passion that the heroic world rightly seeks to avoid. The catastrophe thus leaves the measure of Dido's guilt uncertain. As both a victim of the gods and a victim of her own irrational sensuality, Dido is neither judged by the divine world that manipulates her nor vindicated by the lyricism through which she seeks her freedom.

Yet while Marlowe offers no explicit judgment of Dido's behavior, the play does elicit our forgiveness for those who suffer disproportionately to their faults. If love is subversive to the pursuit of honor, honor attained at the expense of love is, in light of Dido's emotional collapse, indeed questionable. Neither god nor man ought to treat human affections inconsequentially, and as the audience is let to grow critical of the gods, so Achates' judgment against love is let to fail by nature of its own inflexibility. That judgment cannot move beyond the heroic context of the play, while spectator sympathy for Dido clearly does. Although Dido's last words are ones of defiance, perhaps the only form of epic dignity left her, her end retains the spirit of Ovidianism that redeemed her character throughout the Middle Ages. Even Anna and Iarbas elicit a greater sense of sorrow than reproach in their self-destruction. Only Aeneas, whose commitment to *pietas* receives divine sanction, bears the guilt of honor.

In a sense, Marlowe rediscovered classical tragedy in *Dido*. The impulse by Neville and other early translators of Seneca to ignore the workings of fate and assign the origins of tragedy to individual responsibility is replaced in *Dido* by a dramatic scrutiny of the forces of destiny. Marlowe's world moves closer to Seneca's, wherein the question of culpability is complicated by assumptions about man's relationship to his universe and about the limitations of the will. To be sure, Marlowe does not simply replace a sixteenth-century sense of retributive justice with an epic sense of divine purpose. In *Dido*, Marlowe captured for English tragedy a vision of man as a victim, forced to endure the injustices of the gods and simultaneously trapped by his own self-recriminations.[21]

21. In his *Life of Sidney* (ca. 1610–1612) Fulke Greville distinguishes classical tragedy from the tragedy of his own day by noting that the works of the ancients tended to stir "murmur against Divine Providence." See L. G. Salingar, "Tourneur and the Tragedy of Revenge," in *The Pelican Guide to English Literature: The Age of Shakespeare*, ed. Boris Ford (1955; rpt. Baltimore, Md., 1970), pp. 334–354.

The uniqueness of Marlowe's vision derives largely from the relative uniqueness of his dramatic expression, a uniqueness manifested by his avoidance of an explicit moral judgment. Whereas pre-Marlovian dramatists followed native morality traditions and transformed the Senecan chorus into an extradramatic device capable of making authorial value judgments explicit, Marlowe, following Seneca, let the voices of destiny speak as *dramatis personae,* characters who invest the pursuit of honor with divine purpose but whose values do not "frame" the dramatic world and do not dictate absolute judgments. Thus in *Dido* the commonplace notion that love is subversive to honor does not rhetorically outweigh our experience of the Ovidian view that dishonor in love destroys something more valuable than honor through fame. In the absence of authorial comment on action, the dramatic experience generates its own beliefs, creating an argument that refines our judgments without simplifying them.

Dido is worth exploring critically because, in spite of its imperfections, it reaches a maturity of expression that pre-Marlovian tragedy lacks. Certainly John Pickering's attempt in his *History of Horestes* (1567) to understand the tragic universe in terms similar to Marlowe's represents an early failure of English classicism. Writing still in the old "morality" tradition, Pickering moralizes in his play on sure retribution for unrighteousness, but vindicates Horestes (Orestes) while condemning his murder of Clytemnestra and Egistus. Horestes never shows any remorse for his matricide and indeed justifies himself by claiming that the gods commanded the murder, a rationale Pickering lets stand, ignoring its incompatibility with his moral frame. *Horestes* thus absorbs a classical tension between fate and free will without ever reconciling it with its explicit Elizabethan idea of moral failure. And it is in contrast to defective playwriting like this that Marlowe's *Dido* reveals the dramaturgical sophistication two decades had wrought. Indeed, what Marlowe explores superficially in *Dido* crystallizes in his later plays into a more visionary question: to what extent may the superior will and imagination control reality and transcend the suffering reality imposes? Marlowe's answers varied broadly. In *Tamburlaine, Part I*, the will and imagination triumph over tragedy; in *Edward II*, the will fails utterly; and in *Doctor Faustus*, the Christian imagination turns cruelly upon the mind that oversteps its own religious confines.

It is unlikely that audiences will ever regain any interest in *Dido* as a performable entertainment. The dramatic clumsiness of the *dei ex machinae,* the wordiness of dialogue, the often too strict conformity to Vergil's Latin speeches, all detract from what is distinctly original about Marlowe's treatment of the Dido story. In this respect, John Lyly's influence on Marlowe was probably as deleterious to the conception of *Dido* as it was helpful. The Cupid-Ascanius switch, reminiscent of similar ploys in Lylian comedy, does create an emblem of self-confusion as Dido draws closer to her breast the passions that afflict it, yet the imaginative god-man disguise only serves to distract us from the reality of Dido's suffering. Today, as much as in Marlowe's day, *Dido, Queen of Carthage* remains a "bookish" play, better read than viewed. As a literary artifact, it displays the working of an unusual talent who transformed Vergil's conflict between love and honor into an original experience of passion, destiny, and cosmic betrayal.

"The Power of Speech / To Stir Men's Blood": The Language of Tragedy in Shakespeare's Julius Caesar

GAYLE GREENE

> Eloquence hath chiefly flourished in Rome when the common-wealths affaires have been in worst estate, and that the devouring Tempest of civill broyles, and intestine warres did most agitate and turmoile them.
>
> Montaigne, "Of the Vanitie of Words"

WHEN ANTONY CONCLUDES his funeral oration by modestly disclaiming the powers of rhetoric he has so abundantly displayed—

> I am no orator, as Brutus is; . . .
> But (as you know me all) a plain blunt man . . .
> . . . .
> For I have neither wit, nor words, nor worth,
> . . . nor the power of speech
> To stir men's blood; I only speak right on.[1]

---

1. *Julius Caesar*, III.ii.219–225. All textual references are to *The Arden Shakespeare*, ed. T. S. Dorsch (London, 1955).

—he draws attention to the very arts of oratory which have enabled him to seize triumphant control of his world. Indeed, his rhetorical tour de force turns the course not only of the action of the play, but of the tide of times. Effecting the shift of power from Brutus to Antony, it marks the end of the Republic and the beginning of events which will issue in the Empire; and, as his words "inflame" (l. 146) his audience, their "fire" (l. 117) becomes more than metaphorical, to spark the actual blaze that burns Rome. Nor is the oration an isolated instance: it is but one of a series of persuasion scenes on which the play as a whole is structured, wherein language is used to "work," "fashion," "move," "fire," its listeners. Earlier in this scene, Brutus persuaded the crowd to accept a version of the assassination, as, earlier in the play, Cassius persuaded Brutus—his words, too, "struck . . . fire" (I.ii.175–176); and, in soliloquy, Brutus "fashion[ed]" (II.i.30) an argument to persuade himself.[2]

In the Rome of *Julius Caesar*, language is power and characters rise or fall on the basis of their ability to wield words. Their awareness of the importance of language is indicated by terms they associate with it. Words are associated with weapons—"speak, and strike" (II.i.56)—and, at various times, with friendship, love, and life itself.[3] Conversely, powerlessness and incapacitation are suggested by terms such as "silence," "speechless," and "tongue-tied."[4] These Romans identify with their

2. Throughout, these words are associated with persuasion. First, Marullus "moves" (I.i.61) the plebs; then Cassius "works" (I.ii.161, 306) on Brutus, "humors" (l. 312) him; next, Brutus promises to "fashion" (II.i.220) Caius Ligarius, and Decius to "work" on Caesar, to "give his humor the true bent" (ll. 209–210). After the assassination, first Brutus, then Antony, "work" on (III.ii.262) and "move" (l. 231) the crowd. The words "work" and "move" are used by Henry Peacham to describe the effect of language on the passions. *The Garden of Eloquence* (London, 1577), p. 13; quoted in Miriam Joseph, *Shakespeare's Use of the Arts of Language* (New York, 1947), p. 328.

3. See also II.i.47, III.i.76, V.i.27–30. Cassius describes friendship in terms of the proper use of words (I.ii.70–77); Portia describes love in terms of vows (II.i.272–273); and Brutus's dying lines suggest that his life has been a tale told by himself (V.v.39–40).

4. The citizens slink off "tongue-tied" (I.i.62) after the rebukes of the tribunes; Caesar falls down "speechless" (I.ii.250); Marullus and Flavius are "put to silence" (I.ii.286). We hear, also, of Caesar's concern to act in accord with what "our elders say" (I.ii.7) and of "that tongue of his that bade the Romans / Mark him, and write his speeches in their books" (I.ii.124–125). Antony describes his death: "But yesterday the word of Caesar might / Have stood against the world" (III.ii.120–121).

names and reiterate their own and one another's names, "sound[ing]" them almost as though "conjur[ing] with 'em" (I.ii.143, 144).[5] Even the most private scenes, between husband and wife, are characterized by a declamatory style and stance: Portia calls on "vows" (II.i.272) and her Roman virtues to persuade Brutus to tell her what troubles him; Calphurnia, alone with Caesar, argues to prevent him from going to the Capitol.

The markedly rhetorical style has often been noted, and Dr. Johnson's opinion that "Shakespeare's adherence to . . . Roman manners [was] cold and unaffecting" has been echoed by critics such as Mark Van Doren, who characterizes the play as "more rhetoric than poetry" and its characters as "more orators than men."[6] But rhetoric in this play is a theme as well as a style: accorded prominence by structure and imagery, it is integral to characterization, culture, and to the central political and epistemological concerns. In Shakespeare's depiction of Rome as a society of skilled speakers whose rhetorical expertise masks moral and political truth is implied a criticism of rhetoric and of language itself which is central to the play's tragic vision.[7]

I

Problems of language are related—historically and philosophically—to problems of knowledge. Thus an understanding of language in *Julius*

5. R. A. Foakes notes that Caesar's name occurs 211 times (Caesar even once refers to himself as a "name" [I.ii.196]), Brutus's 130, Antony's 68, and Cassius's 39. "An Approach to *Julius Caesar*," *ShQ*, V (1954), 266. See also Madeleine Doran, "Proper Names in *Julius Caesar*," in *Shakespeare's Dramatic Language* (Madison, Wis., 1976), pp. 120–153.

6. *Samuel Johnson on Shakespeare*, ed. W. K. Wimsatt, Jr. (New York, 1960), p. 106; Mark Van Doren, *Shakespeare* (Garden City, N.Y., 1939), p. 153. Granville-Barker also found the play "rather frigid"—these "noble Romans flinging their togas gracefully about them . . . speaking with studied oratory." *Prefaces to Shakespeare* (Princeton, N.J., 1946), II, 218.

7. A number of recent studies of Shakespeare's language—James L. Calderwood, *Shakespearean Metadrama* (Minneapolis, 1971); Terence Hawkes, *Shakespeare's Talking Animals* (London, 1973); Rosalie Colie, *Shakespeare's Living Art* (Princeton, N.J., 1974)—altogether ignore *Julius Caesar*. Some of Lawrence Danson's remarks are suggestive; *Tragic Alphabet: Shakespeare's Drama of Language* (New Haven, Conn., 1974), pp. 50–67.

Caesar begins from a consideration of its epistemological meaning; and both must be seen in relation to the skepticism and nominalism of the late Renaissance. Whereas traditional readings of the play concentrated on its political meaning, attempting to establish Shakespeare's sympathies as republican or monarchical, recent critics have found the ambiguity to be deliberate, concluding that Shakespeare intentionally obscured the political issues in order to emphasize problems of knowledge.[8] The play suggests a sense of the limits of knowledge and fallibility of judgment, of the fatal human tendency to—as Cicero cautions—impose subjective distortions on objective realities:

> But men may construe things, after their fashion,
> Clean from the purpose of the things themselves.
>
> (I.iii.34–35)

Indeed, Cicero, as the representative of rhetoric for the Renaissance, is the most appropriate figure in the play to understand this danger, and seems to appear solely to speak these lines.

Faced with questions of Caesar's nature and potential, Brutus choses to kill him, and though his action plunges Rome into civil war, nothing we are shown of Caesar enables us to assess Brutus's assessment of him. Since our opinion of Caesar determines our views of the justice of his death, the presentation of Caesar as a public man caught up in posturing and posing obscures the central political problem: our inability to know the "real" Caesar confuses our judgment of the assassination and the assassins. Uncertainty is further suggested by a recurrence of the same or similar words to express contradictory points of view about the same subjects: Brutus's view of the conspirators as "sacrificers, but not butchers" (II.i.166) is qualified by Antony's "butchers!" (III.i.255), the discrepancy impugning the valid-

---

8. Ernest Schanzer, *The Problem Plays of Shakespeare: A Study of Julius Caesar, Measure for Measure, Antony and Cleopatra* (1963; rpt. New York, 1965), pp. 10–70; Mildred E. Harstock, "The Complexity of *Julius Caesar*," PMLA, LXXXI (1966), 56–62; René E. Fortin, "*Julius Caesar*: An Experiment in Point of View," *ShQ*, XIX (1968), 341–348, D. J. Palmer, "Tragic Error in *Julius Caesar*," *ShQ*, XXI (1970), 399–409.

ity of both versions.[9] Further ambiguities are created by a pattern in which characters "construe" various phenomena—the omens of blood and fire, the beast without a heart, Calphurnia's dream of Caesar's statue spouting blood[10]—to arrive at contradictory interpretations which reveal more about the characters themselves than the reality they are describing. If we sympathize with Brutus, we will read the omens as signs of Caesar's tyranny and new life to the state, but if we side with Caesar, they signify the conspirators' guilt and civil strife.[11] Thus at the heart of the play is ambiguity of an ultimate sort, uncertainty about what the symbolism is symbolizing. Titinius's comment on Cassius's suicide, "Alas, thou hast misconstrued every thing" (V.iii.84), and Mesalla's apostrophe to "error" as the perception of "things that are not" (l. 69), have resonances beyond their immediate contexts, to reflect on the entire enterprise. Like Romeo, Brutus "thought all for the best" (*Romeo and Juliet*, III.i.104); but, acting with limited awareness of external circumstances and, above all, himself, he incurs tragic consequences. The play suggests a sense of man's tragic blindness—a skepticism comparable to and probably influenced by Montaigne's—which would find further expression, within a few years, in *Hamlet* and *Troilus and Cressida*.

But an attitude toward knowledge implies an attitude toward language, since when truth is thought to be beyond man's reason, it is also usually thought to be beyond his powers of description, and skepticism is utimately skepticism of the word.[12] Thus Montaigne is as wary of the ability of words to represent reality as he is of man's ability to know that reality. A

9. See also I.ii.255 and III.ii.191; I.i.35 and III.ii.144; II.i.173–174 and V.i.39–40; I.i.32–34 and III.ii.90–91. Schanzer describes the sense of *déjà vu* created by these echoes, the feeling "that we have been through all this, or something very like it before" (p. 70).

10. To Calphurnia, the dream is an omen of death, but to Decius—"This dream is all amiss interpreted" (II.ii.83)—it is an omen of new life to Rome. Both are, ironically, right.

11. Maurice Charney discusses these discrepant interpretations of the cosmic imagery: *Shakespeare's Roman Plays: The Function of Imagery in the Drama* (Cambridge, Mass., 1961), pp. 41–78.

12. Ernst Cassirer and Wilbur Urban discuss the relationship of skepticism and nominalism. *The Philosophy of Symbolic Forms* (New Haven, Conn., 1953), I, 122; and *Language and Reality* (London; 1939), pp. 23–24.

corollary to the skepticism implied in *Julius Caesar* is a skepticism concerning language which may be seen against a background of cultural revolution. Written on the eve of the seventeenth century, *Julius Caesar* reflects Shakespeare's awareness of processes at work in the age: the shift from early Renaissance belief in language and eloquence to modern nominalism and an ideal of the plain style, which would lead to the views of Hobbes, Locke, and the Royal Society. [13] The seventeenth century no longer assumed the right relation of language to reality, but, recognizing its arbitrary and conventional nature, saw it as a hindrance to understanding. Similitude (which included analogy and metaphor) was no longer thought to be a reflection of the world's shape and nature, but a source of error and confusion. This sense of the division of language from reality—one of the meanings implied in the myth of the Fall—is expressed most clearly, in Shakespeare's day, by Montaigne and Bacon. Bacon criticizes language as a main source of error, and Montaigne insists on a plain style to compensate for the distortions inherent in the verbal medium. [14]

It may seem strange to attribute to Shakespeare views which prefigure seventeenth-century nominalism; certainly, it is not the most pronounced aspect of his thought. Shakespeare was the supreme expression and embodiment of Renaissance eloquence; he used more words than anyone before or since, reveling in them for their sounds, textures, and rhetorical arrangements as well as for their sense. But in proportion as he knew the power of language, so did he know its danger, and there is another side to

13. For backgrounds on sixteenth- and seventeenth-century attitudes toward language, see R. F. Jones, "The Moral Sense of Simplicity," *Studies in Honor of Frederick W. Shipley* (St. Louis, 1942), pp. 265–287; *The Seventeenth Century: Studies in the History of English Thought from Bacon to Pope* (Stanford, Calif., 1951); Morris Croll, *Style, Rhetoric, and Rhythm*, ed. J. Max Patrick et al. (Princeton, N.J., 1966); Wilbur Samuel Howell, *Logic and Rhetoric in England, 1500–1700* (1956; rpt. New York, 1961); Perry Miller, *The New England Mind: The Seventeenth Century* (New York, 1939).

14. Montaigne's views on language are contained in the essays "On Cicero," "Of Names," "Of the Vanitie of Words" (Vol. I), and "Of Glory" (Vol. II), *The Essayes of Michael Lord of Montaigne*, trans. John Florio, ed. Henry Morley (London, 1886). For Bacon on language, see *The Works of Francis Bacon*, ed. James Spedding, R. L. Ellis, and D. D. Heath (London, 1858): *The Advancement of Learning*, III, 253–491; *The New Organon*, IV, 39–248; *Of the Dignity and Advancement of Learning*, IV, 275–498.

his relation to language, a sense implied in a number of the plays, of its capacity to corrupt, conceal, and misconstrue. In *Julius Caesar*, an ambivalence toward language is suggested, a complex awareness of its potentials, from a number of perspectives—psychological, social, political, and epistemological—which corroborates Montaigne's and Bacon's worst criticisms and casts doubts on the value of poetry itself.

II

An analysis of four crucial "persuasion" scenes will demonstrate how language functions to "work," "fashion," "move," "fire" its listeners, leaving the central political questions veiled in obscurity. Brutus is, as we hear repeatedly from him and from others, an honorable man and a man of reason, a stoic who prides himself on reason and is forever urging "reasons" to others;[15] this leads us to expect that his participation in the conspiracy will be undertaken with deliberation and cause. But if we look to the secnes where we most expect to find cause for Caesar's assassination—the scene in which Cassius "seduces" (I.ii.309) Brutus to come into the conspiracy; the soliloquy in which Brutus "fashions" (II.i.30) an argument for himself to join the conspiracy; the forum scene, where first Brutus, then Antony, "move" (III.ii.231) the crowd, Antony "working" (l. 262) and "inflaming" (l. 146) them to riot and mutiny—we find no reasons, only a rhetoric that obscures questions of Caesar's ambition and the justice of his death.

The "seduction scene" (I.ii.31–175), in which "Cassius first did whet [Brutus] against Caesar" (II.i.60), is the first place where we would expect to hear the case against Caesar, or at least some specific grievance. Yet, as Schanzer observes, "in this crucial scene . . . Cassius . . . does not mention any specific acts of tyrannical behaviour" (p. 26). Schanzer concludes that Cassius is not well suited to his role of guileful seducer. His case against Caesar is made in terms like "this age's yoke" (I.ii.61), "these hard

---

15. Just after the assassination, he offers Antony "reasons" (III.i.224–226). To the mob, he offers "the reason of our Caesar's death" (III.i.237), our "public reasons" (III.ii.7); and, overriding Cassius's plan of battle, he sends them to Philippi and destruction with "Good reasons must of force give place to better" (IV.iii.203).

conditions as this time / Is like to lay upon us" (ll. 172–173)—hardly convincing enough to warrant murder. In fact, on the surface, Cassius and Brutus seem barely to hear or to speak to one another. In the first part of the scene (to line 88), they essay one another, Cassius trying both to ascertain Brutus's feelings and to persuade him of his own point of view, without actually stating that point of view, while Brutus, partly defensive, partly enticed, simultaneously backs off and beckons him on. Twice, Brutus asks directly what Cassius wants of him ("Into what dangers would you lead me, Cassius?" [l. 62]; "wherefore do you hold me here so long?" [l. 82], and twice, Brutus's attention is deflected so that Cassius does not have to reply. On neither occasion does Brutus seem to notice or object. The first time, Cassius merely continues his line of thought, without any indication that he has even heard Brutus's question (l. 65);[16] and the second time, rather than waiting for a reply to his question, Brutus continues his own line of thought (ll. 84–88). Twice, Cassius declares intentions to speak of subjects he never again refers to: Brutus's "hidden worthiness" (l. 56) and "honor." Though he announces "honor is the subject of my story" (in the first of the two long speeches, ll. 91–130, which comprise the second movement of the scene), honor is not his subject; it is, rather, his outrage at Caesar's physical infirmities.

Yet by the end of the exchange, they have communicated, and Brutus indicates, in veiled, vague terms, that he assents:

> What you would work me to, I have some aim:
> How I have thought of this, and of these times,
> I shall recount hereafter . . .
> . . . .
> . . . What you have said
> I will consider; what you have to say
> I will with patience hear, and find a time
> Both meet to hear and answer such high things.
>
> (I. ii. 161–168)

16. "Heterogenium is the vice of answering something utterly irrelevant to what is asked"; Joseph, p. 66. Dudley Fenner explains it as a device of sophism; *The Artes of Logike and Rhetorike* (Middelburg, 1584), Sig. E 2ᵛ; in Joseph, p. 300.

In measured, balanced phrases (as though a control of language could assure a control of reality), he refers the whole matter to another time.

Though Brutus nowhere, here or later, insists on clearer definition of Cassius's suggestions, he is persuaded because something else is going on in the exchange. Cassius's real appeal is made in veiled, allusive terms which communicate, not through what they state but through what they suggest: "thoughts of great value, worthy cogitations (l. 49), noncommital terms with enticing innuendoes which Brutus is echoing by the end of the scene—"such high things" (l. 168). The real argument is made through indirection and insinuation because the actual grounds of Cassius's appeal are not the sort he can state: they are to Brutus's vanity and image of himself as a noble Roman, and are inarticulated because inadmissible.

Cassius reveals these terms in solioquy at the end of the scene, when he describes the petitions he plans to throw in at Brutus's window:

> . . . all tending to the great opinion
> That Rome holds of his name; wherein obscurely
> Caesar's ambition shall be glanced at.
>
> (ll. 315–317)

"Opinion," "Rome," the "name"—and only then is Caesar's ambition "obscurely glanced at." Indeed, these terms are implicit throughout the "seduction," and are the power of an otherwise nonexistent argument. When Cassius offers to be Brutus's "glass" (l. 67) to show him an image of his "hidden worthiness" (l. 56), Brutus's acknowledgment that "the eye sees not itself / But by reflection, by some other things" (ll. 51–52) is an admission of his dependence on the opinions of others for knowledge of himself. A few lines later, Cassius again evokes the imaginary audience he knows is so essential to Brutus's self-esteem, mirrors without which he cannot see and does not know himself: "many of the best respect in Rome / . . . Have wish'd that noble Brutus had his eyes" (ll. 58–61). A similar appeal is contained in his second long speech ("Why, man, he doth bestride the narrow world" [ll. 133–59], where he weaves the words "Rome," "man," "Brutus," "Caesar," "name," "fame," and "shame" into a pattern that creates an ideal of Roman manhood: an ideal represented by the name ("yours is as fair a name," l. 142), by opinion ("When could they say, till now, that talk'd of Rome . . . " [l. 152], by "our fathers" and the first Brutus (ll. 156–157). According to this ideal, Cassius urges Brutus to define himself, and this "works" (ll. 161, 306) more strongly than logical argument.

"Rome," "honor," "name" are words which are loaded with affective connotations that make them capable of kindling powerful responses. Though for the moment Brutus says nothing, their effect on him is obvious later when, again asked to "see thyself!" (II.i.46), he responds with an outburst about Rome and his ancestors (ll. 52–54). These words are powerful because they enshrine the dominant cultural values, the thought and belief of the past—libertarian ideals of republican Rome passed down through what "our fathers say" (l. 156). They contain what Bacon calls "common and general notions," to which "the individual is bound unless he takes care to distinguish them well" (*Dignity and Advancement of Learning*, IV, 431). They "annex to them"—in Locke's terms—"obscure and uncertain notions," implicit assumptions which are confusing because unexamined:

Men having been accustomed from their cradles to learn words . . . before they knew, or had framed the complex ideas, to which they were annexed, or which were to be found in the things they were thought to stand for; they usually continue to . . . [use them] all their lives; and without taking the pains necessary to settle in their minds determined ideas, they use their words for such unsteady and confused notions as they have . . . [which] manifestly fills their discourse with abundance of empty unintelligible noise and jargon, especially in moral matters, where . . . [the words'] bare sounds are often only thought on, or at least very obscure and uncertain notions annexed to them. [17]

These words and notions are bound up with Brutus's conception of himself, determining the way he experiences himself and reality.

The most important of these is "honor." Honor words are used so frequently by Brutus or with reference to him that they become, as Charney notes, "almost an identifying tag for his character" (p. 227, n. 19). Brutus's susceptibility to what touches his honor is indicated by his outburst in this scene:

17. "Of the Abuse of Words, "*An Essay Concerning Human Understanding, The Works of John Locke* (London, 1824), III, 23–24.

> Set honour in one eye, and death i' th' other,
> And I will look on both indifferently;
> For let the gods so speed me as I love
> The name of honour more than I fear death.
>
> (ll. 85–88)

Though his general intention is clear, his language is not,[18] and this is typical of Brutus's confusions when his imagination has been kindled and of his real confusions concerning honor: it is, as he says, "the name of honor" he loves. This conception of honor—as "name" or "reputation"—was associated, by the Renaissance, with classical antiquity, and is an aspect of Shakespeare's depiction of Rome.[19] But the idea of honor as a social attribute conferred by the "opinion" of the community is a notion of which Shakespeare is elsewhere critical, one which he associates elsewhere, as here, with confusion in language. For if honor is reputation, it is "a word," as Falstaff observed (*Henry IV*, Part 1, V.i.134), following—or anticipating—Montaigne, who begins his essay "Of Glory" with the statement that the argument about fame is an argument about language, and the relation of a man to his reputation is as tenuous as that between word and thing:

There is both name, and the thing: the name is a voice which noteth and signifieth the thing: the name, is neither part of thing nor of substance: it is a stranger-piece joyned to the thing, and from it.

(II.xvi, 317)

Brutus's uncritical acceptance of the Roman ideal both results from and reinforces the confusions in language which make him obtuse to the real terms of Cassius's appeal.

18. The lines have occasioned a page and a half of notes in the *Variorum Julius Caesar*, ed. Horace Howard Furness, Jr. (Philadelphia, 1913), pp. 33–35. First, there is the question of meaning: if Brutus loves honor more than he fears death, how can he be said to be indifferent to both of them? Then there is the bizarre quality of the image: one eye with death in it, the other with honor, is not poetically evocative (as, say, Hotspur's " . . . To pluck bright honor from the pale-fac'd moon" [*Henry IV*, Part 1, I.iii.202]). It is merely muddled.

19. For the Renaissance association of fame with classical antiquity, see Curtis Watson, *Shakespeare and the Renaissance Concept of Honor* (Princeton, N.J., 1960).

The real strengths of Cassius's argument are thus weaknesses in Brutus's character—his concern with reputation and appearance, his subtle vanity and pride—and it is on these grounds that the noble Brutus is seduced. Depending on the opinions of others for his image of himself, Brutus does not know himself, and is vulnerable to whoever provides the desired "reflection." Indeed, the entire exchange begins with Cassius's assurance that he loves Brutus, and ends with Brutus's "That you do love me, I am nothing jealous" (l. 160), as though its entire purport had been to assure Brutus only of this—which, in a way, it has. It is Brutus's confusion of real and professed motives that accounts for Cassius's verbal obliquity: Cassius "palters with him in a double sense,"[20] with different meanings for the heart and ear, seeming to appeal to "honor" and concern for "the general good" (l. 84), while actually appealing to vanity. He is, contrary to what Schanzer says of him, an extremely guileful seducer, who looks quite through the words of men to their real concerns and appeals to the one while seeming to appeal to the other.

But Brutus's fatal confusions are most apparent when, in soliloquy (II.i. 10–34), he defends his decision to take part in the murder of a man he protests he loves. He is, as Antony says, the only conspirator not motivated by "envy of great Caesar" (V.v.70), so we look to these lines when he is alone with himself—the only time in the play—for a cause why Caesar should be killed. Yet the issue disturbingly blurs, disappearing into a tangle of strange and disconnected images of uncertain relevance to one another or to their supposed subject, Caesar. Brutus's language, always more metaphorical than the other characters', is even more metaphorical than usual in this speech. Attempts to make sense of the soliloquy—like John Dover Wilson's "Brutus' theme is the effect of power upon character"[21]—probably represent something like what Brutus would have liked to have said, but nothing this coherent emerges until we have supplied certain missing logical links, and in making this much sense of it, we are ignoring what the language is communicating. Its broken rhythms, uncompleted thoughts, and associational movement present a

20. This is Macbeth's term for what the witches do with him: "juggling fiends . . . / That palter with us in a double sense" (V.viii. 19–20).

21. *Julius Caesar: The Works of Shakespeare* (Cambridge, Eng., 1949), pp. xxx-xxxi.

glimpse into the mind of a man who has not slept for weeks and who has never, in his clearest moments, defined the issues that are tearing him. The sequence of thought and statement is not logical, the conscious, active intellect is not in control, and what emerges is a sense of exhaustion, a linguistic image of the "phantasma" (II.i.65) Brutus describes a few lines later.

Brutus begins with "It must be by his death" (l. 10)—words which have more clarity and conviction than any in the soliloquy, until, perhaps, the final "kill him in the shell" (l. 34). Finding "no personal cause to spurn at him" (l. 11), he looks to "the general" (l. 12), but finding no "general" cause either, by the third line, he has shifted to the conditional: "He would be crown'd: / How that might change his nature, there's the question" (ll. 12–13). Now, instead of evidence from Caesar's past or present conduct to answer the "question" he has posed about a hypothetical future, Brutus reaches for a metaphor:

> It is the bright day that brings forth the adder,
> And that craves wary walking.
>
> > (ll. 14–15)

Again he returns to the question of Caesar's potential—"Crown him?— That;—" (l. 15). The broken thought creates the sense of groping, but what Brutus is groping for is not, as we might expect, reasons for supposing that Caesar is like an adder; rather, he develops the metaphor: "And then I grant we put a sting in him" (l. 16).

Brutus's next statement is a generalization, somewhat confusingly worded, about the misuse of power: "Th'abuse of greatness is when it disjoins / Remorse from power" (ll. 18–19). But he has difficulty applying this generalization specifically to Caesar, since he can find nothing in Caesar's conduct to warrant it:

> . . . and, to speak truth of Caesar,
> I have not known when his affections sway'd
> More than his reason.
>
> > (ll. 19–21)

So he makes another generalization—"But 'tis a common proof" (l. 21)— which he supports with a metaphor: " . . . That lowliness is young ambition's ladder" (l. 22). Though he has admitted difficulty in applying his general principle to Caesar, finding an appropriate metaphor seems to suffice and relieve him of having to justify its applicability. The relevance of this image to Caesar is even less obvious than that of the "adder"; perhaps, in view of the associational movement of the lines, it is there because it rhymes. It is startling, as Schanzer points out, "to find Brutus . . . speak of Caesar as if he were still at the beginning of his career" (p. 55). But it seems to satisfy Brutus because he develops it for the next seven lines, until the "climber-upward" attains "the upmost round ' and,

> . . . then unto the ladder turns his back,
> Looks in the clouds, scorning the base degrees
> By which he did ascend.
>
> (ll. 25–27)

Though strangely ineffectual for the weight it carries in the argument, the figure seems to serve Brutus's need, demonstrating his general principle about the effect of power upon purpose, while still not specifying its relevance to Caesar. What follows weakens the argument even further: "So Caesar may; / Then lest he may, prevent" (ll. 27–28). The only possible application of "vehicle" to "tenor" puts the whole case back in the conditional. Since "the thing he is" (l. 29) will not warrant killing him, Brutus states his intention to "fashion," "color," "And therefore think him," and thus takes the leap that clinches the argument—once more, reaching for metaphor:

> And since the quarrel
> Will bear no colour for the thing he is,
> Fashion it thus: that what he is, augmented,
> Would run to these and these extremities;
> And therefore think him as a serpent's egg,
> Which, hatch'd, would as his kind, grow mischievous,
> And kill him in the shell.
>
> (ll. 28–34)

There is the same incongruity about this metaphor as the last: Caesar is not "in the shell"; he is, as Brutus himself calls him, "the foremost man of all this world" (IV.iii.22).

What Brutus has said in this soliloquy is that there is no complaint about Caesar as he is or has been, but, on the basis of what often happens to people when they get power, Caesar might, given power, change. Brutus cites no "reasons," no cause, for supposing that he would change: images of "adder," "ladder," and "serpent's egg" develop his argument, carrying it to the conclusion to which he is committed. His thought moves back and forth between general observations about human behavior and metaphors that illustrate them, and nowhere does he look outside this self-referential linguistic construct to the supposed subject, Caesar himself. Brutus could "think him" anything on the basis of metaphors enlisted to support "common proofs," and his interpretation need bear no more, or less, relation to his subject than "a serpent's egg"; but the progression of tenses in the soliloquy, from the tentative "might" (l. 13) to "may" (l. 17), to the final "would" (l. 33), indicates that he has blurred the distinction between the hypothetical or metaphorical and the actual. The tentativeness of the subordinate clauses and appositions of the last five lines are overriden by the inexorable rhythms of "And since . . . And therefore . . . And kill," with their strong sense of causal necessity; the uncertain, choppy rhythms find release in the smooth, clinching "kill him in the shell." With his conscious mind relaxed, the conceptual controls dulled by exhaustion, the mechanism of Brutus's fatal construing is obvious: his willingness to let words do his thinking for him. A sense of the dangers of figurative language is implied comparable to that expressed by Hobbes, who called metaphors "useful only to deceive."[22] An influence of language on thought is suggested like that described by Bacon:

. . . words plainly force and overrule the understanding and throw all into confusion, and lead men away into numberless empty controversies and idle fancies

(*New Organon*, IV, Aphorism XLIII, 55)

---

22. *Leviathan* (New York, 1958), p. 207. Bishop Sprat asks, "who can behold, without indignation, how many mists and uncertainties, these species Tropes and Figures have brought on our knowledge?" *The History of the Royal-Society of London, for the improving of natural knowledge* (London, 1734), p. 111. This reading of the soliloquy follows my analysis in "The Language of Brutus' Soliloquy: Similitude and Self-Deception in *Julius Caesar*," *Humanitas: Essays in Honor of Ralph Ross* (Claremont, Calif., 1977), pp. 74–86.

For men believe that their reason governs words; but it is also true that words
react on the understanding

(*New Organon*, IV, Aphorism LIX, 61)

The strategies of deception that work privately, between a man and his
friend, and, more insidiously, between a man and himself, are merely
subtler, less obvious versions of the rhetorical tactics used publicly in the
funeral orations. Brutus's oration (III.ii. 12–41), his prose, "attic" statement of "public reasons" (l. 7), is traditionally contrasted to Antony's
impassioned "asiatic" style, and is usually read as an appeal to the intellect
rendered powerless by Antony's more effective appeal to the emotions.
These misreadings of Brutus's lines are extremely revealing, since they are
based on effects which Brutus himself carefully creates. Brutus explicitly,
in the first lines, establishes his authority as a man of reason addressing the
reason of others—

Romans, countrymen, and lovers, hear me for my cause, and be silent, that you
may hear. Believe me for mine honour, and have respect to mine honour, that you
may believe. Censure me in your wisdom, and awake your senses, that you may
the better judge.

(ll. 13–18)

—associating himself, by the repetition of key words, with honor, wisdom, and judgment. The technique is *ethos,* establishing the personal
character of the speaker, on the basis of the principle—stated by
Aristotle—that we are likely to accept the argument of a good man. And
despite the confusions Brutus has manifested, critics seem simply to have
taken him at his word, interpreting the oration, nearly unanimously, as an
appeal to the reason—a "straightforward statement" of "real reasons"
"logically delivered."[23] Yet when we look more closely, no reasons appear, no argument that could appeal to logic. The one accusation of
Caesar—"he was ambitious" (l. 27)—is slipped in among protestations of
Brutus's love for him and is nowhere supported or even referred to again.

23. See M. M. Mahood, *Shakespeare's Wordplay* (London, 1968), p. 180; T. S. Dorsch,
ed., *The Arden Julius Caesar*, p. 78; Ruth Nevo, *Tragic Form in Shakespeare* (Princeton,
N.J., 1972), pp. 119–120; Milton Crane, *Shakespeare's Prose* (Chicago, 1951), pp. 144–
145; John Palmer, *Political Characters of Shakespeare* (London, 1945), pp. 23–27.

Caesar's ambition is again, in Cassius's phrase, "obscurely . . . glanced at" (I.ii.316–317), in a linguistic construction which makes use of formal patterning, abstract terminology, and brevity to gloss over issue and event. Yet critics who have read the oration as an appeal to the reason are taking their cues from actual elements in it, from rhetorical and syntactical effects carefully contrived to create the illusion Brutus desires.

Brutus's most effective device is to present the issue as though it were a choice between two alternatives which leave no choice but to assassinate Caesar, but which rest on unexamined assumptions concerning Caesar: so that, again, the argument is a self-referential construct that makes sense in its own terms but casts no light outside itself to its supposed subject. He is aided in this by rhetorical figures that are related to logical processes and enable him to suggest logical distinctions and relationships, while actually falsifying the distinctions they imply. The first three sentences (quoted above) make use of one such figure, "antimetabole," a figure which "repeats words in converse order, often thereby sharpening their sense" (Joseph, p. 305). But, while seeming to "sharpen the sense," its function in Brutus's speech is simply tautology: "Believe me for mine honor and for mine honor believe." The necessity of choice between two mutually exclusive alternatives, love of Caesar and love of Rome, is asserted in the line, "Not that I lov'd Caesar less, but that I lov'd Rome more" (III.ii.21–22); but nowhere does Brutus substantiate that these were the alternatives, or that they excluded one another. The question he then springs ("Had you rather Caesar were living, and die all slaves, than that Caesar were dead, to live all freemen?" ll. 23–25) again implies logical distinction and the necessity of choice between alternatives suggested to be mutually exclusive—living in freedom or dying in bondage—but again, without evidence that these were the real alternatives. Both these distortions involve "enthymeme," an abridged syllogism, in which the omission of one premise results in "a strong tendency to accept the conclusion without scrutinizing the missing premise on which the argument rests" (Joseph, p. 178). The implicit premise on which all these claims depend is an assumption about Caesar: that Caesar's nature was such that it was necessary to choose between love of him and love of Rome, that Caesar living would have necessitated their "dying all slaves." This is the missing premise, nowhere confronted or supported, on which Brutus bases his entire case. The rhetorical questions which conclude his oration again present a choice between alternatives that again rest on an unexamined assumption regarding Caesar: "Who is here so base that he would be a bondman? If any, speak, for him have I offended" (ll. 30 ff.). Brutus creates a context wherein any objection would be an admission of rudeness, baseness, or vileness—so that, within this circular construct, it is indeed true, "Then none have I offended" (l. 37).

There are, moreover, close-knit causal relationships implied within nearly every line that further this illusion of logic. The first three sentences make use of a construction that twice implies causality—"for" (on account of) and "that" (in order that). The next two lines are conditional clauses setting up "if . . . then" relationships. Brutus uses the figure "taxis"[24] to mete reward and penalty in a syntactical arrangement implying distribution of effect according to cause: the cumulative effect of "as Caesar was . . . so I," repeated three times, lends finality to the concluding "but, as he was ambitious, I slew him" (l. 27). Of the sixteen sentences in the oration, six begin with "if," lending the final "Then none have I offended" a weight that clinches the argument. Even his last lines, which are not part of the argument but merely refer his audience to the records in the Capitol, use a construction that metes out reward and punishment in logical distribution: "his glory . . . wherein he was worthy . . . his offences . . . for which he suffer'd death" (ll. 39–41). Such syntactical arrangements occur from beginning to end of his speech, creating an illusion of irrefutable logic, causing the mind to fill out the pattern suggested by the syntax and to perceive reasons where there are none.

The oration is far from an appeal to the intellect with "real reasons"; nor is it an ineffective piece of oratory showing the intellectual's inability to communicate with the masses, as it has also been interpreted.[25] It is a

24. A figure of division "which distributeth to everie subject his most proper and naturall adjunct" (Peacham, p. 60; in Joseph, p. 319). "As Cicero saith, it helpeth . . . to make things that be compound, intricate, or confused, to appear simple, plaine, and certaine." Blundeville, *Art of Logike*, p. 62; in Joseph, p. 314.

25. Palmer, *Political Characters of Shakespeare*, p. 222. In fact, Brutus's style is not even "attic," as is usually assumed: rather, as R. W. Zandvoort demonstrates ("Brutus' Forum Speech in *Julius Caesar*," *RES*, XVI [1940], 62–66), it is euphuistic. Zandvoort concludes that Shakespeare gives Brutus this style because euphuism is "pre-eminently a style for the

brilliant piece of oratory, brilliantly suited to manipulating a difficult crowd, while resorting to none of the obviously cheap tricks so conspicuous in Antony's performance. Thus it enables Brutus to preserve his conception of himself in his own eyes and others' as a rational man reasonably motivated—an effect he accomplishes with spectacular success, judging from critics' misreadings. In fact, in its use of balance and parallelism to create the illusion of control, it is subject to Bacon's criticisms of Ciceronian rhetoric:

> . . . men began to hunt more after words than matter; and more after the choiceness of the phrase, and the round and clean composition of the sentence, and the sweet falling of the clauses, . . . than after the weight of matter, worth of subject, soundness of argument, life of invention, or depth of judgment.
>
> (*Advancement of Learning,* III, 283)

This is what Bacon calls "the first distemper or learning, when men study words and not matter." As an instrument of "the severe inquisition of truth, and the deep progress into philosophy" (*Advancement of Learning,* III, 284), such language is useless; but as a technique of rhetorical persuasion, it is effective.

All Antony does in the opening speech of his remarkable oration— "Friends, Romans, countrymen" (ll. 75–109)—is to pretend to accept Brutus's claim, Caesar "was ambitious," and then set about undermining it, by twisting a few crucial words. Merely by repeating, at regular and strategic intervals within a subtly changing context, "Brutus says he was ambitious and Brutus is an honorable man," he causes the words "honor" and "ambition" to assume opposite and ironic meanings, and Brutus's claim to redound on itself; the repetition is "antiphrases, or the broad

---

intellect" (p. 65). Actually, euphuism was not considered to be suited to the intellect at all; it was a highly contrived, elaborate prose style, characterized by repetition and antithesis— the "figures of sound" (*schemata verborum*) or Gorgian patterns, which were the mark of Ciceronian rhetoric. In the traditional twofold division which the Renaissance inherited from Quintilian and the *ad Herennium,* the "figures of sound" were associated with rhetorical embellishment and opposed to the "figures of thought" (*figurae sententiae* or *sententiarum*)—which, interestingly, Antony makes more use of than Brutus. Thus Brutus's oration is more Ciceronian than attic, and Zandvoort, like other critics, is misled by accepted notions of it and of Brutus to misclassify the style he so accurately analyzes.

flout . . . irony of one word" (Joseph, p. 139). Thus twenty-one lines into the speech, "Brutus says he was ambitious, / And Brutus is an honorable man" actually means, "Caesar was not ambitious, nor is Brutus honorable," and by line 155, the crowd itself can draw the conclusion which Antony nowhere has to state: "They were traitors; honorable men!" Master of irony, Antony is a master of language who has power to make words mean what he wills.

His power derives from his understanding of irony, his skill in adapting language to audience, and his superior insight into the value of *pathos* in persuasion. The oration is a lurid and dramatic appeal to a whole range of feelings, from grief for the loss of a leader and friend, desire to honor the dead, to curiosity, greed, fury, and revenge. At the end of this first long section, Antony pauses, ostensibly to compose himself, actually to calculate his effect on the crowd, and from this point on, he makes use of techniques and props to supplement the verbal: the will, the bloody mantle, and the body. In the next long speech (ll. 171–199), he "comes down," has the crowd make a ring around the corpse, and, holding up the bloody mantle, reenacts the murder. Antony's language and action are all concentrated on evoking the deed, with effects quite opposite to Brutus's distancing, obfuscating techniques. Injunctions occur at the beginnings of four lines—"Look" (l. 176), "See" (l. 177), "Mark" (l. 180), "Judge" (l. 184)—building to the final moment when he reveals the body itself: "Look you here" (l. 198). His language is characterized by a quality R. W. Zandvoort describes as "animation," the ascription of life to lifeless objects, somewhat in the manner of the pathetic fallacy (p. 65): Caesar's wounds are "poor, dumb mouths" which "speak for me" (ll. 227–228); the "blood of Caesar" followed Brutus's sword "As rushing out of doors to be resolv'd / If Brutus so unkindly knock'd or no" (ll. 181–182); while Pompey's statue "all the while ran blood" (l. 191). This is the key to the vitality of his language, the energy that enables him to seize hold of his world. Finally, sweeping aside the garment to reveal the body, he releases forces of chaos and destruction: "Revenge! About! Seek! Burn! Fire! Slay!" (ll. 206–207).

Having worked them to this pitch, Antony is now so confident that he can afford to play, so audacious that he can disavow the very arts of oratory he has so lavishly displayed—"wit," "words," "power of speech" (ll.

223–224)—in a triumphant flourish of his own showmanship. This gesture is an appropriate conclusion to a performance which is pervaded with irony, for irony is the essence of his oration, from his persona of "a plain blunt man / That . . . speak[s] right on" (ll. 220–225), to the more specific rhetorical forms of "antiphrases" and "paralipsis." "Paralipsis," a mode of irony which works by disclaiming the very things the speaker wishes to emphasize, is one of his most effective techniques. Repeating the word "wrong" six times within four lines (ll. 125–129), he insinuates that wrong has been done in the very process of denying that it has. Pretending to try to quiet the crowd, to dissuade them from "mutiny and rage" (ll. 123–124), he achieves his ends even as he disclaims them. His handling of the will, "which, pardon me, I do not mean to read" (l. 133), similarly makes use of "paralipsis": in enumerating all his reasons for withholding the will, he describes exactly the ways it will "inflame" (l. 146) them.

Not the least of his ironies is his claim to appeal to the reason: "O judgment! thou art fled to brutish beasts, / And men have lost their reason" (ll. 106–107). Yet in a sense, for all his histrionics, Antony does offer more information about Caesar than Brutus did, offering at least the assertions, "He was my friend" (l. 87), he brought captives home to Rome (l. 90), he wept for the poor (l. 93), he thrice refused the crown (l. 99). But at least two of these statements have been contradicted by other characters. With reference to the second, we have Marullus's words, "What conquest brings he home? / What tributaries . . . " (I.i.32–33). And to Caesar's refusal of the crown, we have Casca's wry commentary, "but, to my thinking, he was very loath to lay his fingers off it" (I.ii.237–238)—even without which, we would be a little more judicious than to leap to the crowd's conclusion, "Therefore 'tis certain he was not ambitious" (III.ii.115). Thus nothing Antony says of Caesar leaves us more enlightened than we were as to his character, and though his language evokes the murder visually and dramatically, questions of Caesar's ambition and the justice of his death are, again, "obscurely glanced at."

Antony's last long speech begins and ends with references to mutiny, at the end of which the mob takes its cue and cries, "We'll mutiny (ll. 233), proclaiming it as their own idea. The chaos he has prophesied has come; or rather, he has brought it about. Antony wins the day because he is the greatest actor of them all, his is the greatest show, a play within the play—complete with gesture, action, and props—which reverses the course of the play itself. Unconcerned with morality or truth, his energies are undivided, all geared to the manipulation of others: this is why he so effectively keeps his footing on such "slippery ground" (III.i. 191). The fire imagery associated with his oration (III.ii. 117), his feigned reluctance to "inflame" them (l. 146), suggests that his words spark the actual blaze: "We'll burn [Caesar's] body . . . And with the brands fire the traitors' houses . . . Go fetch fire" (ll. 256–259). In his soliloquy at the end of the scene—"now let it work" (l. 262)—Antony uses the same verb that Cassius used to describe his seduction of Brutus. Though Cassius's persuasion of Brutus was subtler, his words, too, "worked" and "struck . . . fire" (I.ii.306, 175).

III

Thus each oration creates its own Caesar, or its own illusion of Caesar. Both cannot be true, yet nothing we have seen of Caesar enables us to know which to accept. The Roman mob first applauds Brutus, then, under the influence of Antony's oratory, shifts its allegiance to Antony, demonstrating what Montaigne called

. . . that foolishnesse and facilitie which is found in the common multitude, and which doth subject the same to be managed, perswaded, and led by the eares by the sweet, alluring and sense-entrancing sound of his harmonie, without duely weighing, knowing, or considering the trueth of things by the force of reason.
("Vanitie of Words," I, li, 152)[26]

The crowd reflects its rulers, and their behavior is consistent: in the forum,

26. Because of this susceptibility of the common people, eloquence "chiefly flourishes" in republics rather than monarchies, and especially in periods of civil strife: "It [rhetoric] is an instrument devised to busie, to manage, and to agitate a vulgar and disordered multitude, and is an implement imployed but about distempered and sicke mindes, as Physicke is about crazed bodies. And those where either the vulgar, the ignorant, or the generalitie have had all power, as that of Rhodes, those of Athens, and that of Rome, and where things have ever been in continuall disturbance and uproare, thither have Orators and the professors of that Art flocked." ("Vanitie of Words," I, LI, 152).

as with Cinna the poet, they care only for the word, not the reality, and do not bother with fine distinctions between the two—"It is no matter, his name's Cinna. Pluck but his name out of his heart" (III.iii.33–34). Casca's identification of the mob with an audience, "clap[ing]" and "hiss[ing]" as they "do the players in the theatre" (I.ii.255–258), implies, as well, an identification of the audience with the mob. We have, finally, no better basis than they to judge the truth of Brutus's or Antony's claims, and are left as much at the mercy of rhetoric—"led by the ears" rather than the "force of reason." It is this which accounts for the play's central ambiguities: if a point of view is persuasively stated, it passes for truth.

It also accounts for the sense we have of the characters as constantly observing one another, on the alert for unguarded gestures or natural expressions which might afford a truer glimpse than language does into character and motive. Cassius "observes" less "show of love" from Brutus (I.ii.33); Caesar wishes to see the soothsayer's face (I.ii.20); Brutus observes the angry spot on Caesar's brow, the expression in Cicero's eyes (I.ii.180–186); Caesar remarks on Cassius's lean and hungry look and on *his* ability to see "through the deeds of men" (ll. 191, 199). And in fact, such nonverbal physical signs provide, in this play, more reliable bases for knowledge than language does.

Brutus's language functions in several ways to reshape reality. In accepting the issues as Cassius presents them, he accepts words such as "honor" and "Rome" as explaining more than they actually do, substituting them for precise evaluation of complicated realities. His own verbal techniques—the construing figures of the soliloquy, the complex rhetorical patterns of the oration—are ways of distancing and avoiding, of not assigning names to realities. Nor is the soliloquy the only instance of his use of figurative language to support fatal decisions. Brutus similarly envisions the murder as a sacrificial rite (II.i.166–174), defends the decision to spare Antony on the grounds that Antony is "but a limb of Caesar" (II.i.165), and urges the battle at Philippi on the basis of "a tide in the affairs of men" (IV.iii.217)—a particularly compelling image with which he overrides Cassius's objections and any further discussion, assured that the "tide" is "now" (l. 221). Confronted with problems requiring careful assessment, his judgment is confounded by these habits of language.

Julius Caesar follows a pattern familiar in Shakespeare's tragedies: the protagonist's error, his misjudgment of external reality, is related to lack of self-knowledge and to self-deception, and his confusions are facilitated by language. But, as M. M. Mahood observes, the protagonist's disillusionment, his discovery of evil and deception from within and without, usually involves a discovery about language: that words do not necessitate the existence of the things they name (pp. 181–185). Thus Lear understands that "flattery" has been his undoing (IV.vi.96) and Macbeth realizes that "equivocation" has been his (V.v.42). Hamlet and Troilus express skepticism of "words, words, words" (II.ii.192; V.iii.108), and Timon curses language as though it were the root of evil itself: "let . . . language end" (V.i.220). But Brutus dies deluded, consoling himself that no man was ever false to him; and because he does not awaken to his own self-deception, he never awakens to the deceptions involved in language to express a disenchantment like that of the others. His confusions are too deeply sanctioned by a society that assumes honor is a name and rhetoric is reality. In fact, as the consequences of his deeds unravel before him, Brutus shows even less ability to confront the meanings of things, and there is, in these last scenes, a sense of strain and self-righteousness about him that makes him resemble, increasingly, the man he has murdered.[27] And when "Brutus' tongue / Hath . . . ended his life's history" (V.v.39–40), Antony's epigraph preserves the fiction of "the noblest Roman of them all" (l. 68).

But there is another kind of "actor" in the play who does not confuse the self with the role. Whereas Brutus and Caesar are lost in their own language and posturing and beguiled by the rhetoric and role playing of others, Antony and Cassius keep private selves separate from public personae and understand distinctions between words and realities. The pairings are familiar from *Richard II* and *Othello*, where self-deluded word spinners are similarly destroyed by undeluded, unprincipled nominalists.

27. Norman Rabkin discusses a number of similarities in the characters of Brutus and Caesar—a rhetoric that hovers between magnificence and bluster, identification with the name indicative of concern with the public image. *Shakespeare and the Common Understanding* [New York, 1967], pp. 105–114. In the final scenes, this resemblance becomes more pronounced, as Brutus seems even more to be holding himself together with high-sounding terms, speaking in ways which are increasingly reminiscent of Caesar's (IV.ii.38; IV.iii.37, 39–40, 66–69).

Victors are differentiated from victims in these plays by their understanding of words.

If figurative language functions only as an instrument of fatal error, then poetry, too, is deprived of meaning or value in educating. This sense of language casts light on the two "poet" scenes—strange, grotesque little episodes which are so puzzling that the second, at least, is usually omitted in production.

The errors and fates of both poets reflect those of the main characters. Cinna has an intuition of truth, a premonition of disaster, but ventures forth to Caesar's funeral in spite of it. (As with Brutus, the "charging" of "fantasy" is "unlucky" [III.iii.1–2].) Asked his name and warned to "Answer . . . directly . . . briefly . . . wisely . . . and truly" (ll. 9–12), he does not answer directly, and his quibbling enrages the mob. As with the main characters, verbal indirection, along with a fatal confusion of name with reality, cost him his life. The second poet acts according to his "fashion" (IV.iii.134) and "humor" (l. 135) rather than a sense of the "time"—as Brutus can see with him, though not with himself. Bursting in to reconcile the quarreling generals just when they have reconciled themselves, he pronounces his advice:

> Love, and be friends, as two such men should be;
> For I have seen more years, I'm sure, than ye.
>
> (IV.iii.131–132)

Like Cinna, he has some intuition of truth; like Brutus, he is well-intentioned; but his advice is ill-timed, it is bad poetry, it contains a *non sequitur*, and if Brutus's dismissal of him as a "jigging fool" (l. 136) is unkind, it is not inappropriate.

Whatever intuition either character has is beside the point: it has no effect on the action, of others or of their own. Both poets are ineffectual, and their scenes are the closest to anything like "comic relief" in the play. With the second of these episodes, Shakespeare made two significant changes in his source: whereas in Plutarch, a cynic philosopher intervenes and actually stops the quarrel, Shakespeare makes him a poet who bursts in too late. So much for the lofty humanist ideal of the poet, as truth-teller, educator, counselor, and adviser to the prince. The poet in *Julius Caesar* is denied a positive, meaningful function; he is ludicrous, trivial, torn limb from limb. Rome is no country for poets: "What should the wars do with these jigging fools?" (IV.iii.136) Nor will the next age in England be.

In *Julius Caesar*, it is the negative potentials of language that are most strongly emphasized. Rhetoric is an instrument of appearance which can make, as Plato says, the worse appear the better. Stimulating passion and imagination, it disrupts the proper workings of the mind, perpetuating psychological and social disorder which, in Christian terms, repeats the error of the Fall. [28] Its strength is in human weakness, the corrupt will and unreason: pandering vanity in Brutus and Caesar, it kindles worse passions in the mob. Though language is supposedly man's medium for "coming to terms with the objective world" (as Cassirer calls it), [29] it can be enlisted in the service of subjectivity, of seeming rather than signification, to facilitate the perception of "things that are not" (V.iii.69)—to "misconstrue every thing" (V.iii.84). Bacon's criticism of the scholastics for creating verbal systems based on linguistic logic rather than empirical foundations applies as well to these characters and accounts for their tragic confusions. Speaker and listener are locked in what Bacon calls a "contract of error":

> . . . for as knowledges have hitherto been delivered, there is a kind of contract of error between the deliverer and the receiver; for he who delivers knowledge desires to deliver it in such form as may be best believed, and not as may be most conveniently examined; and he who receives knowledge desires present satisfaction, without waiting for due inquiry; and so rather not to doubt, than not to err . . .

> (*Dignity and Advancement of Learning*, IV, 449)

28. Stanley Fish describes the tradition which associated rhetoric with "the verbal equivalent of the fleshly lures that seek to enthral us and divert our thoughts from Heaven, the reflection of our own cupidinous desires"; "through rhetoric man continues in the error of the Fall." *Surprised by Sin: The Reader in Paradise Lost* (New York, 1967), p. 61. This sense of rhetoric is consistent with the conception of Rome as the earthly city, "the world" before Christ, which was traditional in the Renaissance and which Shakespeare draws on in *Julius Caesar*. See T. J. B. Spencer, "Shakespeare and the Elizabethan Romans," *ShS*, X (1957), 27–38; J. Leeds Barroll, "Shakespeare and Roman History," *MLR*, LIII (1958), 327–343; and J. L. Simmons, *Shakespeare's Pagan World: The Roman Tragedies* (Charlottesville, Va., 1973).

29. *An Essay on Man* (New Haven, Conn., 1944), p. 132.

Such confusions account for the chain of events which begins with
Cassius's persuasion of Brutus, leads to Brutus's persuasion of himself,
Caesar's assassination, and Antony's victory—ending in a new age of Caesar.
It was Shakespeare's genius to integrate these criticisms of language into an
epistemological focus which is central to the play's tragic vision.

The Iron World of Sejanus: History in the Crucible of Art

WILSON F. ENGEL, III

MONG THE ANTI-TIBERIAN VERSES which Suetonius cited as evidence of
the public's fear and hatred of Tiberius is this one:

> You, O Caesar, have altered the golden ages of Saturn,
> For while you are alive, iron they ever will be.

If the age of Augustus, portrayed by Jonson in *Poetaster*, is golden, the
world left Jonson by classical records for *Sejanus* is iron. *Sejanus* amplifies
the theme suggested by Suetonius, but its tone and satirical edge derive
from Jonson's richly synthetic quality of mind. Not satisfied to rely on
only one classical account or to borrow from the drama one model for his
plot, Jonson mingled his numerous sources into a pattern that defies an
easy parsing out of "influences," yet at the same time enjoys, as its most
intriguing characteristic, a multiplicity of diverging or even conflicting
points of view. But Jonson's quality of mind, not the variations in the
tone, structure, and content of his sources, is responsible for the frighten-
ing unity of effect of this complex play. Jonson, in combining his often
contradictory sources, somehow remained true to them all and true to his

95

invention. A clear picture of the place of *Sejanus* within Jonson's works and within the drama of his time can only emerge after consideration of his integration of classical sources, his incorporation of diverse voices within an almost mathematical plot structure, and his transformative use of the dramatic tradition. Finally, *Sejanus* emerges as enigmatical but controlled, powerful and menacing, a conflation of historical, satirical, philosophical, and dramatic parts, which form a diverse and sinister whole—the iron world itself.

I

Poetaster, Sejanus, and *Catiline* are Ben Jonson's three Roman plays, each representing different eras in Roman history and marking separate stages in the author's dramatic evolution. *Sejanus* has deservedly received the most critical attention of these plays. Critics have been so intrigued by the historical sources for the play that, until quite recently, they have emphasized Jonson's abilities as a historian at the expense of his drama. Coleridge admired *Sejanus* and *Catiline* as histories, not tragedies, and numerous critics have followed his lead, many going so far as to say that a thorough knowledge of classical history is necessary before the plays may be enjoyed.[1] Others have repeated Hazlitt's compliment that Jonson's tragedies are "admirable pieces of ancient mosaic."[2] The nature of the tragic worlds that Jonson created has been examined by two generations of critics who have digested the notes to the monumental collected works of Jonson

1. Roberta F. Brinkley, ed., *Coleridge on the Seventeenth Century* (Durham, N.C., 1955), p. 645; this departs radically from Dryden's view in "An Essay of Dramatic Poetry," in *Essays of John Dryden*, ed. W. P. Ker (Oxford, 1900), I, 82; for the need of background to understand *Catiline*, see Angela G. Dorenkamp, "Johnson's *Catiline*: History of the Trying Faculty," *SP*, LXVII (1970), 210–220, esp. p. 219; and Joseph Allen Bryant, Jr., "*Catiline* and the Nature of Jonson's Tragic Fable," *PMLA*, LXIX (1954), 272 and 275; for the necessity of historical framework, see Una Ellis-Fermor, *The Jacobean Drama* (London, 1936), p. 110. Recently critics have begun to examine each tragedy on its own merits, e.g., W. F. Bolton, ed. *Sejanus*, The New Mermaids (London, 1965), xiii; and J. W. Lever, *The Tragedy of State* (London, 1971), p. 63, and the work by John W. Velz.

2. W. C. Hazlitt, *Works*, ed. P. P. Howe (London, 1930–1934), VI, 263; see John Palmer, *Ben Jonson* (London, 1934), p. 129. However, compare W. F. Bolton, *Sejanus*, p. xiv.

by Herford and Simpson,[3] the painstaking source studies of Daniel C. Boughner for *Sejanus*,[4] and the writings of Lynn Harris and Ellen M. T. Duffy on *Catiline*.[5] But there have been critical disagreements about the nature of Jonson's tragic vision. Swinburne's complaint that no one can sympathize with the major characters in the plays has been generally accepted.[6] Some critics have suggested that, paradoxically, Jonson so completely captured the atmosphere of the classical world that we have no means of recognizing our worlds as having anything to do with the one he portrayed.[7]

Jonson's Roman plays have been called "tragical satires," "tragedies of state," "Renaissance tragedy," "drama of revelation"; the interplay of Tiberius and Sejanus has even been called satirical comedy.[8] *Sejanus* transcends its historical sources by means of its compression and arrangement of incidents according to familiar literary patterns; its sharp, clear characterization; its reiteration of fearful, vivid images; and its elaborate uses of irony. The Roman world of *Sejanus* is achieved through the transformation of history by art, and it offers a key to Jonson's tragic vision.

Nowhere in his earlier work did Jonson exhibit the method of construction that he used in *Sejanus*. One might guess that his choice of subject was

3. *Ben Jonson*, ed. C. H. Herford and P. E. Simpson, 12 vols. (Oxford, 1925–1952), henceforth cited as H & S. All citations to Jonson's works are from this edition.

4. Daniel C. Boughner, "Jonson's Use of Lipsius in *Sejanus*," *MLN*, LXIII (1958), 247–255; "Juvenal, Horace, and *Sejanus*," *MLN*, LXXV (1960), 545–550; "*Sejanus* and Machiavelli," *SEL*, I, no. 2 (1961), 81–100; *The Devil's Disciple: Ben Jonson's Debt to Machiavelli* (New York, 1968).

5. Lynn Harris, ed., *Catiline His Conspiracy*, Yale Studies in English, Vol. LIII (1919), Introduction; Ellen M. T. Duffy, "Ben Jonson's Debt to Renaissance Scholarship in 'Sejanus' and 'Catiline'," *MLR*, XLII (1947), 24–30.

6. A. C. Swinburne, *A Study of Ben Jonson* (London, 1889), p. 86.

7. Harris, p. li; see also Ellis-Fermor, p. 110.

8. H & S, II, 27: "*Sejanus* is the tragedy of a satirist"; Lever, pp. 63–69; Ralph Nash, "Jonson's Tragic Poems," *SP*, LV (1958), 185: "Renaissance tragedies" because neither "classical" nor "Elizabethan" tragedies; Gabriele B. Jackson, *Vision and Judgment in Ben Jonson's Drama*, Yale Studies in English, vol. CLXVI (New Haven, Conn., 1968), p. 2: "drama revelation"; Boughner, "*Sejanus* and Machiavelli," p. 95: *Sejanus* is a "vulpine comedy of wits engaged in deadly opposition"; and K. W. Evans, "*Sejanus* and the Ideal Prince Tradition," *SEL*, XI (1971), 264: "*Sejanus* is a brilliant satire on the struggle for power."

related to the tyranny exercised by the ministers of the aging Elizabeth, or
the Essex rebellion and its aftermath, or Jonson's own involvement with
the privy council for libels in his plays, or the spies that plagued Jonson
because of his recent conversion to Catholicism, or Jonson's desire to outdo
Shakespeare, who had written *Julius Caesar* and *Troilus and Cressida* with
flagrant disregard for his sources. But these must remain speculations.

As for the approach he took in composing *Sejanus*, it is clear that
Jonson's pattern of thinking was influenced over a long period by William
Camden; his acquaintance with many of the original members of the
Society of Antiquaries might well account for his concern for accuracy in
historical details, as well as his interest in depicting this particular time in
the classical period.[9] When he was composing *Sejanus* he was working
with the best available resources; it was an ideal time to perform the kind
of research required. Given his patrons and the tastes of the newly arrived
King James, a royal pedant who had been tutored by George Buchanan,
himself a writer of historical drama, such a thorough approach as Jonson
took in preparing his play might well have paved the way to preferment.
Just how the temperaments of the antiquaries as a whole influenced Jonson
and the other serious dramatists is a matter for further study.

As to the form which *Sejanus* took, it is clear that Jonson at this time
had no sure allegiance to the French Senecans and their English imitators,
like Samuel Daniel, Fulke Greville, and Sir William Alexander. Further,
the popular tradition of Roman plays from Bower's *Appius and Virginia*
(1564) to Shakespeare's *Julius Caesar* (1599) with the authors' imprecision
of historical details could only have angered him. The English history play
offered a more attractive framework, but the providential theory of history
behind the writings of Hall and Holinshed did not suit a just presentation
of Tiberian Rome. Jonas Barish was right in suggesting that in writing
Sejanus Jonson departed from both the Senecans and the popular dramatists, though he exhibited some elements from the drama of each.[10] But he
also drew upon Greek and Roman tragedy, medieval drama, and Renais-

---

9. Palmer, p. 69; *Dictionary of National Biography*, 4: 1234; Joan Evans, *A History of the
Society of Antiquaries* (Oxford, 1956), p. 11.

10. Jonas Barish, ed. *Ben Jonson: Sejanus*, The Yale Ben Jonson (New Haven, Conn. &
London, 1965), pp. 2–4.

sance revenge plays, as will be shown. Jonson's eclecticism in his use of
dramatic conventions, evident in the footnotes to competent modern
editions of his works, has never fully been explored, and it has a direct
relation to Jonson's antiquarian interests. *Sejanus* is no mere ragbag of
borrowings from various contexts, but, thanks to Jonson's genius for
synthesis, it is an organic and original whole.

More important than any of the theatrical traditions to the genesis of
Sejanus was the way Jonson drew on his classical sources. That *Sejanus*
"follows *all* its sources," has been noted by Barish; that it does so in a
manner "as accurate as contemporary historical scholarship could provide"
is the conclusion of Joseph Allen Bryant, Jr. [11] Jonson's choice of the time
of Tiberius and the tragical pattern of Sejanus's life as his subjects dictated
a focus on the degeneracy of the time, but he explored it in different voices
and with different levels of indignation. Renaissance scholars saw that
time as a decadent age, a viewpoint justified in the classical sources themselves.

Jonson drew mostly from Tacitus's *Annales* in the first three acts of
Sejanus; the play opens in the sinister Tacitean and Machiavellian atmosphere which was known by name to Elizabethans but which had never
before been given such direct expression. Tacitus's terse language had
conveyed outspoken loathing of everything in Tiberius's reign. After
complaining that the era he examined had no great material, such as wars
and conflicts of classes, Tacitus wrote:

My theme is narrow and inglorious: a peace unbroken, or disturbed only by petty
wars; a distressful course of events in Rome; a prince with no interest in the
expansion of the empire. It may serve some good purpose, nevertheless, to look
closely into these things, at first sight so unimportant; since it is often from such
beginnings that mighty movements take their rise. [12]

11. Barish, p. 4; Bryant, p. 275; this is a prevailing view; see Peter Ure, "On Some
Differences Between Senecan and Elizabethan Tragedy," in *Elizabethan and Jacobean Drama*,
ed. J. C. Maxwell (Liverpool, 1974), p. 69, no. 9: "Jonson's knowledge of *romanitas* was
exceptionally fruitful." Jonson viewed classical texts through the perspective of Renaissance
commentators, such as Justus Lipsius; see Boughner, "Jonson's Use of Lipsius," pp.
247–255.

12. Tacitus, *The Annals of Tacitus*, Books I–VI, trans. G. G. Ramsay (London, 1904),
IV.32, p. 291; all citations to Tacitus in the text are from this translation.

He continued:

My task is to record a succession of cruel edicts, of prosecutions heaped on
prosecutions; to tell of friends betrayed, of innocent men brought to ruin, of trials
all ending in one way, with a uniformity as monotonous as it is revolting.

(IV.33, p. 293)

Tacitus rarely missed an opportunity in the *Annales* to editorialize on the
depravity of the time he scrutinized, and we can see reflections of the fears
Jonson himself felt about the dangers in producing such a work:

There are many living now whose ancestors suffered punishment or incurred
disgrace, under Tiberius; and even if the families concerned have died out, there
are those who deem an attack upon the vices akin to their own to be an attack
upon themselves.

(IV.33, p. 293)

Tacitus's moralizations appear in *Sejanus* mostly in the mouths of
Agrippina's party, especially Arruntius. In other words, the pattern of
commentary-atrocity-commentary in Tacitus is carried over into Jonson's
play through the separation into factions of commentators and committers
of atrocities. Jonson skillfully compresses Tacitus's horrors within the
limits of his play, without losing the impression that every crime is a
direct result of the plotting of Tiberius, Sejanus, or Macro. It has been
argued that Tacitus, for all his condemnation of Tiberius, still made him
human, but Jonson acknowledged the humanity of his titanic characters as
only a dim possibility in the mouths of credulous men. [13]

Jonson looked to Cassius Dio's *Roman History* for the basis of Acts IV
and V of *Sejanus*. This was a practical necessity, for Tacitus broke off just
short of the denouement of the Tiberius-Sejanus relationship. Yet where
Tacitus made Tiberius somewhat human, Dio made Tiberius a calculating
manipulator, and he directly attributed to Tiberius's management all that
happens in the history. He almost delighted in giving the minute details
of Sejanus's fall from favor, especially when he could show the grim irony

13. H & S, II, 25.

of Sejanus's self-deception.[14] His comments on the history were given by Jonson to Arruntius and Lepidus, and his cool, detached descriptions of every vicious act are mirrored in the casual cruelty of the powerful persons in the play. Dio recorded the savage death of Sejanus and the deaths of his children with the outrage of his virgin daughter by the public executioner, the wild accusations of Livia by his wife Apicata, the great uproar of the people, and the fall of all Sejanus's former supporters. Tiberius's role in the proceedings was made very clear in the *Roman History*, as the people realized "that their former woes were the work of Tiberius, quite as much as the work of Sejanus."[15]

Suetonius's Life of Tiberius portrays a man of apparent modesty progressing to extreme tyranny, seclusion, debauchery, and open plunder. Suetonius reported that Augustus said of Tiberius, "Alas for the Roman people, to be ground by jaws that crunch so slowly,"[16] a quotation assimilated by Jonson and amplified again and again in the insistent imagery of devouring.[17] Suetonius's account of Tiberius's most bloodthirsty years epitomizes the atmosphere which Jonson reflects:

Not a day passed without an execution, not even those that were sacred and holy; for he put some to death even on New Year's day. Many were accused and condemned with their children and even by their children. The relatives of the victims were forbidden to mourn for them. Special rewards were voted the accusers and sometimes even the witnesses. The word of no informer was doubted. Every crime was treated as capital, even the utterance of a few simple words.[18]

The portrayal of Tiberius in the rumors that are spread after his withdrawal in *Sejanus* owes much to Suetonius's account. Unlike Tacitus and Cassius Dio, Suetonius rarely commented on the events he so calmly related. The

14. Cassius Dio, *Dio's Roman History*, trans. E. Cary (London, 1914–1927), VII.lviii. 10 ff.

15. *Ibid.*, LVIII.xvi.

16. Suetonius, "Tiberius," in *The Lives of the Caesars,* trans. J. C. Rolfe (London and Cambridge, Mass., 1924), III.xxi.325.

17. Christopher Ricks, *"Sejanus* and Dismemberment," *MLN*, LXXVI (1961), 301–308.

18. Suetonius, III.lxi.379.

horror of the events was intensified by the vehicle that projected them. The conscienceless main figures in *Sejanus* and the cool flow of utterly inhuman words and actions resemble the detached Suetonian account.

But the historians were not the only recorders of the iron regime of Tiberius. Boughner was right in suggesting that Juvenalian influence is pervasive in *Sejanus*.[19] The unspeakable delight of the populace in tearing Sejanus's flesh into fragments, a recurrent figure in the imagery of the play, is from Juvenal's Tenth Satire, which has Juvenal's characteristic energy and moral indignation. Juvenal's love of graphic but outrageous details and obscure historical references, his cruel rage and biting ironies, are present throughout *Sejanus*, often in Arruntius's malcontented outbursts. Just as laughter is impossible in Juvenal's satires when they touch on heinous crimes, so in Jonson's play we are repelled by criminal ideas, yet fascinated by the energetic language that bodies them forth. Because of Arruntius's moral posture, he can be made to mouth Juvenal and the historians' moralistic commentaries; his range of tones is broader than nearly any other figure of his kind on the Elizabethan or Jacobean stage, and this range is derived from Jonson's combination of sources.

In *Sejanus* Jonson brought together these and other classical sources, assimilating their various aspects into a coherent atmosphere of his own. Critics fascinated by this coherency include Swinburne, Herford and Simpson, L. C. Knights, Bamborough, and Barish.[20] Barish noticed "a thick atmosphere of delation and cloaked collusion" (p. 17) in a play where crises have "the jolting impact of geological cataclysms, the product of centuries of shifting of subterranean rock" (p. 24). Lindsay has seen the play as "a total, black, universal tragedy" on three separate but related levels, each qualifying the others: Sejanus's personal tragedy; the tragedy of the Roman state; and a cosmic tragedy, where the impression of the

---

19. "Juvenal, Horace, and *Sejanus*," pp. 545–550.

20. H & S, II, 27. L. C. Knights, *Drama & Society in the Age of Jonson* (London, 1937), pp. 180–185. J. B. Bamborough, *Ben Jonson* (London, 1920), pp. 50–65; see Geoffrey Hill, "The World's Proportion: Jonson's Dramatic Poetry in *Sejanus* and *Catiline*," in *Stratford-upon-Avon Studies*, I (1960), 113–132; *Sejanus* presents a world "bent awry." Barish, p. 11.

futility of human existence is unrelenting.[21] Clearly, the idea of levels complements the kind of integration of disparate but related classical materials that Jonson employed. The unity of effect arises not from a single strand of simple actions strung together but from the inevitable collision of numerous complex variables with profound bearing on the human situation.

II

Sejanus is brilliantly plotted so as to sharpen the issues and characters gradually while increasing the speed of events toward their inevitable final horror. The effects of the formal strategy complement the effects of the conflation of disparate source materials. The logical unity of cause-and-effect is allowed to remain simple and clear, a brutal surface order resembling an imperial chess game; causes may be widely separated from their effects, but the effects will come, we are assured, inexorably. Paradoxically, the clear, unsullied plot contains a complexity of characters, rhetorical stances, and secondary effects, marshaled to show in unabashed detail the grim tone of tyranny. The paradox is compounded by the fact that the audience is never sure of the working of Tiberius's complex mind.

Sejanus begins with the suspicions of members of the Germanicus party who are doomed to become victims of the state. Division, mistrust, factionalism, and unrest are carefully developed in the first act. Drusus is eliminated and the Germanicus party is isolated in Act II, as Sejanus's character begins to emerge, and his actions are curiously sanctioned by the apparently weak but politically aware Tiberius. Act III shows the triumph of Sejanus's politics, the betrayal of his ambitions before Tiberius, and Tiberius's answer to the problem—his giving power to Macro. Act IV

21. Barbara N. Lindsay, "The Structure of Tragedy in *Sejanus*," *ES*, L (1969), Supp., xliv-l. J. A. Bryant contends—though few would agree—that the wisdom gained by the survivors of the tragedy "encourages the hope of a season of civic health"; see Bryant, *The Compassionate Satirist: Ben Jonson and His Imperfect World* (Athens, Ga., 1972), p. 59, and Claude Lee Finney, "The Nature of the Conflict in Jonson's *Sejanus*," in *Vanderbilt Studies in the Humanities*, ed. R. C. Beatty, J. P. Hyatt, and M. K. Spears (Nashville, Tenn., 1951), I, 197–219.

portrays the political consequences of Sejanus's power and the growing personal concern of Macro to maintain his place. Sejanus does not appear in Act IV, but he opens Act V with a prideful soliloquy. The action accelerates toward the inevitable trap sprung in a swift succession of reversals and surprises, which finally slow for the grave interplay of the messenger and moralizers in the closing lines. The choral Germanicus party gradually assumes a focus in Lepidus and Arruntius as key spokesmen. Throughout the play images of cobwebs, nets, snares, and weaving emphasize the intricacy of the plotters' designs. These designs, the ironical and often pathetic commentary, the workings of Fortune, and the impression of inevitability of ruin implicit both in the language and action, indicate an even darker significance for these images: that man is caught not only in his own evil webs but also in the webs of fortune and of universal history.

The rigid and predictable structure of the plot, with its increasing clarity of focus, provides a framework within which human figures are ground down. A simple Machiavellian decision not only achieves its end, but also strangles an entire population. Crowded with more characters than either *Julius Caesar* or *Antony and Cleopatra, Sejanus* gives the impression of moral chaos in a larger framework that is under rigid artistic control.[22] Jonson has used his classical sources to fashion numerous types of characters who fall into two political groups: the Germanicus faction and the Sejanus faction. Drusus is eliminated before we are convinced of his reportedly noble nature, and Macro's followers, like Laco, are malleable at best and can be grouped with Sejanus.

The Germanicus faction has seeds of virtue but seems unable to act without its leader. Agrippina is the typical Roman matron, Lepidus the stoical but politically adept adviser, Arruntius the vacillating yet passionately cynical commentator, Silius the mildly corrupt man of action, ennobled by his resolute suicide, Cordus the forthright historian, whose reasonable defense of his work only forestalls his tragedy, and Sabinus the unwary confidant, ensnared by informers. By defining character according to Roman philosophical and moral types, Jonson has differentiated members of the Germanicus faction, but the virtue that we see in these characters is always carefully limited. Arruntius is allowed to live because his

22. Barish repeatedly refers to the "mathematical" structure of *Sejanus*.

cynical remarks paradoxically dull rather than sharpen the edge of suspicion. White-haired, stoical Lepidus gives sound advice for living long, but he can only do a little to abate the corruption of the prince he serves. Germanicus, slain before the action begins, is universally praised, but the accuracy of accounts of his godlike virtue is always in question in a world where the mob takes Macro for a savior and Sejanus for a martyred saint. Indeed Jonson has gained much by his choice of a starting time for his play's action. True heroism is a vague past dream, always hedged about by the pragmatic and ruthless men of power. Those who contain particles of goodness lack the will to make their goodness grow.

Good in *Sejanus* is always overshadowed by evil, and the grim engines, practicers, organs, and informers—the physician Eudemus, the orator Afer, the judge Vertumnus, and the rest—are members of that same, distant, lost world of the classical mold that yielded to the worship of Fortune, the statues of heroes, the intricate and corrupted legal practices, and the formulas for the lady Livia's cosmetics. They are all known by scant references in the Roman histories, some by name alone, and they are made agents of unscrupulous powers in the play, as were their dramatic ancestors, the soldiers, mockers, scourgers, and nailers at the Cross in the mysteries or the assailants or tempters in the moralities. There, like here, these figures work in the open air with an implied official sanction that is chilling. G. B. Jackson has shown the elaborate manner by which Jonson drew characters, known only by name in the histories, by exhausting the meanings of their names.[23] This suggests a larger order in this sinister world than the one apprehended by the characters within it; it also suggests the play's very close link with the morality tradition. The sinister figures, colored by images of machines or hounds, have a mindless instinct for evil; unlike the morality figures, they move in a wholly pagan context that offers no possibility of redemption.

Sejanus's rise, self-deception, and fall are a familiar pattern in medieval and Renaissance drama, but Sejanus is doomed never to rise to the summit of his ambition. His fall is intricately bound up with his fatal blindness, but he is never pictured as one of the mettle of the typical tragic hero. He

---

23. G. B. Jackson, pp. 63–64: Fulvia, Curius, Lentulus, and Bestia from *Catiline* are examined, but Macro will certainly serve as well.

seems curiously destined to follow a plan laid out for him by Fortune, who
is his goddess. His quarrel with Drusus only gives a public cause for the
removal he has already plotted. Tiberius has already conceived of the
extermination of the Germanicus party when Sejanus tells him of his plan
for a final solution. Macro has completely arranged the confrontation in
the Senate when Sejanus hurls down his unruly statue, once owned by a
Roman king. Sejanus's pride in his rise is undercut everywhere by our
broader vision. His successes are admired by his followers and disbelieved
or grudged by the Germanicus faction. It is surprising that he is allowed to
proceed as far as he does. In Act III Sejanus is shown as wholly misjudging
Tiberius, whom we finally see as devious as well as decisive. Though his
presumptuous petition to marry Drusus's widow Livia evokes Tiberius's
ominous grunt, Sejanus does not suspect mistrust. Instead he swells with
pride each time Fortune smiles on him. This master of flattery penetrates
neither Tiberius's profession of friendship nor Macro's later promise to live
to serve him. Sejanus's blindness provides occasion for some of the biting
ironies in the play; in one sense the play may be a satirical portrait of the
mind of an ambitious man, but if this sense is elaborated, comedy and
satire must part ways—we do not laugh at Sejanus, ever.

It is possible to argue that we glimpse for a brief moment the humanity
of Sejanus, as for no other character, when, thwarted by Fortune, he hears
of Macro's arrival amid a plethora of lesser portents. But his momentary
admirable humility, carefully emphasized by Cotta and the others,
vanishes when Sejanus believes the lie about the tribunicial power and
quickly swells again with disdainful pride. His humble wish to divide
himself among his followers is granted in his dismemberment, perhaps the
most grotesquely ironical detail in the whole play.

Tiberius, cunning, yet cautious, associated with the image of the
ravenous wolf, is ever inscrutable and all-powerful, because of his almost
superhuman knowledge of how his people will act. No one stands on an
equal base with him, and his intelligence and political finesse are not only
impressive, but they assure his survival through the holocaust. Perhaps the
most brilliant portrait of the Machiavellian Prince in the drama, Tiberius
equivocates in a public world that is an Argus of eyes and a Rumor full of
tongues. In private he seems to play with Sejanus like Sejanus's catlike

statue of Fortune, "the eternal game and laughter." He has countenanced Germanicus's death and capitalized on Drusus's fall. He will break laws to serve his servants and lie endlessly to cover his deceits or fears. His masterful politics are nowhere more evident than in his conjuration of Macro in Act III, after Sejanus's ambitions are clear to him. Having provided this "aconite" to purge his "Scorpion's" poison, he vanishes into godlike seclusion, only referred to afterward by conflicting rumors, the delaying incident at Spelunca, and the oracular letter in the Senate. From Macro we learn that Tiberius has been given false information; from Sejanus that he is surrounded with spies; from Arruntius and others that he is gratifying his outrageous lust. To stay in Rome spelled fear. To go to Capreae meant not only immunity (Capreae was like a charmed circle, outside of which the evil magic worked), but isolation from true report-age. Macro was, indeed, in retrospect timely, if not divinely, thought upon. The emperor who refused the honors of a god assumed the role of one, and the play from Act III to its conclusion resembles no model more closely than Euripides' *Bacchae,* in which the punishment of Pentheus's people far exceeded their crimes. Sejanus's mistake, like Pentheus's, was not to recognize the god.

Tiberius's use of the metaphor of poison for his two henchmen not only underscores the emphatic use of the imagery of poison in the play, but also suggests that the state itself is a body stung by a scorpion and in need of a desperate remedy. Jonson's concern for the theory of humours provides an avenue for approaching this metaphor of the body politic, where the state is a single body and within it the faculties of the mind seem to be warring for the possession of its soul. The slaughter of the finest mental faculties—of the possibility of integral wholeness in Germanicus, or of the power to perceive and act in Silius, or of the power to remember exemplary figures of the past in Cordus—clears the way for undermining the rest of the character. Sejanus, the infected will, given power by Tiberius, the waver-ing and defective wit, its divine power only dimly discerned through its depravity, seeks to corrupt the body or body politic absolutely. Rome, by this crude model, becomes a kind of Renaissance version of the Castle of Perseverance, and the progressive deterioration of the state, an analogue for the increasing depravity of man himself. This allegorical reading is supported by the insistent use of the imagery of bodily parts as well as of division and disintegration.[24] As his friend Donne transformed the death of Elizabeth Drury into an Anatomy of the Whole World and of Man in his *Anniversaries*, so Jonson showed that the personal and historical developments in his drama are mutually reflective. Human degeneracy and the progressive decline of the world are as immutable laws.

The beadle of Tiberius, the visible scourge Macro, is a ruthless self-seeker whom we remember from an often-quoted soliloquy that may reach the moral nadir among forthright statements in the play:

> I will not ask why CAESAR bids me doe this . . .
> Were it to plot against the fame, the life
> Of one, with whom I train'd; remoue a wife
> From my warme side, as lou'd, as is the ayre:
> Practice away each parent; draw mine heyre
> In compasse, though but one; worke all my kin
> To swift perdition, leave no vntrain'd engin,
> For friendship, or for innocence; nay, make
> The gods all guiltie: I would undertake
> This, being impos'd me, both with gaine, and ease.
> The way to rise, is to obey, and please.
>
> (III.iii.714, 726–735)

This speech with its stops and turns, and its cool progression through a list of increasingly atrocious deeds, is in unobtrusive rhyme, and mirrors the cool and narrow mind that gives it such exquisite form in the same way that the form of the play is related to its content. We look forward from this speech to Lodovico of *The White Devil:* "I limned this night piece and it was my best," and to Bosola of *The Duchess of Malfi:* "Look you, the stars shine still," but Macro, unlike Bosola, does not mock to ennoble,[25] and seems thinly drawn next to Webster's eloquent and ambivalent creations. Macro's evil is grotesquely refined and transcends mere politics. He, not Suetonius's executioner, gratuitously ravishes Sejanus's innocent daughter

24. Norbert H. Platz, *Ethik und Rhetoric in Ben Jonsons Dramen* (Heidelberg, 1976), pp. 200–202, sees the chorus as anatomizing the body politic.

25. Travis Bogard, *The Tragic Satire of John Webster* (Berkeley, Calif., 1955), pp. 144–145, on "integrity of life."

on the scaffold to slake his lust. Amplified from a mere name in the histories, Macro becomes a symbol in *Sejanus*, the visible extension and externalization of the will of the Machiavellian Prince. His obedience is to Caesar alone; he is controlled by a clear knowledge of his ambition and its limitations.

The world Jonson created has been repeatedly called "Machiavellian." One interpretation even calls Tiberius the Ideal Prince.[26] Numerous parallel passages have been adduced to show Machiavelli's influence. However, most of Jonson's Machiavellism can be explained by his classical sources, especially Tacitus.[27] Toffanin has shown that Machiavelli and Tacitus were fused in the Renaissance Continental imagination, and that *Tacitismo* had grave political overtones.[28] It is probable that Jonson drew from Tacitus and Machiavelli simultaneously (in *The Magnetic Lady* he joined the two names as a matter of course), not in order to advocate any political theory as such, but to illustrate a more problematical and even tragic political condition.

Many political "lessons" have been drawn from *Sejanus*,[29] and numerous attempts have been made to relate the play to contemporary politics in England. J. W. Lever's cogent account of the politics of *Sejanus* in *The Tragedy of State* emphasizes that "Jonson's devastating satire portrays not the tragedy of one man but of a whole society in the political inferno of its own creation" (p. 69). Jonson has not written either a political treatise or an ethical code. What he shares with Tacitus and Machiavelli is a fundamental skepticism about the possibility of virtue triumphing either in

26. Evans, pp. 239–264; see Boughner, "*Sejanus* and Machiavelli," p. 95.

27. E. Meyer, *Machiavelli and the Elizabethan Drama* (Weimar, 1897), p. 101, first showed that Jonson got his Machiavellianism from the classics; see also G. K. Hunter, "English Folly and Italian Vice: The Moral Landscape of John Marston," in *Stratford-upon-Avon Studies*, I (1960), 96, n. 18; and see Dorenkamp, p. 215, for "Machiavellianism" in *Catiline*.

28. Giuseppe Toffanin, *Machiavelli e il "Tacitismo" la "politica storica" al tempo della controriforma* (Padua, 1921). Jonson himself fused Machiavelli and Tacitus in *The Magnetic Lady*, I.vii.29–32: "A crysolite, a Gemme: the very Agate / Of State and Politie: cut from the Quar / Of Machiavel, a true Carnelian / As *Tacitus* himself!"

29. Evans, p. 249, enumerates some of these. For implications of Republicanism in *Sejanus*, see Platz, pp. 180–202.

human nature or in world history. The play extolls no viable philosophical system as satisfactory—there is no effectual man of virtue in the play; instead it huddles proponents of various systems in a larger skeptical framework, which remains problematical rather than conclusive. For all of Jonson's didacticism, *Sejanus* is the least overtly didactic of his plays.

III

Critics trying to dissociate *Sejanus* from the medieval tradition of the "Wheel of Fortune" play have debated whether the Romans' faith in Fortune is a red herring.[30] The portents, statue of Fortune, and *sententiae* are real, but the evil forces operating in the play are in the hearts of its characters too, and the certainty of disaster overrides apparent freaks of Fortune in the life of any single man. Some force, larger even than Tiberius, is working in the play, but its operations are inscrutable, and it seems to be guiding Rome toward the universal ruin that Augustine saw as metaphorical of a final end to the world. Innocent and guilty alike fall prey to the battling titans. Suspicion and informing breed an atmosphere of danger, and in this atmosphere aspects of character that may promise survival, such as sleepless plotting, endless railing, or stoical withdrawal, are not altogether admirable. Law is subject to a tyrant's whim, and a mob is ready to destroy anyone at the word of an orator. Even skepticism will not guarantee survival.

In earlier English drama there are a few precursors to the atmosphere of *Sejanus*, but no previous play presents an impression of such unrelieved disaster: a poisoned body politic actively destroying itself. The rigid structure, the interplay of Fortune's little jokes and great tragedies, the multiple sententious voices all crying different philosophies, and the stark, morality-play villains, convince us that the world of *Sejanus* is a successful re-creation not simply of the Tacitean-Machiavellian world, but rather of a

30. Gary D. Hamilton, "Irony and Fortune in *Sejanus*," *SEL*, XI (1971), 265: Jonson's use of fortune is "basically ironic"; Boughner, "Juvenal, Horace, and *Sejanus*," p. 547, n. 5: it is "misleading to regard Fortune as the predominant concept in *Sejanus*"; and Barish, p. 221: "Fortune, at base, is a metaphor, a desperate trope whereby men shirk the consequences of their own folly."

world in which Machiavellian politics can thrive because its whole structure seems to be without a sure foundation.

This atmosphere—where rational, stoical, cynical, and Machiavellian
positions are given voice, but undercut by one another within a larger
skeptical framework where grim ironies are the only truths available—
justifies a reappraisal of the genre of *Sejanus.* Its mixture of history,
tragedy, and even satire perplexes. Doubt is pervasive in the play, which
demands a skeptical, but certainly not comic or sardonic, reaction.

If the morally critical implications of the play suggest a satiric perspective, it is satire without laughter; yet its tragic dimensions lack the
ennobling qualities that Travis Bogard has explored in Webster's more
reflective "tragical satires." Dryden thought that the interchange between
Eudemus and Livia was comic; but the scene is darkly ironical, not comic.
Its purpose is to help us realize the inhumanity of characters whose conversation coolly mingles cosmetics and poisons. To associate the chesslike
movements of Tiberius with the comic ingenuity of Volpone or Subtle is
to take the influence the wrong way. Sejanus's blindness is not laughable,
though his actions are certainly criminal; and his death is unnaturally
horrible and awesome, revealing the fearful power of Tiberius and Macro
and the furious mob. Arruntius, whose forced laughter has been an expression of rage throughout the play, is so struck by Sejanus's fall that he can
immediately and sincerely meditate on the frailty of human life in the
hands of Fortune.

There is a tension between the over-all form of the play and the hid-
eously deformed characters and actions within that form. We are reminded
of the fashionable Mannerist grotesques on quasi-classical façades, like
those of Giulio Romano, with their massive and contorted bodies and
savage, leering faces, discordant over their precisely delineated windows.
The precision of the design of the whole play is in tension with the crowds
of bothersome characters. Neither the grotesques nor the over-all geo-
metric form of the play are human, the former too monstrous, the latter
too perfectly mathematical, like the content and form of Macro's soliloquy.

Other aspects of the drama cause unrest. We can neither ignore nor
sympathize with Tiberius, Macro, Sejanus and his party, the Germanicus
party, Drusus, or the mob. We may marvel at the ingenuity and power of

the titans, and we may find attractive the philosophical posture of one of the
Germanicus faction, but we cannot accept the consequences of any choice.
The paradoxes in the play are not resolved for us, and we dare not resolve
them for ourselves. We are forced to accept or to reject the whole action
and all its characters as mirrors of aspects of ourselves, as members of
mankind. *Sejanus* is satiric in the way all tragedies are: it mocks the thing
it feeds on; here, however, the tragedy is not of a single man or of a
society, but of the pervasive state of mind of a whole age. Although
satire generally provides or implies standards, those offered by Lepidus,
Arruntius, and Terentius at the play's end are unsatisfactory. Times have
changed. The center will not hold. The compass is broken. In the pattern
of world history, centuries must pass before the new Golden Age can
come, and individual men in this historical framework seem insignificant.
Jonson's attention to historic details suggests a tragic view of history as an
entropic process, a continual decline. The Providential and Hesiodic views
of history intersect only in Revelation, and Apocalypse is the only answer
to the world Jonson presents.

Sir Philip Sidney had placed the poet above the philosopher and the
historian. *Sejanus* partakes of both philosophy and history, but transcends
both, though Jonson clearly presents no "golden" but an iron world. The
philosophy is evident in the individual voices and in the darkly inquisitive
nature of the atmosphere of the whole play. History has been arranged to
force the audience to a higher awareness of the tragedy of a world being
ground between gigantic forces in a historical cycle that shows no relief.
The artistic form evokes an emotional, not a contemplative response. For
all its pretensions to historical accuracy (see the 1605 Quarto and its
sidenotes), *Sejanus* is a powerful tragedy with a poetry brilliantly conceived
to reflect both irony and tragic grandeur. Surely Jonson would have liked
his readers to investigate the histories from which he took his material,
but *Sejanus* has more than a narrowly pedantic purpose, as Jonson's removal of the 1605 marginal notes in the Folio of 1616 implied. Jonson's
tragedy is revolutionary in ways undreamed of by the privy council.
Historically a tragedy for the fitful few, *Sejanus* has value not in its
historical accuracy but in the enormous burden it places on the man who
once enters and for a moment utterly accepts its statement about the
condition of mankind.

Sejanus did not entirely satisfy Jonson, and for eight years he produced only comedies and masques, but the play troubled his contemporaries and had an immediate impact on his fellow dramatists. When we recall Jonson's feud with Dekker and Marston at the turn of the century in the theater war, we are not surprised that they were the first to attack Jonson's scrupulous use of historical details. Marston had dedicated *The Malcontent* (1604) to Jonson and collaborated with Jonson and Chapman on *Eastward Ho!* (1604), but took him to task for the notes to the 1605 *Sejanus* in the introduction to his *Sophonisba* (1606). Later Webster and Chapman had to part ways with Jonson on the matter of historical details, though both had praised *Sejanus* in commendatory poems in the 1605 Quarto. The burden of historical accuracy was too heavy to bear; nevertheless, the serious dramatists, especially in their tragedies of revenge, revealed a significant debt to the *atmosphere* of *Sejanus*. That is, although Jonson's effects were in large part derived from his use of a multitude of sources, the play which emerged could be taken as standing apart from the method used.[31]

Sejanus's closest relatives are the French tragedies of Chapman.[32] The France of *Bussy D'Ambois* has the same distant quality as the Rome of *Sejanus*, only its landscape is more restrictive. The court is corrupt, but our sympathies are likely to be engaged on account of the love intrigues and the genuinely heroic temper of Alcides-like Bussy. John Webster's *The White Devil*, whose introduction is nearly a copy of Jonson's 1605 introduction to *Sejanus*, and *The Duchess of Malfi* are set in worlds apart, and in them we see our deepest fears about government, gods, and our own darker nature. But, in the latter, alongside the spidery operations of the

31. W. F. Bolton, p. xi, describes its more specific influence after its revival between 1605 and 1616: "in its revived esteem (*Sejanus*) provided a quarry for poets from Fletcher and Drayton to Milton, who adopted its language"; see E. Koeppel, *Ben Jonsons Wirkung auf zeitgenossische Dramatiker,* Anglistische Forschungen, vol. XX (Heidelberg, 1906), especially his praise of *Sejanus* on p. 146. But *Catiline*, not *Sejanus* was "the premier English tragedy in the minds of seventeenth-century writers," according to G. E. Bentley, *Shakespeare and Jonson: Their Reputations in the Seventeenth Century Compared* (Chicago, 1945), I, 111–12; cf. W. D. Briggs, "The Influence of Jonson's Tragedy in the Seventeenth Century," *Anglia*, XXXV (1924), 277–337.

32. H & S, II, 4; see K. M. Burton, "The Political Tragedies of Chapman and Ben Jonson," *Essays in Criticism*, III (1952), 397–412.

villainous characters, especially the Cardinal, is the genuine nobility of the Duchess.

Jonson's great contribution to the drama in *Sejanus* may have been made unawares. Trying for scrupulous honesty in his use of sources, he did not invent a moral envelope that might mitigate the ruthless attitudes embodied in them. He might add speeches, choose a character to mouth choral asides, put two trials of innocents side-by-side for contrast and compound this by having one commit suicide on the stage, but he could not reform Tiberius entirely or gloss over Sejanus's character, or make Macro the savior of the country. Jonson's fidelity to history in *Sejanus* brought forth a self-contained universe that was multifaceted, distant, and coherent. That universe was narrow and fearful, but mirrored another world deep in all our minds, ready to degrade us when we recognize its presence as separate, inviolable, containing all the possibilities of crime, deception, superstition, and fear, which move us, however remotely, in reading the Roman histories themselves.

Emblem and Antithesis in
The Duchess of Malfi

CATHERINE BELSEY

T HE TENSION between realism and abstraction which characterizes much Renaissance drama is strikingly displayed in *The Duchess of Malfi*. Critical discussions of the play's psychological realism, on the one hand, or its moral instruction, on the other, have proved largely unproductive. Though critics have recognized an elusive power in Webster's text, they have reluctantly concluded that it is ultimately flawed—psychologically incoherent or morally anarchic. Meanwhile, however, we are becoming increasingly aware that the qualities of plays like *Tamburlaine*, for instance, or *The Revenger's Tragedy*, are more readily understood in the context of an approach to Renaissance drama which takes account of its patently nonrealist antecedents. *The Duchess of Malfi*, I want to suggest, is a play poised, formally as well as historically, between the emblematic tradition of the medieval stage and the increasing commitment to realism of the post-Restoration theater.

The realist tradition, which becomes dominant in the eighteenth century and culminates in the well-made play of the nineteenth, places a high premium on individual psychological analysis, narrative enigma, and a dramatic structure which facilitates the unfolding of a coherent action.

115

The medieval tradition, by contrast, deals in the much more generalized psychology of representative moral types (in the cycles) or of "Mankind" (in the moralities), and develops a structure which promotes moral understanding in the audience rather than suspense. Realism (in the sense in which I have defined it) invites close audience involvement in the action; the medieval tradition distances the audience from the narrative, repeatedly arresting the action for the sake of moral analysis or debate.

Renaissance drama inherits this tradition of analysis and debate, while at the same time moving toward new conventions of verisimilitude and narrative tautness. The realist element has been the subject of extensive critical discussion, of course, but we have paid rather less attention to the continuing use of the medieval techniques of emblem and antithesis to focus the attention of the audience on the solution to the moral questions raised by the play, as opposed to the resolution of the narrative and psychological enigmas it poses. Dieter Mehl has drawn attention to the prominence of the emblematic tradition in Renaissance drama,[1] and I think that we may extend his argument to find evidence of the tradition not only in stage properties and allegorical dumb shows, but in the structural patterns of the plays themselves.

Emblem books use picture and text to propose an *interpretation* of a *concept* (opportunity, constancy), or the *relationship between concepts* (truth and error, wisdom and experience). In this they are the direct heirs of the medieval allegorical tradition. On the medieval stage the spectacle of Mankind flanked by Good and Bad Angels constitutes a "speaking picture" and its interpretation, an emblem of the human condition, divided between good and evil impulses. In this sense emblematic drama employs a mode of representation which is radically different from the realist quest for lifelike imagery.

At the same time, the tradition of debate in the medieval drama— between Cain and Abel, or Noah and Mrs. Noah in the cycles, for instance, or between virtues and vices in the moralities—depends on a pattern of antitheses. The spectators participate actively in the process of moral analysis to the extent that they evaluate the arguments, behavior,

---

1. Dieter Mehl, "Emblems in English Drama," *RenD*, II (1969), 39–57.

and fates of the contrasted figures. At the structural level the pattern of antithesis appears in the introduction of contrasted episodes, or of comic episodes which parody the main action. The conjuring of the clowns in *Doctor Faustus* is descended from the tradition which finds its most elaborate form in *The Second Shepherd's Play*.

Renaissance drama displays a conflict of interest between the new search for the reproduction of outward appearances and the concomitant commitment to narrative form, and the inherited tendency to interpretation and analysis of what seems to lie behind appearances. Glynne Wickham finds in the contemporary disputes over the adequacy of Renaissance staging conventions evidence of "a head-on collision of two fundamentally opposed attitudes to art: the typically medieval contentment with emblematic comment on the significance of the visual world versus a new, scientific questing for the photographic image."[2] It is my hypothesis that we may find evidence of a similar collision within the structures of the plays themselves, and that the existence of this collision necessitates a critical approach to Renaissance drama which is not content with the discussion of psychological realism or the moral values of the dramatist.

Contradictory structural elements in *The Duchess of Malfi* generate a tension between its realist features—psychological plausibility and narrative sequence—and the formality of its design. Close analysis of the text reveals that the audience is repeatedly invited by the realist surface to expect the unfolding of a situation or the interplay of specific characters, only to find that the actual constantly resolves into abstraction, the characters into figures in a pattern. The imagery, both visual and verbal, often functions in a way that is emblematic rather than realistic, arresting the movement of the plot and placing the emphasis on significance rather than experience. The effect is a play that presents an anatomy of the world rather than a replica of it.

The tension between realism and abstraction informs the construction of the play from the beginning. Act I opens with Antonio's account of the "fix'd order" established by the judicious king of France (I.i.4–22).[3] What

2. Glynne Wickham, *Early English Stages* (London, 1959 ——), II, i. 209.
3. References are to the Revels text, ed. John Russell Brown (London, 1965). There is no need to suppose that the speech is an interpolation (Brown, pp. xxv-xxvi).

is remarkable about this speech is that it tells the audience little about
Antonio and nothing at all about the situation which provides the plot of
the play. This is unusual in the *extent* to which the speech is isolated from
the narrative sequence. The openings of Elizabethan tragedies, though
they often do much more, normally offer at least some information concerning the ensuing action. The first scene of *King Lear* introduces Lear's
intention to divide the kingdom as well as Edmund's bastardy; the opening scene of *Othello* establishes Iago's hatred of the hero. *The Revenger's
Tragedy* begins with Vindice's commentary on the court as it passes over
the stage, and his subsequent meditation with the skull explains the
sources of his impulse to revenge; the opening of *The Changeling* shows
Alsemero in love with Beatrice-Joanna and so points toward the central
situation of the play. On the other hand, in each of the first three cases the
opening scene has the important function of defining not only the relationships between individual characters, but also a state of society within
which the ensuing action is intelligible.

Other instances resemble *The Duchess of Malfi* more closely. The opening
of *Bussy D'Ambois* functions fairly obviously as a prologue to the theme of
courtly corruption and has something of the static and defining quality of
Antonio's speech. But it also serves to identify Bussy's own initial position
of Stoic virtue, which is immediately threatened by the entry of Monsieur.
It is thus not external to the action in quite the same sense as Antonio's
description of the French court. The Andrea-Revenge prologue to *The
Spanish Tragedy* is outside the central events of the play, but it frames
them, giving an account of the preceding action and leading into the main
plot.

Antonio's speech, however, brings sharply into focus a mode of construction which is very different from that of the realist tradition. The
speech defines an ideal of government which emphasizes by *contrast* the
courtly corruption of the world of the play. It forms not only an integral
but an important part of the whole: the play refers back to it many times,
as I shall suggest. But it works by establishing an external and static
model, not by leading into a sequence of events.

The entry of Bosola (l. 22) and of the Cardinal (l. 28) leads us to expect
that the world of the play's action will now be introduced. And to some
extent this expectation is fulfilled. Bosola is seen to be a recognizable

dramatic type, the malcontent, and his opening exchanges with the Cardinal indicate a specific situation: he is neglected and resentful. At this point several possible developments suggest themselves to the audience: a quarrel, an account of the crime which has led Bosola to the galleys, or the employment of Bosola for some specific purpose. Instead the Cardinal gives three brief and noncommittal replies to his complaints and then goes out, leaving Bosola in mid-generalization about the pursuit of honesty (ll. 42–44). Antonio again invites us to expect an account of Bosola's situation: "He hath denied thee some suit?" But Bosola does not answer the question directly. Instead he offers an image of the court:

He, and his brother, are like plum-trees, that grow crooked over standing pools; they are rich, and o'erladen with fruit, but none but crows, pies, and caterpillars feed on them.

(ll. 49–52)

The plum trees and the stagnant pools are stationary, their relative positions fixed in an image which functions like an emblem, simultaneously delineating and commenting morally on the world of the play. There is a specific contrast here with Antonio's account of the French court, which is a fountain nourishing the state (l. 12), and which is purged of parasites like those which "feed" on Ferdinand and the Cardinal (ll. 7–9). There follows a series of images, equally vivid and equally emblematic (ll. 52–69), and all amplifying Bosola's analysis of the Italian court. When Bosola leaves the stage at line 69 we have learned no more of the plot than we knew at line 30.

There follows the entry of the court (ll. 82 ff.), and by analogy with *Hamlet* or *Lear*, or even *The White Devil*, the audience might now expect the main lines of the action to be drawn up. What they are offered is a quasi-realistic conversation concerning horsemanship, and a series of double entendres at the expense of Castruchio. The episode gives us no significant information at the level of action. Instead it amplifies further Bosola's images of the court. It is idle (ll. 91–92) like the stagnant pools, and it nourishes flattering sycophants like those dismissed by the French king (l. 8).

The figure of Ferdinand is dominant:

Why do you laugh? Methinks you that are courtiers should be my touch-wood,
take fire, when I give fire; that is, laugh when I laugh, were the subject never so
witty.

(ll. 122–125)

This court has none of the reciprocity of France, where the king relies on a
council "who dare freely / Inform him the corruption of the times" (ll.
17–18). In contrast to the French court the Italian one is dramatized, not
described: action and interaction between figures on the stage replace an
account. But at the same time the episode shares something of the static
quality of Antonio's description or Bosola's images. It displays and defines:
it does not develop.

The entry of the Duchess and the Cardinal (l. 147) provokes not a
situation but further description, Antonio's "characters" of the Cardinal,
Ferdinand, and the Duchess. Like the Overbury *Characters* these define a
series of types: they are in no sense psychological portraits. [4] They make no
attempt to account in terms of motive or past experience for the qualities
they identify, nor are they offered as a basis for moral or psychological
development. In this sense they are analogous to Antonio's opening speech
and Bosola's images of the court, and like them they are related to one
another by specific antitheses:

> the spring in his face is nothing but the engendering of toads
> (ll. 158–159)

> the law to him
> Is like a foul black cobweb to a spider—
> He makes it his dwelling, and a prison
> To entangle those shall feed him
> (ll. 177–180)

> She stains the time past, lights the time to come.
> (l. 209)

While light radiates from the Duchess, what issues from the Cardinal and

4. Cf. Monticelso's "character" of a whore, John Webster, *The White Devil*, ed. John
Russell Brown (London, 1966), III.ii.78–101; cf. also Vindice's opening account of "four
excellent characters," Cyril Tourneur, *The Revenger's Tragedy*, ed. R. A. Foakes (London,
1966), I.i.5.

Ferdinand is dark, repulsive, and finally deadly. The contrast evokes the antithesis within Antonio's opening speech:

> a prince's court
> Is like a common fountain, whence should flow
> Pure silver drops in general: but if't chance
> Some curs'd example poison 't near the head,
> *Death and diseases through the whole land spread.*
>
> (ll. 11–15)

The emblematic fountain radiates purity and life, or death and diseases. Antonio's equally emblematic portraits of the Duchess and her brothers echo these contrasting possibilities, and the rest of the play amplifies the antithesis, juxtaposing the Duchess's world of innocence, reciprocity, and fertility with Ferdinand's sterile darkness, isolation, and death.

These metaphors of spreading and radiating are oddly analogous to Webster's own dramatic technique. After over two hundred lines the play still has no semblance of plot. Commentary has alternated with episodes which fail to develop a situation, leaving the audience with its expectations unfulfilled in terms of events, but with a strong and expanding sense of certain polarities which the text defines in outline and then in detail, in imagery and then in action.

The long-delayed creation of a situation now follows very rapidly. In only eight lines Cariola arranges a meeting between the Duchess and Antonio, and Ferdinand secures the provisorship of the horse for Bosola (ll. 210–218). His appointment of Bosola as intelligencer follows, and the details of the situation begin to emerge: Bosola is to "observe the duchess" (l. 252); she is a young widow (l. 255); Ferdinand "would not have her marry again" (l. 256). The dialogue now has a strong flavor of realism. Bosola's harsh cynicism is expressed in the language and rhythms of ordinary speech:

> Whose throat must I cut?
>
> (l. 249)

> what's my place?
> The provisorship o'th'horse? say then, my corruption
> Grew out of horse-dung.
>
> (ll. 285–287)

At the same time, however, a curiously archetypal quality in this episode underlies the realism of the surface:

> 　　　　　　　　　　　Take your devils
> Which hell calls angels . . .
> 　. . . should I take these they'd take me to hell.
> 　　　　　　　　　　　　　　　　　　(ll. 263–266)
> 　　　　　　　　　　Thus the devil
> Candies all sins o'er . . .
> 　　　　　　　　　　　　　　　　　　(ll. 275–276)

The language recalls the pattern of temptation analyzed allegorically in countless morality plays. Bosola is "lur'd" to Ferdinand (l. 231) and is entangled, through his own desire to "thrive" in the world (l. 261; cf. l. 37), in a web of false reasoning, deception, and self-deception which leads to his damnation. The specific hiring of a spy simultaneously evokes the temptation and fall of Mankind, and the episode hovers disturbingly between realism and abstraction. Bosola's closing *sententia* seems to resolve it into abstraction:

> Let good men, for good deeds, covet good fame,
> Since place and riches oft are bribes of shame—
> Sometimes the devil doth preach.[5]
> 　　　　　　　　　　　　　　　　　　(ll. 289–291)

The instruction to the Duchess follows logically in terms of the play's action, but this time it is the ritualistic nature of the dialogue which is surprising. The play itself draws attention to the "studied" quality (l. 329) of the patterned, formal, joint monologue of the brothers, which is punctuated by the strikingly more natural interjections of the Duchess: "Will you hear me?" (l. 301); "This is terrible good counsel" (l. 312). At the literal level the episode tells the audience nothing that Ferdinand has not already told Bosola. It fails to resolve the enigma of his motivation, already apparently deliberately created by the play ("Do not you ask the reason," l. 257). Instead it establishes a contrast between the natural

---

5. The devil or the Vice conventionally "preaches" in the morality plays.

behavior of the Duchess and the curiously contrived, "studied" world of the brothers. Subsequently, Ferdinand's motives remain obscure: his examination of the "cause" (IV.ii.281–287) explains nothing to our satisfaction, and his dying words preserve the enigma—*"Whether we fall by ambition, blood or lust . . . "* (V.v.72). But the polarity established here is amplified in the rest of the play, which consistently aligns the Duchess with the freedom of nature, and Ferdinand and the Cardinal with a world of artifice, embodied in the waxworks, the masque of madmen, and the violent ritual of the divorce. In Act IV the Duchess is "plagu'd in art" (IV.i.111) until she becomes like her "picture":

> A deal of life in show, but none in practice;
> Or rather like some reverend monument
> Whose ruins are even pitied.
>
> (IV.ii.32–34)

The two parts of the comparison taken together ironically evoke her own previous assertion:

> This is flesh, and blood, sir;
> 'Tis not the figure cut in alabaster
> Kneels at my husband's tomb.
>
> (I.i.453–455)

The effect of Webster's technique is to define good and evil by antithesis, at first in broad terms (the fountain and the poison) and then more specifically (domination and reciprocity, radiance and cobwebs, nature and artifice), and at the same time to show through the sequence of events the processes by which evil reduces good to a semblance of itself. Ferdinand's "artifice" envelops the Duchess, reducing her to a lifeless work of art; his darkness progressively reduces her radiance; his mental hell is realized in the tortures of the Duchess and brings her close to despair.

Further detailed analysis of the mode of construction in *The Duchess of Malfi* would, I suggest, reveal that the technique I have described is consistently maintained. The quasi-realistic surface repeatedly dissolves into *sententiae*, meditations, and fables. Not only does the imagery form a network of echoes, antitheses, and amplifications: whole episodes refer to and parody each other. The distribution of the central characters shows

more concern with pattern than with any kind of psychological probability.[6] As Antonio is to the Duchess, so the Cardinal is to Ferdinand—
cautious, prudent, restrained. They are figures in a design, not character
studies. The high points in the action of the play are realized precisely by
arresting the action and drawing the audience's attention to a visual
tableau: the Duchess unconsciously isolated on the stage, abandoned by
Antonio and threatened by Ferdinand (III.ii); the spectacle of the Duchess
confronting the spectacle of the waxworks (IV.i). During the dance of the
madmen (IV.ii) the Duchess does not speak; the emphasis is not on the
psychology of her reactions but on the contrast between her solitary still-
ness and the grotesque caperings which are an image of the tyranny she is
"chain'd to endure" (IV.ii.60). The dumb show of the Cardinal's arming
and the divorce (III.iv) distances what in another play would be a cue for
passionate individual response. The commentary of the pilgrims bears
precisely the same relation to the visual spectacle as the explanation to the
picture in an emblem.[7]

> 1ST PILGRIM
> What was it with such violence he took
> Off from her finger?
> 2D PILGRIM
> 'Twas her wedding ring,
> Which he vow'd shortly he would sacrifice
> To his revenge.

                                        (III.iv.36–39)

The key words "violence," "sacrifice," and "revenge" focus attention on
the nature of the evil, not on the experience of the characters. The same
principle is more sharply evident in the preceding exchange: "But by what
justice?" "Sure, I think by none" (III.iv.34). Abstraction repeatedly prevails over actuality, pattern over situation, structure over event.

6. For the death blow to the quest for probability see Christopher Ricks, "The Tragedies of Webster, Tourneur and Middleton: Symbols, Imagery and Conventions," *English
Drama to 1710,* Sphere History of Literature in the English Language, III (London, 1971),
306–351.
7. Mehl, p. 47.

Instead of tracing further the details of the play's construction, however, I should like to consider more closely the nature and the implications of the patterns which the technique establishes. As I have suggested, the central pattern is one of antitheses whose function is to identify and define. Thus, for instance, Cariola's terrified efforts to escape death emphasize the Duchess's fortitude (IV.ii). Julia acts consistently as a foil for the Duchess. Her relationship with the Cardinal forms a (rather slight) subplot which intensifies by contrast the effect of the main plot, drawing attention to the moral distance between Julia's fruitless and distrustful adultery and the Duchess's marriage. Act II, scene iv, offers a display of reciprocal accusations of inconstancy, which concludes with the Cardinal's extraordinarily ambiguous reassurance ("for my affection to thee, / Lightning moves slow to 't," II.iv.40–41), and Julia's ambivalent response to Delio's overtures. By Act V the Cardinal is weary of her; Julia betrays him to Bosola; he poisons her. This sequence is in direct contrast to the increasing fertility and reciprocal trust of the Duchess's marriage.

It has long been recognized that Julia's proposition to Bosola parodies the Duchess's proposal to Antonio both in language and action. Gunnar Boklund complains that this episode comes too late to clarify the moral question whether the Duchess's second marriage is innocent or wanton, willful, and base.[8] It seems to me, however, that this is a question raised by twentieth-century criticism anxious to locate the Duchess's tragic flaw, and not by the play itself, which owes nothing to the Aristotelian concept of tragedy. The function of the intrigue between Julia and Bosola is to reenact in caricature the entire life of the Duchess, and not merely her wooing. As a result of her wanton overtures to Bosola, Julia hurries to her ruin (V.ii.258) by coming to participate in "a prince's secrets" (l. 260). In doing so she ties a dangerous knot (l. 264): the Cardinal warns her that possession of the secret may cause her death (l. 266). He poisons her, and she dies exclaiming, "I go, / I know not whither" (ll. 288–289). The Duchess's wooing, by contrast, leads to the "sacred Gordian" of her secret marriage which is the cause of her death. She dies certain of heaven. Julia's

8. Gunnar Boklund, *The Duchess of Malfi: Sources, Themes, Characters* (Cambridge, Mass., 1962), p. 158.

intrigue is like a negative photograph of the Duchess's marriage, and part of its effect is to "place" the Duchess in the minds of the audience so that the values she represents are reemphasized after her death. The echo scene, which follows this one, achieves a similar effect by positive means, offering Antonio (and possibly the audience)[9] a momentary vision of the Duchess herself (V.iii.45).

During the wooing scene (I.i.361–503) Antonio accuses himself of ambition (ll. 412–413) and calls it "madness" (ll. 420 ff.). In case the audience should be tempted to any absolute evaluation and judgment, the following scene opens with Castruchio's grotesque version of the same vice and Bosola's instructions on how to satisfy it (II.i.1–20). Earlier in Act I Bosola has displayed the more serious implications of ambition: in order to "thrive" in the world he knowingly chooses a course which leads to damnation. Thus placed between exemplum and satire, Antonio's "ambition," which leads to faithful marriage, is seen to be artless and transparent, dangerous in the corrupt world of the play, but morally innocent in the sense that, unlike Bosola and Castruchio, Antonio defies the values of that world.

Similarly, the painted Old Lady serves to reinforce the Duchess's purity. Bosola's "meditation" (II.i.45–60) and his sardonic imperative, "you two couple" (II.i.61), reduce humanity to the level of the beasts. The scene follows the declaration of Antonio and the Duchess that their marriage is to emulate the music of the spheres (I.i.481–484). Far from "tainting" the Duchess as Berry suggests,[10] the contrast defines her, and the juxtaposition of the two scenes embraces the paradox of human nature.

This paradox, that human beings may aspire to heaven or sink to the level of the beasts, is among the main implications of the play's pattern of contrasts. The central antithesis in the play is, of course, between the Duchess who, valuing life, is able to die (III.ii.71) and the predatory Ferdinand, man as wolf, destroying others. That the play establishes a polarity between the values of life and death, fertility and destruction is widely agreed. What is not, I think, so commonly recognized, is the

9. A lighting effect may have revealed the Duchess herself within a grave (Brown, p. xxxv).

10. Ralph Berry, *The Art of John Webster* (Oxford, 1972), p. 42.

number of points at which the pattern of the play apparently calls this antithesis into question by establishing parallels between Ferdinand and the Duchess, only to resolve them again into further polarities. The Duchess's dissimulation, her equivocation, her double entendres, her cursing and her "madness" are in a sense *like* Ferdinand's. (That they are twins, of course, invites a director to draw attention in visual terms to the ironic parallels.) At the same time, however, examination of these points of likeness proves in each case to emphasize the moral distance between the Duchess and Ferdinand. The play thus constitutes an exploration of the nature of evil, setting out to discover whether it is synonymous with particular patterns of behavior, and concluding, I believe, that it is not. Just as the form of the play constantly raises expectations that its focal point will be a series of events, only to resolve situation into pattern or abstraction, so the pattern itself draws parallels between Ferdinand and the Duchess, only to resolve them into new contrasts. As the construction of the play undermines its realism, so its thematic pattern undermines Antonio's self-accusation:

> The great are like the base—nay, they are the same—
> When they seek shameful ways, to avoid shame.

> (II.iii.51–52)

Dissimulation is the characteristic method by which Ferdinand and the Cardinal achieve their aims.[11] Ferdinand "will seem to sleep o'th'bench / Only to entrap offenders" (I.i.174–175); the Cardinal, who would have become pope by bribery "without heaven's knowledge" (I.i.166), would appoint Bosola an intelligencer and "not be seen in't" (I.i.225). Even in his fury Ferdinand determines to "study to seem / The thing I am not" (II.v.62–63), and thereafter he consistently seems generous when he is most dangerous. He tortures the Duchess with waxworks, ingenious counterfeits designed to bring her to a real despair. In P. F. Vernon's view, "the actions of the Duchess and Antonio in the first three acts of the play are as culpable as those of their persecutors. They are up to their ears

---

11. For a detailed analysis of the theme of dissimulation in the play see P. F. Vernon, "The Duchess of Malfi's Guilt," *Notes and Queries*, N.S. X (1963), 335–338.

in secrecy and disguise." [12] But while it is true that the play establishes an analogy in terms of action, it goes to some lengths to make distinctions in terms of causes and consequences. The mode of behavior which is *chosen* by Ferdinand and the Cardinal is *imposed* on the Duchess and Antonio. The text stresses the reluctance with which they dissemble:

> O misery! methinks unjust actions
> Should wear these masks and curtains, and not we
>
> (III.ii.158–159)

It also stresses the inadequacy of innocence obliged to dissimulate. The Duchess has succeeded in "plotting" a "politic conveyance" for the mid-wife (II.i.163–165), but the suddenness of her labor leaves the guileless Antonio helpless, convinced that they are "lost" (II.i.160). It is Delio who suggests how to cover the situation by giving out the information that Bosola's apricots have poisoned the Duchess, and then devises a way to keep the physicians at bay, while Antonio complains, "I am lost in amaze-ment: I know not what to think on't" (II.i.173). In the same way it is Bosola who suggests the feigned pilgrimage. There is considerable irony in the Duchess's assertion that she can thus "wisely" forestall her brothers (III.ii.322).

While the dissimulation of Ferdinand and the Cardinal is designed to entrap and destroy, the schemes of the Duchess and Antonio cloak not "unjust actions" but childbirth and the flight from tyranny. The *mag-nanima menzogna* (III.ii.180) of Antonio's dismissal injures no one but Antonio, whom it is designed to protect. In the case of the stolen jewels the Duchess is said to be anxious that her device should give no offense, far less do harm: "She entreats you take't not ill . . . " (II.ii.61). The judg-ment that condemns the Duchess and her brothers as equally culpable is too simple. Webster shows that the great are like the (morally) base only to display that they are far from "the same." Similar behavior springs from antithetical impulses—to protect or to destroy.

---

12. *Ibid.*, p. 337. The Duchess's dissimulation is also noted as a moral weakness by Clifford Leech, *Webster: The Duchess of Malfi,* Studies in English Literature No. 8 (London, 1963), p. 54; Peter B. Murray, *A Study of John Webster,* Studies in English Literature No. 50 (The Hague, 1969), pp. 148–150; Berry, p. 111.

Ferdinand "as a tyrant doubles with his words, / And fearfully equivocates" (I.i.443–444). Again the play itself draws attention to the parallel
between the Duchess's equivocation and Ferdinand's:

> so we
> Are forc'd to express our violent passions
> In riddles, and in dreams, and leave the path
> Of simple virtue, which was never made
> To seem the thing it is not.
>
> (I.i.444–448)

For Ferdinand language is part of the mist which obscures the true nature
of evil. His equivocation is designed to entangle his victims: "*Send Antonio
to me; I want his head in a business*" (III.v.28); "*I had rather have his heart than
his money*" (III.v.35–36). His offer of the dead hand to the Duchess is a
grotesque and cruel caricature of the wooing scene:

> I will leave this ring with you for a love-token;
> And the hand, as sure as the ring; and do not doubt
> But you shall have the heart too; when you need a friend
> Send it to him that ow'd it; you shall see
> Whether he can aid you
>
> (IV.i.47–51)

His double entendres are a form of antagonism directed against Castruchio
(I.i.105 ff.) or offensive to the Duchess (I.i.336–337). The equivocation
of the Duchess, by contrast, is designed to communicate with Antonio. It
is not an expression of hostility but a means of reestablishing and reinforc-
ing relationship. Its object is first marriage, and later praise, mitigating
the dramatic effect of her simulated rage as she dismisses Antonio: "I have
got well by you . . . " (III.ii.183); "I would have this man be an example
to you all" (III.ii.189). Her double entendres are similarly transparent and
domestic, secret references understood by Antonio and the audience to her
secret marriage (II.i). The mist generated by Ferdinand envelops the
Duchess's behavior, but the effect is to emphasise the contrast between
them: parallel again resolves into antithesis.

Ferdinand curses the Duchess: "Damn her!" (IV.i.121). And the tortures
of Act IV are intended as a means of realizing his curse, "To bring her to

despair" (IV.i.116) and so to damnation. Ferdinand's efforts are finally ineffectual, but he succeeds in creating for the Duchess a world which resembles hell (IV.ii.25–26). Ferdinand's curse "places" the Duchess's:

> DUCHESS
> I could curse the stars.
> BOSOLA
> O fearful!
> DUCHESS
> And those three smiling seasons of the year
> Into a Russian winter, nay the world
> To its first chaos.
> BOSOLA
> Look you, the stars shine still:—
> DUCHESS
> O, but you must
> Remember, my curse hath a great way to go.
>
> (IV.i.96–101)

Bosola's mockery and the Duchess's ironic reply draw attention to the inefficacy of this curse. The stars shine still: human beings are powerless to affect their courses;[13] and the Duchess is aware of their remoteness. Unlike Ferdinand's, this is a curse which she can make no attempt to realize. It is an expression of anguish not of a desire to destroy. She compares the stars to tyrants (IV.i.103), but she does not curse the tyrants themselves. The result of Ferdinand's attempts to envelop the Duchess in his own evil is to produce patterns of behavior which externally resemble his own, but it is an empty resemblance, the form without the substance.

The play invites a similar consideration of the Duchess's "madness" in conjunction with Ferdinand's. Ferdinand's is indicated in Act II, scene v (ll. 2, 46, 66). It is destructive and self-destructive (ll. 63–64), "deform'd," "beastly" (l. 57). It is finally established in the lycanthropy of Act V. The Duchess's "madness" is her marriage (I.i.506), mad only in the terms of the world she lives in. Ferdinand nonetheless offers her the masque of madmen as an emblem of her state (IV.i.124 131). Despite the

13. Job 38: 31–33. For parallels between the Duchess and Job see Murray, pp. 130–134.

references in the dialogue to madness (IV.ii.7, 17), the Duchess reiterates that she is not able to escape in this way (ll. 24, 26), and the masque itself creates an antithesis between the silent Duchess and the chattering madmen. Ironically, they function dramatically as transformations not of the Duchess but of Ferdinand. Like Ferdinand, who would damn the Duchess, the First Madman would draw doomsday nearer (IV.ii.73). He would "set all the world on fire" (IV.ii.74–75), just as Ferdinand would "have their bodies / Burnt in a coal-pit . . . " (II.v.66–70), and would despatch Bosola

> To feed a fire, as great as my revenge,
> Which ne'er will slack, till it have spent his fuel.
>   (IV.i.140–141)

The Second Madman sees hell as a glass house "where the devils are continually blowing up women's souls" (IV.ii.77–78). His vision is a demonic caricature of Ferdinand's readiness to imagine the Duchess "in the shameful act of sin" (II.v.41). His statement that "the law will eat to the bone" (IV.ii.94–95) recalls the image of Ferdinand using the law "to entangle those shall feed him" (I.i.180). The Third Madman's insistence that "He that drinks but to satisfy nature is damned" (IV.ii.96–97) functions as a parody of Ferdinand's attitude to the Duchess's natural impulse to marry again. If the Third Madman is referring here to the eucharistic wine, there is an additional parallel with Ferdinand's behavior: the Duchess tells Ferdinand, "You violate a sacrament o'th'church / Shall make you howl in hell for't" (IV.i.39–40). [14] The Fourth Madman is a companion to the devil (IV.ii.107): Ferdinand is the devil's own child (V.iv.21). Like Ferdinand, the madmen are condemned to a perpetual hell of the mind, a sleepless world of perverted sexuality and death. It is Ferdinand, and not the Duchess, who finally escapes into madness.

Thus in each case a seeming parallel resolves into a new antithesis. The effect is not simply to extenuate the Duchess's behavior: rather, the play identifies evil itself—not in terms of individual motive or intention but as a concept—by locating it within a pattern, defining it with increasing

---

14. I am indebted for this suggestion to G. K. Hunter.

precision by a series of contrasts. *The Duchess of Malfi* invites the audience
to consider evil as a mode of behavior, only to suggest in the end that it is
something anterior to this, at once more mysterious and more substantial.
Ferdinand's evil denies all reciprocity: " . . . you that are courtiers should
be my touch-wood, take fire, when I give fire . . . " (I.i.122–123); "Do
not you ask the reason . . ." (I.i.257); "Distrust doth cause us seldom be
deceived" (I.i.241). He incorporates the world into himself, feeding on it
like a spider (I.i.177–180), a tiger (III.v.86), or a shark (III.v.123–141),[15]
or transforms it in his own image, "Rotten, and rotting others"
(IV.ii.320). Both impulses have their origins in an egoism that verges on
solipsism:

> He that can compass me, and know my drifts,
> May say he hath put a girdle 'bout the world
> And sounded all her quicksands.

(III.i.84–86)

His object is "a general eclipse" (II.v.79) which will envelop the world in
his own darkness, and the recurrent imagery which aligns Ferdinand with
the devil draws attention to the parallel between this and the Satanic desire
to transform paradise into hell.[16] The play explores, too, the power of evil,
challenging the audience to question the extent of its capacity to destroy.
Ferdinand murders the Duchess but he cannot damn her. A corrupt world
can darken the Duchess's outward behavior but it cannot touch her soul.

These two areas of exploration, the nature of evil and the extent of its
power, are finally fused in the climactic antithetical emblems of Act V,
Ferdinand as wolf and the Duchess as echo. The grim comedy of
Ferdinand's "treatment" shows the Doctor trying to tame him through
fear as Ferdinand has tried to frighten the Duchess into obedience. Like
Ferdinand, the Doctor fails. Ironically, Ferdinand is "studying the art of
patience" (V.ii.45), but his concept of the virtue is a travesty of the

---

15. For images of the Duchess as his prey see III.v.110–113, IV.ii.237, V.ii.341.

16. Cf. D. C. Gunby, *"The Duchess of Malfi:* A Theological Approach," in *John Webster,*
Proceedings of the 2d York Conference, ed. Brian Morris (London, 1970), pp. 181–204,
Gunby's argument that the Cardinal and Ferdinand are possessed by the devil seems to me
an overliteral interpretation of the play's imagery.

Duchess's: "To drive six snails before me, from this town to Moscow . . . " (V.ii.47–48). The parallel and contrast between Ferdinand and the Duchess is thus kept before us. Ferdinand as wolf embodies all the qualities we have come to associate with him throughout the play: the symbol evokes a world of isolation, darkness, and destruction. In his quest for total "solitariness" (V.ii.29), Ferdinand would destroy his own shadow (V.ii.31–41). Evil that preys on the world is reduced finally to preying on itself.

The echo scene shows how the Duchess, too, is reduced: the echo is powerless to protect Antonio; it is insubstantial, "*a dead thing*" (V.iii.39). The Duchess's grave is appropriately among ancient ruins where good men hoped in vain to outlast the storms of the world (V.iii.9–17). Paradoxically, however, though the abbey is in ruins, it evokes a "reverend history," and equally paradoxically the ruined Duchess survives as a light which shows "a face folded in sorrow" (V.iii.44–45). Bosola's final pessimism is thus not entirely synonymous with the play's conclusion:

> We are only like dead walls, or vaulted graves,
> That ruin'd, yields no echo
>
> (V.v.97–98)

It is evil which finally destroys itself and seeks to be "laid by, and never thought of" (V.v.90). Innocence survives as an echo, a reverend history, or a momentary light revealing the sorrow which is its inevitable experience in a fallen world.

It is true that the play offers no answer to the problem of how to survive in a corrupt world. Bosola's solution is to submit to its values, and he is finally neglected. The Duchess goes her own way (I.i.321) and is murdered. Service to Ferdinand is deadly, opposition vain. The play suggests no way of reaching the ideal of the French court, cleansed and life-giving.

It is presumably for this reason that Webster has so consistently seemed to critics incoherent, morally anarchic, or nihilistic. In reality, I suggest, the play constitutes a rigorously coherent exploration of the nature of evil in a fallen world, and the coherence is the paradoxical product of its contradictory structure. The values of the play are implicit in the analysis it offers, and in the formality by which it repeatedly distances the audience from imaginative absorption in the plot to challenge examination of its analysis. The tension between realism and abstraction alternately involves the spectators and draws their attention beyond the intensity of the play's action to its anatomy of the world, inviting them to perceive the world as a deep pit of darkness, irradiated by the memory of innocence, Antonio's recollection of the French court, an echo of the Duchess's reverend history.

In an essay of this length it has not been possible to introduce detailed comparisons between Webster and contemporary dramatists at each stage of the argument. My hypothesis is, however, that if *The Duchess of Malfi* is unusual in the period, it is so only in the sharpness with which it displays the effects of the contradictory pressures on Renaissance drama. In Tourneur, for instance, on the one hand, we see the emblematic mode in dominance; in Middleton, on the other hand, the formal patterns are present but are more fully masked by the realist surface. Shakespeare, as always, is a case apart, and here it is perhaps harder for us to perceive the emblematic elements in the plays because of our rich heritage of realist critical analysis. But in Webster, and in *The Duchess of Malfi* in particular, we are able to identify a precise and productive instance of the conflict between the contrary pressures of residual and emerging dramatic conventions.

Diabolical Realism in Middleton and Rowley's The Changeling

J. L. SIMMONS

MIDDLETON'S PARADOXICAL GENIUS was affirmed by T. S. Eliot in 1927 in a way that modern criticism tends to vulgarize into simple contradiction. Middleton was, for Eliot, an "impersonal" artist with "no point of view," "no message"; he was "merely a great recorder," his work grounded by "a strain of realism underneath."[1] With those characteristics, however, and perhaps even because of them, he wrote in *The Changeling* a play of "profound and permanent moral value and horror"; here "Middleton is surpassed by one Elizabethan alone, and that is Shakespeare." Eliot apparently saw no dichotomy: in *The Changeling* Middleton objectively exposed "fundamental passions of any time and any place"; he was not distracted from reality by the Elizabethan deduction that God's revenge triumphs over the crying and execrable sin of murder. The playwright's masterpiece exhibited to Eliot the perennial tragedy, beyond historical pieties, of "the immoral nature, suddenly trapped in the inexorable toils of morality—of morality not made by man but by Nature—and forced to

---

1. "Thomas Middleton," in *Selected Essays* (1932; rpt. London, 1951), pp. 161–170.

135

take the consequences of an act which it had planned lightheartedly." The horrible discovery of these moral toils, Eliot asserted, reveals a "truth permanent in human nature." With his impersonal genius Middleton recorded the tragic progression, thereby transcending (as Eliot thought Shakespeare had transcended) the inferior thought of his age. One nevertheless discovers in Eliot's criticism the potentiality for apparent contradiction: Middleton's tragedy, even if impersonally observed, surely establishes a point of view and even, one would infer from such horror, a message.

Unwisely we have come to see the temporal and the timeless Middletons as problematically opposed. One of the most reputable critics of Middleton's early comedies speaks of "the struggle between satiric observation and determined moralizing."[2] With the tragic Middleton the dichotomy opposes the historical moralist—the author who could bear to read Reynolds's *The Triumphs of God's Revenge* in the first place—against the modern psychological realist who breathed life into the dead weight of his source. Obviously, these oppositions are insidious if we must choose between a moralized Middleton indistinguishable from contemporary hacks and a Middleton modernized for all time, vaguely, as a realist, a naturalist, or a psychological dramatist.[3] Eliot went too far in isolating Middleton from his age, but historical criticism has had little success in accounting for the impulse that distinguishes Middleton and Rowley's mutual enterprise from Reynolds's novella. We end up either with the

2. R. B. Parker, "Middleton's Experiments with Comedy and Judgement," in *Jacobean Theatre,* ed. John Russell Brown and Bernard Harris, Stratford-upon-Avon Studies, No. 1 (London, 1960), p. 179.

3. For the opposition see Helen Gardner, "Milton's 'Satan' and the Theme of Damnation in Elizabethan Tragedy," *ES,* N.S. I (1949), 46–66; and T. B. Tomlinson, "Poetic Naturalism—*The Changeling,*" *JEGP,* LXIII (1964), 648–659, expanded in his *A Study of Elizabethan and Jacobean Tragedy* (Cambridge, Eng., 1964). Gardner acknowledges the psychological realism in the play but insists that "there is more than realism here" (p. 57). Tomlinson, however, is doggedly insensitive: "there is no mention in this play of 'damnation' (certainly not in the *Faustus* sense)"—*A Study,* p. 187, n. 1. The historical approach can also be needlessly limiting: Robert Jordan, in "Myth and Psychology in *The Changeling,*" *RenD,* III (1970), 157–165, sees the play as based on the myth of beauty and the beast; what is apparent psychological subtlety is for him merely the by-blow of literary conventions at work.

moral vision that every Jacobean playwright can be blindly made to share or with the recording realism that is discomfited by any pressure from beyond the natural or, in a modern sense, the psychological realm. And precisely how Rowley could have adapted himself so completely to Middleton's psychological genius is a mystery that no critic, not even Eliot, has touched.

The word *psychology* should itself beg the question; as Robert West observes, it was not a word or, in our conception, a science known to Elizabethans. He continues:

similarly, perhaps, they lacked our conception of the cleavage between the objective and the subjective. But it was not that they were without a theory of mental process, or neglected to distinguish the forms impinged upon the intellect by the outside world from combinations of these forms which the soul itself originated. It was rather that they were not so sure as we of the inviolability of the personality, not sure that alien personalities could not come into the mind in a manner much more immediate than anything our theories of suggestion and hypnotism admit of. The subjective . . . was an uncertain category in a day when authorities held that a percept might indeed be peculiar to a man as shared with no other and having no existence outside his mind, yet originate with and represent a foreign substance.[4]

It is this foreign substance that I intend to investigate, as well as the artifice whereby the two collaborators were able to exhibit and, simultaneously, to incorporate the alien within the violated personality. As J. Leeds Barroll has argued in relation to Shakespeare's characterizations, a playwright of another age may very likely have discovered truths of human nature acceptable to modern psychology; but "the structure of ideas by which he sought to account for such phenomena would have been quite importantly different."[5]

In order to reach this conceptual structure, I shall begin with the sexual fantasies of Beatrice-Joanna and De Flores as projections of an alien and demonic order peculiarly rationalized in the characters themselves. I shall proceed to the major sources of the play where we can discover, as did

4. Robert West, *The Invisible World: A Study of Pneumatology in Elizabethan Drama* (Athens, Ga., 1939), pp. 165–166.

5. *Artificial Persons: The Formation of Character in the Tragedies of Shakespeare* (Columbia, S.C., 1974), p. 21.

Middleton and Rowley, this connection between demonology and those sexual fantasies. I shall give new consideration to an important topical matter alluded to in the play; indeed I shall urge that the Essex divorce or nullity trial and the scandal following the murder of Sir Thomas Overbury are sufficiently influential for these events to be considered an inspiration for the play and even a source. Finally, I want tentatively to trace in the works of Middleton and of Rowley before 1622 a few signs that these two playwrights would prove uniquely compatible for what may be the greatest of all dramatic collaborations. By going over some old material in a new light, I hope to establish a meeting ground between our preoccupation with the psychological in sexual matters and the Jacobean preoccupation, in such matters, with the demonic. Perhaps we can thereby get closer to what Eliot saw in the play as fundamentally true, even if the two centuries approach this truth from different directions.

I

Wherein lies the essential tragedy of *The Changeling*? "The *habituation* of Beatrice to her sin," answers Eliot, emphatically. But that fact, one would have to say, does not in itself distinguish her from a bustling company of impudent Jacobean heroines. Eliot's conclusion is succinct but, for purposes of definition, uncritically reticent: "The tragedy of Beatrice is not that she has lost Alsemero, for whose possession she played; it is that she has won De Flores." I think, however, that Eliot considered *The Changeling* to be more than a tragedy of ironic retribution. What tragedy, after all, is not? It is grimly appropriate that Eliot's intelligent modesty would prevent his further specification; for, if the tragedy has any message, it is that such delicacy in human sexuality, even when proceeding from a morally vacuous nature, is in some way self-protective and therefore genuinely ethical. The mask of modesty, facially and linguistically, hides a reality that is death to explore—a bawdy death, but death nevertheless:

> Speak it yet further off that I may lose
> What has been spoken, and no sound remain on't.
> I would not hear so much offence again
> For such another deed.
> . . . .

> Why, 'tis impossible thou canst be so wicked,
> Or shelter such a cunning cruelty,
> To make his death the murderer of my honour!
> Thy language is so bold and vicious,
> I cannot see which way I can forgive it
> With any modesty.
>
>   (III.iv. 102–125)[6]

The tragedy of winning De Flores does not lie merely in the irony of the retribution but in the sexual nightmare of it, a sexual hell both horrible and fascinating. In this respect the popular wisdom of our day is the same as in Middleton's. One recent critic, inspired by the BBC Television production in 1974, has called the play "the tragedy of an arrogant self-indulgent nature, hell-bent on total appetite, total experience, total destruction." He acknowledges that now more than ever, with our alluring delusions of sexual liberation, we are able to perceive the real focus of the tragic experience: "many young Beatrices of today would recognize, rather more readily than literary scholars, their affinity with the Jacobean teenager,"[7] But we will only convict ourselves once more of the modernist's fallacy unless in the psychological perception we take seriously the literal force of *hell-bent*. The total loss of sexual control, the complete abandonment of the self to eros, leads to eternal death; therefore Beatrice-Joanna justly loathes De Flores "As much as youth and beauty hates a sepulchre" (II.ii.67). Her revulsion is not only "the obverse of a fascination";[8] it also represents a ghost-guessed apprehension of her infinite capacity for damnation when that damnation is perceived, as Beatrice-Joanna perceives everything, sexually.

The Changeling uniquely dramatizes the progression of a diabolically psychosexual nightmare, a progression in which the sexual drive is not tamed, sublimated, and legitimized within the conventions of courtship

---

6. All references are to N. W. Bawcutt, ed., *The Changeling*, The Revels Plays (London, 1958).

7. S. Gorley Putt, "The Tormented World of Middleton," *TLS*, 2 August 1974, pp. 833–834.

8. Dorothy M. Farr, *Thomas Middleton and the Drama of Realism* (Edinburgh, 1973), p. 56.

and marriage. Middleton and Rowley show a yielding to the wild and
naked thing itself, a yielding that plunges one into a sexual abyss:

> if a woman
> Fly from one point, from him she makes a husband,
> She spreads and mounts then like arithmetic,
> One, ten, a hundred, a thousand, ten thousand. . . .
>
> (II.ii.60–63)

Arithmetically spreading and mounting, Beatrice physically and psychi-
cally conjoins the feminine abandon and masculine aggression that lead
toward a grotesque infinity. When she embraces the horror, as dreadful as
it is, she is ensnared in the damnable satisfaction of a world-without-end:

> Thy peace is wrought for ever in this yielding.
> 'Las, how the turtle pants! Thou'lt love anon
> What thou so fear'st and faint'st to venture on.
>
> (III.iv.169–171)

The peculiar fascination of the tragedy is not that it shows the wages of sin
to be death but that it discloses in Beatrice the whispering allure of being
"undone . . . endlessly" (IV.i.1). We see through her the horror that
Joseph Conrad's Marlow saw through Kurtz, the result of losing all re-
straint, of yielding to the diabolic darkness in a voracity for its "unspeakable rites." To look upon that depravity, as to look upon the face of God,
is to die; and Beatrice, when she is united with De Flores, cannot avoid the
final obscene *Liebestod*. "I'll be your pander now," says Alsemero, closeting
the doomed lovers for their sexual as well as their dramatic catastrophe:

> rehearse again
> Your scene of lust, that you may be perfect
> When you shall come to act it to the black audience
> Where howls and gnashings shall be music to you.
> Clip your adult'ress freely, 'tis the pilot
> Will guide you to the Mare Mortuum,
> Where you shall sink to fathoms bottomless.
>
> (V.iii.114–120)

Beatrice's nature is in both sexual and Calvinistic terms reprobate from the beginning, before the confirmation with De Flores that she is bent on hell. Her change of affection from Alonzo to Alsemero was, as De Flores charges, "a kind / Of whoredom in thy heart" (III.iv.143–144); but her forbidden desires are not to be domesticated by either the civil Alonzo or Alsemero. It is obscenely appropriate that, as she moves toward her deadly satisfaction, De Flores returns to her "the first token" given Alonzo in their courtship, her ring upon his severed phallic digit;[9] and all feeling for the pallid Alsemero is transcended in the erotic and murderous excitement of her pact with De Flores. The Edenic chances for Beatrice are lost in her fascination for the serpent that will deflower her:

> This ominous ill-fac'd fellow more disturbs me
> Than all my other passions.
>
>   (II.i.53–54)

The ugly face, which "Blood-guiltiness becomes," represents her destiny, as she is finally able to see when, in his arms, she looks not to heaven but to his prodigious visage:

> Beneath the stars, upon yon meteor
> Ever hung my fate, 'mongst things corruptible;
> I ne'er could pluck it from him: my loathing
> Was prophet to the rest but ne'er believ'd.
>
>   (V.iii.154–157)

Beatrice's sexuality, then, has demanded a literal phallic worship, with the meteoric face ultimately adored for all its loathsomeness. In elevating her Florentine admirer to her service, this perverted Petrarchan lady is a witch raising her familiar devil.[10] In metaphor she fondles and arouses the

9. The finger image is employed sexually in both plots (I.i.231–234; I.ii.27–31). In the Dumb Show preceding Act IV, "Alonzo's *ghost appears to* De Flores *in the midst of his smile, startles him, showing him the hand whose finger he had cut off.*" This obscene gesture manqué indicates not only the phallic obsession of the lovers but also the sexual nature of their nemesis.

10. For discussions of the parody of courtly love in the play see Robert Ornstein, *The Moral Vision of Jacobean Tragedy* (Madison, Wis., 1960), pp. 179–190; Thomas L. Berger, "The Petrarchan Fortress of *The Changeling*," *RenP* (1969), pp. 37–46. For the importance of sexual innuendo in the language of the play—particularly in the word *service*—see Christopher Ricks, "The Moral and Poetic Structure of *The Changeling*," *Essays in Criticism*, X (1960), 290–306.

tumescent instrument of her destruction and her desire, though it is the
same object she has loathed "to a hair and pimple":

> BEATRICE
> Hardness becomes the visage of a man well,
> It argues service, resolution, manhood,
> If cause were of employment.
>   DE FLORES
>   'Twould be soon seen,
> If e'er your ladyship had cause to use it.
> I would but wish the honour of a service
> So happy as that mounts to.
>
> (II.ii.92–97)

The result of raising the turgid face for her service is that it must finally, in
exchange, become her god:

> How heartily he serves me! His face loathes one,
> But look upon his care, who would not love him?
> The east is not more beauteous than his service.
>
> (V.i.70–72)

The sadomasochistic alliance rhetorically identifies each of the demonic
lovers as both subject and object: "His face loathes one"; "one loathes his
face." The rhetoric penetrates the pat explanation Alsemero gives for
Beatrice's "infirmity": "There's scarce a thing that is both lov'd and
loath'd" (I.i.125). It is this duality in Beatrice—the love in the loathing,
the loathing in the love—that is most striking in *The Changeling*: not
exactly that she becomes habituated to sin or that, losing Alsemero, she
gains De Flores; rather that she comes to acknowledge the love of what she
hates at the same time that she is able to see fully her own degradation:

> Oh come not near me, sir, I shall defile you:
> I am that of your blood was taken from you
> For your better health; look no more upon't,
> But cast it to the ground regardlessly:
> Let the common sewer take it from distinction.
>
> (V.iii.149–153)

These lines are among the most terrifying in dramatic literature and the recognition lifts Beatrice—a most unlikely candidate—among the great tragic figures. Her recognition, furthermore, clearly distinguishes this tragedy of damnation from *Macbeth* or *Paradise Lost*—though, as Helen Gardner has shown, the common pattern is clearly present.[11] Beatrice is distinct because her damnation depicts the fascination of evil as it is manifested in forbidden sexual fantasies loathed and loved, fantasies which, pursued to their sadistic and masochistic climax, annihilate the self. In this process, as De Flores insists, there is indeed eternal rest. Beatrice's loss of identity—a tenuous distinction at best—is quintessentially the Jacobean dissolution of personality in the face of erotic evil.

II

Within the period of Middleton and Rowley's inspiration, where could one find an expression of these sexual fantasies mingling eros and evil in an alliance that leads to physical and spiritual death? That a conceptual structure of ideas for such an experience was extant I take to be self-evident from the close collaboration: Rowley contributed not only the subplot that physically reflects the spiritual grotesquerie of Beatrice-Joanna and De Flores; the minor playwright also fashioned the opening and closing scenes, initiating and resolving the tragic main plot. No doubt Middleton's genius was inspiriting; but clearly the two men conceived the tragedy together or at least shared, as a communicable point of reference, a concept of sexual damnation that became a source both for the characterization and for the metaphoric pattern of the tragic experience. This psychological structure was a nightmare that captured the sexual imagination of Europe during the sixteenth and seventeenth centuries—the fascination with witchcraft and demonology. The specific source of the play in fact points to this frame of reference; and, if we take seriously the structural pattern that informs the exemplary tales in *The Triumphs of God's Revenge*, we can discover this more general source of the play.

The tale of Beatrice and her De Flores, like the other stories in the collection, is the tragedy of individuals "seduced partly by sin, but chiefly

11. In addition to Helen Gardner's important essay, see Penelope B. R. Doob, "A Reading of *The Changeling*," *English Literary Renaissance*, III (1973), 183–206.

by Satan, who is the author thereof." [12] In these stories of lust and murder, the absolutes of good and evil exert their force externally upon the tortured psyche; but, while they remain outside the mind, they manifest their power within: "how can wee giue our selues to God, when in the heat of lust and fume of reuenge, we sell our hearts to the deuill?" (p. 106). When Beatrice is plotting to rid herself of Alonzo, Reynolds didactically exposes the supernatural pattern underlying the scene in the play: "And now, after shee had ruminated, and runne ouer many bloody designes: the deuill, who neuer flies from those that follow him, proffers her an inuention as execrable as damnable" (p. 127). At this crucial point Middleton and Rowley diverged from Reynolds's conventional account by their transformation of De Flores. Instead of externalizing the devil's proffered "inuention" as the De Flores who is "a Gallant young Gentleman," they internalized and rationalized the process by creating in their De Flores a demonic creature, "as execrable as damnable," who offers himself to be her instrument. The playwrights nevertheless retained the idea of a pact between a woman, ingenuously evil, and the fiend conjured by her bloody designs.

In the sadomasochistic fantasy of the demonic pact, Middleton and Rowley found the sexual labyrinth into which Beatrice descends. In the English witch-hunts the sexual nature of the alliance was never explored so eagerly as on the Continent; but by the end of Elizabeth's reign the work of Reginald Scot and King James had given notoriety to the erotic elaborations of Continental demonologists. [13] Both Scot and James, whether

12. John Reynolds, *The Triumphs of Gods Revenge, Against the crying, and execrable Sinne of Murther* (London, 1621), sig. B2. Subsequent references are included in the text. Bawcutt reprints most of the relevant material.

13. The most authoritative work on English witchcraft in its social and intellectual setting is Keith Thomas, *Religion and the Decline of Magic* (New York, 1971), pp. 435–583. See also Alan Macfarlane, *Witchcraft in Tudor and Stuart England* (London, 1970); and Wallace Notestein, *A History of Witchcraft in England from 1558 to 1718* (Washington, D.C., 1911). Before the date of *The Changeling* the Continental ideas of erotic devil-worship were disseminated in England, with varying degrees of modesty and credulity, by the following: Reginald Scot, *The Discouerie of Witchcraft* (London, 1584); Henry Holland, *A Treatise Against Witchcraft* (Cambridge, Eng., 1590); George Gifford, *A Dialogue Concerning Witches and Witchcraftes* (London, 1593); King James, *Daemonologie* (Edinburgh, 1597); William Perkins, *A Discourse of the Damned Art of Witchcraft* (Cambridge, Eng., 1608); Alexander Roberts, *A Treatise of Witchcraft* (London, 1616); Thomas Cooper, *The Mystery of*

attacking or supporting the tradition of the *Malleus Maleficarum*, describe the "carnall copulation with *Incubus*" as the chief capital crime of witch-craft, a crime confirming idolatry and apostasy. [14] Since the evidence of *The Witch* argues that Middleton derived his knowledge of witchcraft from the skeptical *Discoverie of Witchcraft*, it is significant to observe that Scot concludes his account "of such abhominable lecheries" with a rationaliza-tion: "Thus are lecheries covered with the cloke of *Incubus* and witch-craft." [15] Even when deemed self-serving exculpations, in other words, the diabolic rationale of sexual depravity remained psychologically as well as morally the most persuasive fantasy. The essential characteristic of the diabolic alliance is also that of the unrestrained sexual urge. As Thomas Cooper explained in his *Mystery of Witch-craft* (1617), the witch is moti-vated to make this "desperate covenant" by "the earnest and unsatiable desire to accomplish our lusts";[16] but the devotee, signaling this insa-tiability, at once loses the will to act independently and yields to all that was once deemed ugly, degrading, and evil. If the forbidden fruit turns to ashes, it nevertheless remains perpetually compelling. In the fantasy, then, lies the fascination with the horror, the love in the loathing, that Beatrice manifests; and this ambivalence is notable in almost all testimo-nies. Although Scot simplistically assumes that women have "more plea-sure and delight (they say) with *Incubus* that waie, than with anie mortall man," those more intimately associated with the experience report differ-ently. As Henry Charles Lea observes, "while the demonologists tell us that the gratification of lust was one of the leading incentives to witch-craft . . . yet the women with singular unanimity everywhere describe the relation as painful and distasteful." [17] But this masochistic confusion in the accounts of pain and pleasure is of course precisely at the source of the

---

Witch-craft (London, 1617). According to Keith Thomas, the Continental ideas of witch-craft were primarily adopted in England by intellectuals and theologians (p. 441).

14. Reginald Scot, *The Discoverie of Witchcraft* (1584), ed. Brinsley Nicholson (London, 1886), p. 56 (III.xix).

15. *Ibid.*, p. 67 (IV.x).

16. *The Mystery of Witch-craft* (London, 1617), p. 32.

17. Henry Charles Lea, comp., *Materials Toward a History of Witchcraft*, ed. Arthur C. Howland (1939; rpt. New York, 1957), II, 916–917. See Scot, p. 60 (IV.iii).

fantasy: "His face loathes one, / But look upon his care, who would not love him?"

Of course if the origins of De Flores were satanic only, the educated might expect the sexual drive of the character to be unimpressive. Cooper describes the arch-fiend as sexually rather passive, though the physical act of intercourse religiously seals the spiritual union: "Lastly, to gratifie them somewhat for this their dutiful seruice, it pleaseth their new Maister oftentimes to offer himselfe familiarly vnto them, to *dally and lye with them*, in token of their more neere *coniunction*, and as it were *marriage* vnto them." Then follows the orgy of the witches' sabbath, ending with that infamous kiss the witch bestows, kneeling in adoration, upon her master: "The baser and vnseemelier the homage is, the more it binds."[18] But the sexual capacity of Satan need not deter one from indulging in demonic fantasies because lower orders of demons were at hand—incubi, succubi, satyrs—which monomaniacally lusted after humans. Authorities offer little in rigorous definition of these beings, their names and origins; but St. Augustine had affirmed for the Christian era their continued existence as progeny of the fallen angels who shortly after the loss of Paradise began to fornicate with "the daughters of men." The power of love affects "the spirits of the air, and devils of hell themselves," writes Robert Burton, whose *Anatomy of Melancholy* preceded *The Changeling* by only a year and, like the play, scientifically observes a psychophysiological morbidity ultimately satanic in origin: these demons "are as much enamoured and dote (if I may use that word) as any other creatures whatsoever. For if those stories be true that are written of incubus and succubus, of nymphs, lascivious fauns, satyrs, and those heathen gods which were devils . . . or those familiar meetings in our days, and company of witches and devils, there is some probability for it."[19]

Though demonic, De Flores is not portrayed as precisely satanic. With his perpetual "hardness" arguing "service," he is also the jovial and scurvy satyr or incubus.[20] "To a hair and pimple" he is a phallic creature who

18. Cooper, pp. 92, 119.

19. *The Anatomy of Melancholy* (1621; rpt. London, 1932), III, 45–46 (III.2.i.1).

20. S. Gorley Putt observes "a degree of nymphomania in the heroine as marked as De Flores's resemblance to a satyr" (p. 834).

"dotes" on Beatrice. Suffering from a diabolic satyriasis in his lust for her, De Flores has the potency to undo the nymphomaniac endlessly. In his scientific *Historie of Foure-Footed Beastes,* Edward Topsell assures the reader "that the deuils do many waies delude men in the likeness of Satyres." Because of their all-consuming lust "the auncient Graecians coniecture their name to be deriued as it were of *Stathes,* signifying the yarde or virile member: and it is certain that the deuils haue exercised their praestigious lust, or rather their imagination of lust vpon mankind, whereof commeth that distinction of Fauni, that some are *Incubi* defilers of Women, and some *Succubi* defiled by men." Satyrs abuse their victims "in most odious and filthy manner . . . not onely in that part that nature hath ordained, but ouer the whole body most libidinously."[21] Not only does the sexual nature of De Flores find its origin in the popular idea of this demon; the character's comic powers of satiric observation also reflect the literary concept of the satyr, etymologically confused with *satura.* Rough and crude in the Juvenalian manner, full of sexual envy, De Flores exposes the hypocrisy of the modest world around him and has a moral conscience in his corruption. Satyr figures had been preoccupied with sexuality since their development in the 1590s, first in verse satire, then in the drama; and De Flores is surely in this regard the culmination of the type.

A representation strongly suggesting Beatrice's satyric captivation is in Book III of *The Faerie Queene,* in the episode of Hellenore's rapture. Seduced and deserted by Paridell, the sexually frustrated wife finds satisfaction in the enthrallment of satyrs. Her husband, the impotent Malbecco, witnesses her grotesque ecstasy:

> At night, when all they went to sleep, he vewd,
>   Whereas his louely wife emongst them lay,
>   Embraced of a *Satyre* rough and rude,
>   Who all the night did minde his ioyous play:
>   Nine times he heard him come aloft ere day,
>   That all his hart with gealosie did swell;
>   But yet that nights ensample did bewray,
>   That not for nought his wife them loued so well,
> When one so oft a night did ring his matins bell.[22]

21. Edward Topsell, *The Historie of Foure-Footed Beastes* (London, 1607), pp. 14, 12, 13.
22. *The Works of Edmund Spenser,* A Variorum Edition, ed. Edwin Greenlaw et al. (Baltimore, Md., 1934), III, 150 (III.x.xlviii).

Spenser's comedic moralism in this episode is directed toward the aged husband and toward the adulterous courtly love that, stripped of all delusions, leads the lady to this sexual abandon. In addition to the satiric matter, the pastoral setting also encourages Spenser in a mood very close to Ovidian humor: between a *malbecco* and the satyr's virile member there is little contest. Nevertheless, the depiction of Hellenore's bestiality is comically grim. Malbecco has difficulty arousing his wife from her contented sleep and then must plead with her not to alert her protective satyr:

> Tho gan he her perswade, to leaue that lewd
> And loathsome life, of God and man abhord,
> And home returne, where all should be renewed
> With perfect peace, and bandes of fresh accord,
> And she receiu'd againe to bed and bord,
> As if no trespasse euer had bene donne:
> But she it all refused at one word,
> And by no meanes would to his will be wonne,
> But chose emongst the iolly *Satyres* still to wonne
>
> (III.x.li)

Middleton and Rowley keep the satyric joviality of the paganized satyr, but De Flores also becomes demonic—possessed and possessing—in his transformation to a tragic human sphere. And Beatrice, whose name like Hellenore's ironically evokes an idealization of the sexual impulse, must face a metamorphosis far more horrific than anything dreamed of in the Ovidian realm.

Like De Flores, Beatrice has the sexual monomania attributed to demons of the pagan world and its folklore, the world that Christianity incorporated into the infernal. Beatrice is the nymph who, once deflowered, suffers hysterical annihilation. She is an alternate Eve, the Lilith who leaves her Eden to copulate with the serpent and who in a later manifestation as lamia hides her ugliness with the illusion of beauty and lures mortals to their destruction. Edward Topsell, in his account of this infinitely lustful creature, relates the story from Philostratus that in Burton's *Anatomy* was to inspire Keats's poem: Menippus becomes enamored of a beautiful phantasm, and only the wisdom of Apollonius, penetrating the illusion, saves the lover from a serpentine marriage. The word *lamia,* writes Topsell, "hath many significations," one of which is the Lilith of Hebraic tradition. These demons are "wonderfull desirous of copulation with men." They can transform themselves, like witches, into other shapes; or, more precisely, they can give the illusion of transformation, for they have in their beautiful appearance "no matter or substance." If they do not actually exist, they are meaningful as fantastic projections of a diabolical reality:

These and such like stories and opinions there are of Phairies, which in my iudgement arise from the praestigious apparitions of Deuils, whose delight is to deceiue and beguile the minds of men with errour, contrary to the truth of holye Scripture, which doeth no where make mention of such inchaunting creatures; and therefore if any such be, we will holde them the workes of the Deuill, and not of God, or rather I beleeue, that as Poets call Harlots by the name of *Charibdis*, which deuoureth and swalloweth whole shippes and Nauies, aluding to the insatiable gulph of the Sea, so the *Lamiae* are but beautiful alligories of beautifull Harlottes, who after they haue had their lust by men, doth many times deuour and make them away.

In case a lamia should be more than allegorical, however, Topsell offers an antidote: the best way to expose the true nature of the diabolic creature, as Apollonius knew, is to "rate it with very contumelious and despightfull words."[23] The reality of language dispels the false appearance, and the phantasm either vanishes or reassumes its terrible shape.

This demonic myth underlies the psychic metaphor when Alsemero discovers Beatrice's true nature. When he tells her "You are a whore," she exhibits all the pain of a supernatural being whose passionate world of illusions has been destroyed by a moral and rational voice:

> What a horrid sound it hath!
> It blasts a beauty to deformity;
> Upon what face soever that breath falls,
> It strikes ugly: oh, you have ruin'd
> What you can ne'er repair again.
>
> (V.iii.31–35)

One aspect of Beatrice's characterization that has not been fully appre-

---

23. Topsell, pp. 452–454.

ciated is her truly desperate concern with appearances, with her reputation and honor:

> Let me go poor unto my bed with honour,
> And I am rich in all things.
>
> (III.iv.158–159)

This fear, totally divorced from any genuinely moral awareness, is perhaps the psychological sign of a spoiled child or a limited intelligence; it is also the apprehension of a real changeling—a fairy who, left in place of a human child, has no moral sense except insofar as appearances are concerned. Appearance, for her, is truly the only reality, and we cannot dismiss as merely fatuous her struggle against the exposure that will effectively spell her dissolution.[24] As indicated in her waiting-woman's name, these nymphs—whose virginal nature exists only in the membrane—are diaphanous, without any substantiality.

The discovery of Beatrice's diabolic alliance, like the discovery of Duessa's true nature in *The Faerie Queene* (I.viii), dispels illusory appearances; unmasked, both witches are so ugly as to be unfit for heaven or earth. As Alsemero says of Beatrice's disguise, "there was a visor / O'er that cunning face, and that became you" (V.iii.46–47). But when the "fair-fac'd saints" have been exposed as "cunning devils" (V.iii.108–109), the concealing beauty is itself recognized as ugliness:

> The black mask
> That so continually was worn upon't
> Condemns the face for ugly ere't be seen.
>
> (V.iii.3–5)[25]

Alsemero finally sees the full extent of her depravity—"Oh, thou art all

---

24. For the psychological analysis to which I refer, see Una Ellis-Fermor, *The Jacobean Drama* (London, 1936), pp. 146–149. The only critics to take seriously the fairylike nature of Beatrice Joanna are William Empson, *Some Versions of Pastoral* (London, 1935), p. 50; and Richard Levin, *The Multiple Plot in English Renaissance Drama* (Chicago, 1971), p. 45.

25. See the perceptive discussion of this and related passages in George Walton Williams, ed., *The Changeling*, Regents Renaissance Drama Series (Lincoln, Nebr., 1966), pp. 92–93.

deform'd!" (V.iii.77): the beautiful witch is now seen as the hag she is. These psychic demons have been made subjective and rationalized; but, although the playwrights have incorporated the objective evil into the poetic characterization, the alien substance is sufficiently activated for Beatrice to warn her father, echoing the caution that the *Malleus Maleficarum* gave to examiners of witches, "Oh come not near me, sir, I shall defile you" (V.iii.149).[26]

Beatrice's warning, along with the whole of the terrifying catastrophe, is universally attributed to Rowley. It is a scene far surpassing anything else he ever wrote. When we assert that *The Changeling* is also Middleton's masterpiece, we are clearly confronted with "the fact that the play's triumph is first and last a triumph of collaboration."[27] The aesthetic and the practical feat of such a partnership, I have tried to suggest, can best be comprehended if the essential aspects of the result—the psychosexual drama of the main plot and the reverberations between the subplot and the main tragic plot—are seen to arise from the sources of the play; and one must include among those sources a conceptual frame of reference for characterization to which the playwrights in their cooperative labor could appeal. Working from the hint in Reynolds, both Rowley and Middleton animated the broomstick figures in the source by internalizing and developing the demonic compulsion that didactically the prose work externalized. And the subplot, dissonantly counterpointing the tragic drama, offers supporting evidence that Rowley had studied Reynolds as respectfully as Middleton had and doubtlessly in close association with him.

No precise source for Rowley's subplot has been discovered,[28] but the situation of the jealous husband who confines his wife and sets a spy upon her occurs in a section of Reynolds's story which Middleton and Rowley discarded in fashioning the main plot. In the prose tale, after the murder of Alonzo permits the marriage, "*Alsemero*, like a fond husband, becomes ielous of his wife; so as hee curbes and restraynes her of her libertie, and

---

26. *Malleus Maleficarum*, trans. Montague Summers (1928; rpt. New York, 1970), pp. 227–230 (III.15).

27. Cyrus Hoy, "Critical and Aesthetic Problems of Collaboration in Renaissance Drama," *RORD*, XIX (1976), 5.

28. See Bawcutt, p. xxxviii; and Williams, p. xiii.

would hardly permit her to see, yea, farre lesse to conferre or conuerse with any man" (p. 132). This jealous passion is entirely unmotivated; merely a "fearefull frensie." There is cause for jealousy in the play, because De Flores enforces the sexual alliance immediately following the death of Alonzo. In the tale, however, the gallant murderer only receives "many kisses" for his reward and then disappears from the scene until he returns as a messenger to the guarded lady. Beatrice, now resentful of her husband's irrational passion, is at last eager to be unfaithful: "shee considering what [De Flores] hath done for her seruice, and ioyning therewith her husbands ielousie, not onely ingageth her selfe to him for the time present, but for the future" (p. 134). This incoherent turn of events, eliminated by the playwrights' alteration of De Flores, found its place with different characters in Rowley's subplot. For the name of this alter Alsemero, Rowley dipped into the next tale in Reynolds's collection and took the name of Alibius. As the playwrights discovered with Beatrice, De Flores, and Diaphanta, the name of Alibius—"being in another place"— was fortuitously a happy one. In the play Alibius, like Alsemero in Reynolds, "sets spies" upon the wife: Lollio in the play, Diaphanta in the source. In Reynolds, Diaphanta eventually discovers Beatrice and De Flores's "beastly pleasures" and betrays the lovers to the jealous husband; but of course Lollio, who yearns like De Flores in the main plot to take his "fool's share," oversees a wife who, although tempted, keeps her virtue intact.

Rowley and Middleton thus found leftover material in the primary source to cut a pattern in grotesque but ultimately happy contrast to the tragedy. Although Isabella feels the attraction of the changeling, she refuses to join the mad world of the black sabbath:

> Luna is now big-bellied, and there's room
> For both of us to ride with Hecate;
> I'll drag thee up into her silver sphere,
> And there we'll kick the dog, and beat the bush,
> That barks against the witches of the night.
>
> (III.III.79–83)

The madmen who, as Isabella seems about to yield, cross the upper stage "*some as birds, others as beasts,*" conjure more fearful images than those of men descending the great chain of being. These illusory transformations, shaped by the malignant fantasies of sexual lunatics, suggest most compellingly the power of diabolic metamorphosis, the power of witches and demons to take any shape the depraved imagination can project. Those captivated by the flesh discover that, as Reynolds cautions in his preface to the reader, "the best of its beauty is but vanity and deformity" (sig. A4).

III

We must now consider the origin of another concatenation of events in the main plot of *The Changeling*, the substitution of Diaphanta for Beatrice-Joanna on her wedding night and the subsequent murder of the waiting-woman. In 1924 Bertram Lloyd identified the most immediate source for this episode as a novel by Leonard Digges, *Gerardo the Unfortunate Spaniard*, translated from the Spanish of G. de Cespedes y Meneses.[29] Published in 1622, Digges's work was entered in the Stationers' Register on 11 March 1621/22; since *The Changeling* was licensed on 7 May 1622, the collaborators must have worked, as all the evidence indicates, with notable dispatch. I would like to suggest that something more urgent than a casual and random process of selection was involved. Middleton may have stumbled onto the Digges translation, but he selected the episode from the novel because of an impulse already disposing the plot in this direction. Before he discovered the events as ordered in the Spanish translation, Middleton was shaping the fable in response to yet another source. It can be identified if we isolate a crucial aspect of the plot not derived either from Digges or from Reynolds—the tripartite virginity test.

The climactic virginal trial is of course that of Beatrice on her wedding night, for which she substitutes Diaphanta. This test is similar to the one reported in Digges but there is an important difference: the husband in the source, unlike Alsemero, has no cause for suspicion; it is not, therefore, primarily and most immediately a judicial encounter, as metaphorically it is in the play:

29. Bertram Lloyd, "A Minor Source of *The Changeling*," *MLR*, XIX (1924), 101–102.

> The more I think upon th'ensuing night,
> And whom I am to cope with in embraces,
> One that's ennobled both in blood and mind,
> So clear in understanding (that's my plague now),
> Before whose judgment will my fault appear
> Like malefactors' crimes before tribunals. . . .
>
>   (IV.i.3–8)

But before "th'ensuing night" Beatrice-Joanna discovers Alsemero's fantastic "closet"; and with the plot's gratuitous disclosure that her new husband is a physician of the occult, she correctly fears that he will make a preliminary test of her virginity with "glass M." The following two examinations—first, of Diaphanta by Beatrice; second, of Beatrice by her husband—have no connection with Digges, where the "honesty" of neither woman is doubted.[30] These two comical tests, as they lead to the substitution of Diaphanta in Beatrice's wedding bed, are more important dramatically than the material in the Spanish novel, and Middleton indicates his inspiration with a topical allusion identified long ago but never investigated as, at the very least, a remarkable analogue to the events of the play: "She will not search me, will she," muses Diaphanta as Beatrice fetches the liquid, "Like the forewoman of a female jury?" (IV.i.100–101).[31] The complex of topical events to which Middleton alludes is much more relevant to *The Changeling* than is Digges: included among those events were a juridical examination for virginity and the substitution of a virgin for a wanton; the intrigue also involved the murder of one who stood in the way of a lustful alliance. Finally, and most importantly for my purposes, the morbidity of these notorious crimes was attributed to the literal workings of witches and demons.

No ghost need come from the grave to tell us that Middleton was attuned to the life of his time, and in the London of 1613 only a ghost could have been deaf to the infamous divorce of the Countess of Essex and her marriage at the end of the year to the king's favorite, the newly created Earl of Somerset. Two years later the scandal deepened with the discovery

---

30. See the reprinted selection from Digges in Bawcutt, pp. 127–129.

31. First noted by A. H. Bullen, *The Works of Thomas Middleton* (London, 1885), VI, 73.

that Sir Thomas Overbury, having stood in the way of Frances Howard's divorce from Essex and her remarriage to Somerset, had been secretly murdered in the Tower. These events, we can believe, touched Middleton intimately. Both Overbury and Middleton were of Queen's College, Oxford; Middleton matriculated in the university early in 1598, at the end of which year Overbury graduated B.A.[32] This collegial connection would urge at least a subsequent acquaintance, given their friends in common and their mutual participation in the literary life of London. As a part of the City's celebration of the Somerset marriage Middleton had written the *Masque of Cupid* for the scandalous lovers.[33] Unfortunately, this work, performed at the Guildhall on 4 January 1613/14, has not survived, but we can be certain that the masque idealized the marriage according to fashion. For such a master of dramatic irony as Middleton, the effect on him when the full corruption of the alliance became known must have been terrific. In *The Changeling* and *Women Beware Women*, when evil makes a mockery of the ideal, it was therefore not the first time that Middleton had celebrated corrupt nuptials with an ironic masque.

It has been suggested that Frances Howard was for Middleton a prototype of the evil but beautiful heroine of the later plays.[34] "Those that saw her Face," wrote one historian with an eye for drama, "might challenge Nature of too much Hypocrisy, for harbouring so wicked a Heart under so sweet and bewitching a Countenance."[35] But, as gossip would have it, the exhibition of her second wedding could not be so convincing as to disguise entirely the black truth: "She thinking all the World ignorant of her sly Practices, hath the Impudence to appear in the Habit of a Virgin, with her Hair pendant almost to her Feet; which Ornament of her Body (though a Fair one) could not cover the Deformities of her Soul."[36] Because white

32. See David George, "Thomas Middleton at Oxford," *MLR*, LXV (1970), 734–736; and "Overbury, Sir Thomas," *Dictionary of National Biography*.

33. R. C. Bald, "Middleton's Civic Employments," *MP*, XXXI (1933), 65.

34. William Power, "Middleton's Way with Names," *N&Q*, N.S. VII (1960), 96. Power does not, however, mention the topical reference to Frances Howard in *The Changeling*.

35. Arthur Wilson, *The History of Great Britain, being the Life and Reign of James I* (London, 1653). I have used the reprint in White Kennett, *A Complete History of England* (London, 1706), II, 687.

36. Kennett, II, 693.

devils like Vittoria Corombona were already making such spectacles of themselves, we can see how, with all the world a stage, the most impudent lady of real life was viewed within the same moral and dramatic frame of vision: one pattern informs both the actual and the reflecting theater of God's judgment, as Sir Francis Bacon declared at Lady Frances's trial. In "the theatre of God's justice," he proclaimed histrionically, "Overbury's blood cried for revenge":

the great frame of justice, my lords, in this present action, hath a vault, and it hath a stage: a vault, wherein these works of darkness were contrived; and a stage with steps, by which they were brought to light.[37]

Bacon's metaphor imposes upon the playhouse its traditional metaphysical mysteries. The vault, of course, is Hell. The stage discloses those secret workings and the subsequent retribution that Heaven exacts. The Somerset tragedy of adultery and murder was viewed as the exemplary Jacobean tragedy of blood revenge, a tragedy which a contemporary pamphlet entitled *The Bloody downfall of Adultery, Murder, and Ambition, presented in a black seane of Gods iust Iudgements in reuenge of the Inocent blood lately shed in this Kingdome*.[38] This drama was also literally a tragedy of state, because James's part in the events implicated the monarchy.[39] His injudicious role in the nullity proceedings and his own part in the imprisonment of Overbury probably damaged his reputation, according to Samuel R. Gardiner, more than his rupture with the House of Commons.[40] William McElwee asserts that "It is doubtful if the popularity and prestige of the Stuart monarchy ever entirely recovered from the damage done by the Somerset case."[41]

37. Thomas B. Howell, ed., *Cobbett's Complete Collection of State Trials* (London, 1809–1826), II, 955, 958.

38. I.T. (London, [1616?]).

39. For the argument that the Jacobean drama topically reflected fatal symptoms in the Jacobean court, see J. W. Lever, *The Tragedy of State* (London, 1971).

40. *History of England, 1603–1642* (London, 1899), II, 174.

41. *The Murder of Sir Thomas Overbury* (London, 1952), p. 261. For the Somerset scandals, see also the account in Gardiner, vol. II, chaps. xvi, xx; and, for its excellent bibliography, Beatrice White, *Cast of Ravens: The Strange Case of Sir Thomas Overbury* (New York, 1965).

In 1622 London witnessed an event that might well explain Middleton's recollecting the tragedy of the previous decade for transposition in *The Changeling*. Middleton, having celebrated their marriage with the *Masque of Cupid*, would not likely overlook the release of the Earl and Countess of Somerset from the Tower on 18 January 1621/22.[42] In 1615 both had been judged guilty of murder (though the earl almost certainly was innocent); but James, while committed to their prosecution and conviction, had never intended that the sentence of death be executed. Instead they were confined for nearly a decade, awaiting the royal pleasure. The release of the fallen great ones, with their retreat into obscurity, was nevertheless a fitting dramatic conclusion to a crime that confirmed the mysteries of God's justice. The stories in Reynolds, having at this same time caught Middleton's dramatic appreciation, are of course based upon the same mysterious structure; Reynolds in fact tells the reader in the preface that but for the author's discretion and compassion exemplary tales of God's triumphant revenge could be included from the English scene. Certainly the first such example to come to mind in the London of 1622 would be the Somerset story, the postscript to which had just been added:

I haue purposely fetched these Tragicall Histories from forraine parts: because it grieues me to report and relate those that are too frequently committed in our owne country, in respect the misfortune of the dead may perchance either afflict, or scandalize their liuing friends; who rather want matter of new consolation, then cause of reuiuing old sorrowes, or because the iniquity of the times is such, that it is as easie to procure many enemies, as difficult to purchase one true friend: In which respect, I know that diuers, both in matters of this, and of other natures, haue beene so cautious to disguise and maske their Actors, vnder the vayles of other names; and sometimes become inforced to lay their Scenes in strange and vnknowne Countries.

(sigs. B2^v-B3)

Reynolds's testimony regarding the veiled transpositions of cautious dramatists is to the point. We are coming more and more to see the topical relevance of the Jacobean drama, disguised though the relevance might be

---

42. *State Trials*, II, 966. McElwee (p. 265) misleadingly gives the date as 1621.

by foreign settings and names.[43] The problems of censorship that arose in the first decade of the century made it clear that, for the deeper disillusionment of the time, some metaphoric mode would be required. "The Plays do not forbear to present upon their Stage the whole Course of this present Time," wrote Samuel Calvert to Winwood in March 1605; "not sparing either King, State or Religion, in so great Absurdity, and with such Liberty, that any would be afraid to hear them."[44] Such a state of affairs could not continue. A drama that truly gave the age its form and pressure would have to be a drama controlled by Reynolds's circumspection.[45]

The Somerset affair offered Middleton more than Diaphanta's comparison of her examination with one like that of Lady Essex, for Frances Howard like Beatrice had to pass her test—at least according to all accounts—well after she had lost her virginity. In 1606 she had been married to the Earl of Essex in an effort of the royal peacemaker to promote harmony between two powerful families. While the young earl was away in France for several years and before the immature couple had been permitted to cohabit, the Jacobean court thoroughly corrupted the young wife, and she became enamored of Robert Carr—Lord Rochester, favorite of the king and soon to become Earl of Somerset. Upon her husband's return she had no intention of giving up her romance and consummating a marriage with one she now loathed. All attempts by the earl at sexual intercourse were repelled; and finally, with the husband loathing his wife in return, both agreed to testify before an ecclesiastical commission set up by the king to nullify the union. In order to prove her virginity the commission appointed a jury of four noble ladies and two midwives to

43. See Lever; and G. K. Hunter, "English Folly and Italian Vice," in *Jacobean Theatre*, ed. John Russell Brown and Bernard Harris, Stratford-upon-Avon Studies, no. 1 (London, 1960), pp. 85–111.

44. Sir Ralph Winwood, *Memorials of Affairs of State in the Reigns of Queen Elizabeth and King James I*, ed. Edmund Sawyer (London, 1725), II.64. Cited in Daniel B. Dodson, "King James and *The Phoenix*—Again," *N&Q*, N.S.V (1958), 436.

45. It is a telling commentary that in 1661 an unidentifiable T. M., Esq., "digested" Reynolds's collection as *Blood for Blood: or Murthers Revenged* and added to the group an account of the murder of Sir Thomas Overbury, along with four other tales, to show "the sad Product of our own Times."

examine the countess. She was deemed *virgo intacta et incorrupta.* Had the judgment been made according to rumor, however, her divorce from Essex and her subsequent marriage to Somerset would have been aborted. Although Archbishop Abbot thought that the jury had probably been tampered with, rumor offered a more dramatic explanation, the substitution of a virgin for the adulterously deflowered woman:

The Countess being ashamed, and bashful, to come to such a Tryal, would not expose her Face to the Light; but being to appear before the Matrons under a Veil, another young Gentlewoman, that had less offended, was fobbed into the Place; and she passed, in the Opinion, both of Jury and Judges, to be a Virgin.[46]

Like Lady Essex, Beatrice has to undergo a test of her virginity or else she will not succeed in her murderous plot to change lovers. Beatrice plans, like her topical counterpart, to fob a virgin into her place for that test; but first she must herself examine the substitute—who wittily evokes for the audience a gossipy recollection of the scandalous episode.

The lustful murder finally charged against Frances Howard was, like the evil in *The Changeling,* partially objectified as abetted by a literally demonic force. The prosecution was thereby able to present a coherent and satisfactory explanation for such sensational depravity, all without an extraordinary violation of judicial and rational experience and without compromising, despite their possession by an objective and alien evil, the moral culpability of the human agents. Even during the nullity trial, when Lady Essex was arranging the murder of Overbury and therefore before the facts of her evil proceedings transpired, demonology became a titillating part of the psychological and physiological explanation for the couple's sexual morbidity. Only evil could account for the abnormal situation, even if no human agent was available to indict.

The Earl of Essex was not willing to forgo the chance of a future marriage by confessing that he suffered a general condition of impotence; he only admitted that it was so with his wife, *impotentia versus hanc.* Archbishop Abbot, who had been led to believe that Essex simply had "no ink in his pen," was alarmed to hear his peculiar testimony and did not

46. Kennett, II, 692.

intend to establish a precedent that would encourage collusion between married partners who had merely ceased to care for each other.[47] Aware of the weakness of their case, the lawyers for the countess suggested that the earl had been bewitched. Later there would be evidence to support a charge of *maleficium*, but in 1613 the Archbishop was dubious of the supposition and argued that, even were it true, church law would not allow the devil to put asunder what God had joined together. King James, however, was entirely convinced: "if the Devil hath any power," he assured his prelate, "it is over the flesh, rather over the filthiest and most sinful part thereof, whereunto original sin is soldered." Had King James not existed, dramatists would have had to invent such a monarch to preside over the Jacobean fascination with phallic evil: "and if the power of witchcraft may reach to our life," the king told his archbishop, "much more to a member . . . wherein the Devil hath his principal operation."[48] James insisted that Abbot defer to the author of *Daemonologie*; and, when the archbishop showed no sign of doing so, the king packed the commission and suppressed the minority opinion.[49]

In 1613 the sober proceedings of Abbot's commission amused the public with its speculations; but, if these matters "were then smiled at, and since that time much sport had been made at the court and in London about them,"[50] the humor darkened in 1615 when the drama moved from the vault to the platform stage and revealed a true Jacobean tragedy of lust, murder, and revenge. Lust does indeed lead to murder, and neither is accomplished without demonological assistance. Murder, however, cannot be concealed, and God's vengeance will triumph at last. Real life is just as the didactic Reynolds and the dramatic structure would have it.

47. *State Trials,* II, 806.

48. *Ibid.*, p. 801.

49. Thomas Cooper, in *The Mystery of Witch-craft* (1617), perhaps reflects the Essex nullity in discussing Satan's power to "hinder the operations of nature": "But *particularly* also, though the party may haue ability to others, yet to serue one, for the like reasons, he may be impotent, not able to performe the worke of Generation, and so deny that duety of marriage, and so happily produce a nullity thereof, vnlesse by *Phisicke*, or some spirituall means his power may be ouerruled, for which some time is to be graunted, and meanes vsed" (pp. 260–261). To the end Abbot protested that the Earl and Lady Essex had not resorted to prayer and fasting.

50. *State Trials,* II, 816.

The lawyers for Lady Essex no doubt stumbled independently onto *maleficium* as a cause of her husband's impotence; but, when the prosecution tried Mistress Anne Turner as an accomplice in the murder of Sir Thomas Overbury, the evidence ironically supported the satanic speculations of the nullity trial. The agent of witchcraft and sorcery turned out to be the countess herself. As anyone could know from a glance at James's *Daemonologie,* the devil had the power "of weakening the nature of some men, to make them unable for women: and making it to abound in others, more then the ordinary course of nature would permit." [51] The frustrated Lady Essex, initiated by the unsavory Anne Turner, called upon those powers by consulting the notorious Dr. Simon Forman in his physician's closet in Lambeth. [52] Becoming disciples of the devil and Forman's "daughters," Lady Frances and Mistress Turner pursued their amorous strategies with forbidden secrets of nature, Mistress Turner to maintain Sir Arthur Mainwaring's love for her, Lady Frances to increase Robert Carr's passion for her with aphrodisiacs and to deter her husband's sexual advances with anaphrodisiacs. At Anne Turner's trial Sir Edward Coke exhibited a fascinating collection of obscene and phallic paraphernalia employed in Forman's devilish mischief, including "certain pictures of a man and woman in copulation, made in lead." At this moment in the crowded Guildhall, so charged was the pornographic atmosphere that an amazing phenomenon occurred: "there was heard a crack from the scaffolds, which caused great fear, tumult and confusion among the spectators, and throughout the hall, every one fearing hurt, as if the devil had been present, and grown angry to have his workmanship shewed, by such as were not his own scholars." [53] Perhaps vexed by the years of her husband's sexual activity with his fashionable clientele, Dr. Forman's widow testified about the strange events that took place behind closed doors:

51. *Daemonologie* (1597), ed. G. B. Harrison, The Bodley Head Quartos (London, 1924), p. xiii.

52. The fantastic dissonance of Alsemero's "physician's closet," along with the arcane virginity test, has disturbed many critics (see Bawcutt, p. lvii); I think that these original and somewhat extraneous details, whether successfully integrated with Reynolds or not, have their inspiration in the topical scandals.

53. *State Trials,* II, 932.

There was . . . enchantments shewed in court, written in parchment, wherein were contained all the names of the blessed Trinity, mentioned in the scriptures; and in another parchment, + B. + C. + D. + E. and in a third likewise in parchment, were written all the names of the Holy Trinity, as also a figure, in which was written this word Corpus; and upon the parchment was fastened a little piece of the skin of a man.—In some of these parchments, were the devils particular names, who were conjured to torment the lord Somerset and sir Arthur Ma[i]nwaring, if their loves should not continue, the one to the countess, the other to Mrs. Turner.[54]

After Dr. Forman's sudden death on 8 September 1611, the two women procured the services of Dr. Savories, who "practised many sorceries upon the earl of Essex's person."[55] No doubt with the wily assistance of Lady Frances, the sorcery and witchcraft proved successful.

The prosecutors showed the pornographic objects again at the countess's trial, "which made them appear more odious as being known to converse with witches and wizards."[56] The strategy must also have been to render for the Jacobean jury a convincing psychological explanation for such impudent crimes. With a judicious use of demonology as a structural rationale, the prosecutors made a coherent and persuasive drama out of the case. The usual pattern of sexual and murderous intrigue had its inception and causality in an evil partially objectified but not entirely so: the devil, after all, merely comes to claim those already his own. In his closing speech at the earlier trial, Coke proclaimed Anne Turner "a whore, a bawd, a sorcerer, a witch, a papist, a felon, and a murderer, the daughter of the devil Forman," desiring her "to become a servant of Jesus Christ, and to pray to him to cast out of her those seven devils."[57] Objectifying the woman's psyche, these "devils" are all deviant oppositions to Jesus Christ in the service of whom are perfect freedom and mental health. If in moral terms of black and white the point of view is simple and absolute, Middleton and Rowley's *The Changeling* and Burton's *Anatomy of Melancholy* prove that the masterly tracing of the mind within that frame of reference can be satisfyingly subtle and variable to a modern vision. We

54. *Ibid.*, p. 933.
55. *Ibid.*
56. *Ibid.*, p. 951.
57. *Ibid.*, p. 935.

can as easily be startled by the psychological disorder of evil as those witnesses in the Guildhall who felt the demon as a palpable thing.

Middleton and Rowley's fantasies of total sexual abandon, of possession by erotic desire, were almost inevitably projected, during the Jacobean period, with images of demonology. Even in his pagan world, King Lear perceives rapacious sexuality, the source of life itself, to be an inferno of devils:

> But to the girdle do the Gods inherit,
> Beneath is all the fiend's: there's hell, there's darkness,
> There is the sulphurous pit—burning, scalding,
> Stench, consumption. . . .
>
> (IV.vi.125–128)[58]

The only alternative lay in the virtue of chastity, as exemplified in the famous character of *A Wife* which Overbury had reputedly written to dissuade his friend from marrying Lady Frances:

> *One* is *loves number*: who from that doth fall,
> Hath lost his hold, and no *new rest* shall find.[59]

Beatrice falls; but, spreading and mounting to infinity, she gains a kind of peace in the assurance of the damned.

IV

"The essential critical point about a collaborative work is that it is the product not of one dramatic vision but of two or more; and the critic of a play like *The Changeling* who attempts seriously to account for its achievement must seek its roots not only in the Middleton canon but in the canon of William Rowley's plays as well."[60] Cyrus Hoy's challenge is a happy one, because for too long Rowley's contribution has received little more than apologetic justification. Although criticism from this negative stance

58. *King Lear,* ed. Kenneth Muir, The Arden Shakespeare (London, 1972).

59. *The Miscellaneous Works . . . of Sir Thomas Overbury,* ed. Edward F. Rimbault (London, 1856), p. 35.

60. Hoy, p. 6.

has taught us much about the multiple plot in Renaissance drama,[61] we might still hesitate to address ourselves to a subject so humble as that of William Rowley's dramatic vision. It will always be an exceptional fact that this most successful of collaborations brought together two play-wrights of such disparate abilities and achievements. No doubt one symptom of their congeniality is that each could adapt himself to different modes or genres so completely as almost to become anonymous. This negative capability certainly would contribute to a talent for collaboration, a method of creation that has itself been described as "the great Elizabethan disappearing act."[62] More positively, however, both Middleton and Rowley had evinced, before *The Changeling*, a notable interest in the dramatic possibilities of demonology, and this in an age when such an interest is not especially remarkable.

The most comprehensive book on the occult in Renaissance drama calls Middleton's *The Witch* (ca. 1615) "the most informative play of the period on the topic of contemporary witchcraft."[63] Almost all of that lore concerns the obscene sexuality of the diabolic world, a black sabbatism of incest, sodomy, and other uninhibited fantasies. "The man that I have lusted to enjoy," says Hecate of the approaching Almachildes; "I've had him thrice in incubus already."

> ALMACHILDES
> Is your name Goody Hag?
> HECATE
> 'Tis anything:
> Call me the horrid'st and unhallow'd things
> That life and nature trembles at, for thee
> I'll be the same.
>
> (I. ii. 197–200)

---

61. See Levin, pp. 34–48; and Empson, pp. 48–52; Muriel Bradbrook, *Themes and Conventions of Elizabethan Tragedy* (Cambridge, Eng., 1935), pp. 213–224; Karl Holz-knecht, "The Dramatic Structure of *The Changeling*," *RenP* (1954), pp. 77–87; Bawcutt, pp. lxii–lxviii; Williams, pp. xiii–xxiv.

62. Norman Rabkin, "Problems in the Study of Collaboration," *RORD*, XIX (1976), 12.

63. Robert R. Reed, Jr., *The Occult on the Tudor and Stuart Stage* (Boston, 1965), p. 171. I have cited the text of *The Witch* in Bullen, V, 351–453.

The Witch does not go very far in suggesting the horror of the thing without a name, but the play is of considerable import in showing Middleton's more than common interest in the subject and in the moral permeation of the diabolical into the everyday world of evil. Furthermore, as R. C. Bald pointed out in a classic essay, *The Witch* appears to have been influenced by the diabolic nature of the Somerset scandal: "In Sebastian's scheme to prevent Antonio from consummating his marriage with Isabella, and in the charms he seeks from the witches to effect his purpose, there is a clear allusion to the notorious Essex divorce case of 1613." [64]

In addition to Sebastian's request for an anaphrodisiac, Bald might have observed Almachildes' visit to the witches for an aphrodisiac; and a third visitor, the Duchess, petitions Hecate to effect a "sudden and subtle" death (V.ii.4) for one who, because he thinks her an unchaste murderess, stands in the way of her marriage to the Lord Governor. All three interactions between the court and the witches thus reflect the evil meditations that led Frances Howard to consort with witches and demonologists. One might also consider, among the intricacies of bed tricks in the play, the instance in which the blindfolded Almachildes has been led to believe that he is deflowering Amoretta when actually "a hired strumpet" has been put in her place. This "examination" reveals to Almachildes what a true test of Frances Howard or Beatrice-Joanna would have exposed, a woman already possessed of sexual knowledge:

> This you that was a maid? how are you born
> To deceive men! I'd thought to have married you:
> I had been finely handled, had I not?
> I'll say that man is wise ever hereafter
> That tries his wife beforehand. 'Tis no marvel
> You should profess such bashfulness, to blind one,
> As if you durst not look a man i' th' face,
> Your modesty would blush so.
>
> (III.i.1–8)

64. R. C. Bald, "The Chronology of Middleton's Plays," *MLR*, XXXII (1937), 41. The topicality of *The Witch* has not been given careful study, but scholars following Bald have been dubious: W. W. Greg and F. P. Wilson, eds., *The Witch*, Malone Society Reprints (London, 1948), p. vi; Power, pp. 96–97; David George, "The Problem of Middleton's *The Witch* and Its Sources," *N&Q*, N.S. XIV (1967), 210. Although I believe that Bald was correct, he perhaps overstated the case when he declared that "there is a clear allusion."

Rowley's *The Birth of Merlin* (ca. 1608) has "the most decisive role assigned to an incubus or a succubus," [65] although the demon who assumes the form of Helen for the damnation of Faustus is more famous. Both Middleton and Rowley were clearly fascinated by these sexual demons, and each playwright stumbled independently onto a highly ingenious theatrical doubling of such demons in their human form. In Middleton's *A Mad World, My Masters* (1606) the actor playing Mistress Harebrain is also required to play a succubus (IV.i) who tempts Penitent Brothel in the form of Mistress Harebrain. Critics have not stopped making faces over this impingement of the supernatural upon what they take to be the realism of the city comedy: does Middleton didactically bungle in this episode, or is the moral pattern of temptation, of sin and salvation, itself rendered with satiric irony? The questions so posed completely miss the real viability of the dramatic experience—that is, that the audience, not having the advantage of the stage direction (*Enter the devil [as Succubus] in her shape*), can no more know than Penitent Brothel that the form of Mistress Harebrain is not, strictly speaking, Mistress Harebrain. Penitent Brothel, in his moral resolve, considers Mistress Harebrain metaphorically a bewitching devil whom he conjures away; but not until three scenes later—after he has questioned his servant, Harebrain's servant, and finally the woman herself—does he know literally that "Then was the devil in your likeness there":

> The very devil assum'd thee formally,
> That face, that voice, that gesture, that attire,
> E'en as it sits on thee, not a pleat alter'd,
> That beaver band, the color of that periwig,
> The farthingale above the navel, all,
> As if the fashion were his own invention.
>
> (IV.iv.28–33)[66]

With Penitent Brothel we experience in retrospect the *frisson* of the visitation—something like what Edward Alleyn felt, prompting his conversion,

---

65. Reed, p. 229.

66. I have cited the text of Standish Henning, ed., *A Mad World, My Masters*, Regents Renaissance Drama Series (Lincoln, Nebr., 1965).

when he recognized that an unaccountable devil had joined in a performance of *Doctor Faustus*:

> What knows the lecher when he clips his whore
> Whether it be the devil his parts adore?
> They're both so like that, in our natural sense,
> I could discern no change nor difference.
>
> (IV.iv.55–58)

This blurring of the natural and the supernatural, indistinguishable to
"our natural sense," suggests *mutatis mutandis* the metaphoric and psychological blurring of the supernatural into the natural conceptions of character. In the city comedy, written for a children's company, the blurring
or doubling has no small effect on the characterization, for Mistress
Harebrain is responsible for the demonic use of her form: "Be honest,"
Penitent advises her, "then the devil will ne'er assume thee" (IV.iv.44).
For the greater verisimilitude of tragedy, written for adult actors, characters could be similarly developed according to the phenomenology of
demons and witches, but with a subtlety more than satisfactory to our own
popular conceptions of human nature.

The only other instance I have found of a doubling such as Middleton
employed in 1606 is in *The Witch of Edmonton*, Rowley's collaboration just
the year before *The Changeling*. There is general agreement on the division
of labor among Rowley, Dekker, and Ford, and no one has questioned
Rowley's responsibility for the comic Cuddy Banks scenes.[67] Parodying
both serious plots, Rowley's clown engages Mother Sawyer's familiar spirit
to make Katherine Carter return his love: "I am bewitched already. I
would have thee so good as to unwitch me, or witch another with me for
company" (II.i.251 ff.). The result is the brief appearance of a devil
disguised as Katherine who leads Cuddy to a drenching. For a feeble joke
the doubling of roles is a *coup de théâtre*, complicating the instance in *A
Mad World*. In *The Witch of Edmonton* the actor playing Katherine is also

---

67. See H. Dugdale Sykes, "The Authorship of *The Witch of Edmonton*," *N&Q*, CLI
(1926), 435–438, 453–457; and Mark Stavig, *John Ford and the Traditional Moral Order*
(Madison, Wis., 1968), p. 47. I have cited the text in *Stuart Plays*, ed. Arthur H.
Nethercot et al. (New York, 1971), pp. 805–843.

required to play a demon who, when he discards his "real" demonic face, has assumed the form of Katherine. Again the audience does not have the advantage of the stage direction: *Enter Spirit in shape of Katherine, vizarded, and takes it off.* The actor's speech accompanying this action, however, makes clear that the stage direction is wholly misleading as far as the conception of the bit part is concerned:

> Thus throw I off mine own essential horror,
> And take the shape of a sweet, lovely maid
> Whom this fool dotes on.
>
> (III.i.107–109)

The theatrical disguise of the horrible mask is not, conceptually, the disguise but the reality; the actor's own face—Katherine's own face—is the deceptive form. Something very close to this confused and confusing disguise informs the complex conception of Beatrice-Joanna's "mask." Her beauty at once hides her essential horror ("there was a visor / O'er that cunning face, and that became you") and at the same time reveals it:

> The black mask
> That so continually was worn upon't
> Condemns the face for ugly ere't be seen.
>
> (V.iii.3–5)

Rowley's part in *The Witch of Edmonton* may have been small, but I think he learned a great deal from the enterprise. With penetrating psychological realism, that remarkable play rationalizes the witch hysteria by showing the persecution of Mother Sawyer which drives her in revenge to call upon the powers of darkness: "'Tis all one / To be a witch as to be counted one" (II.i.151–152). But when the fantastic Dog answers her call we see that the rationalization of evil does not mean that the supernatural power of evil is a delusion.[68] The Dog is rather, as Mark Stavig has shown, "an instructive illustration of the ways in which symbolism, realism, psychology, and morality are often linked in seventeenth-century plays."[69] The final emphasis, however, is upon the more than metaphoric applicability

---

68. See West, pp. 104–108, 144–154, and passim.
69. Stavig, p. 48.

of witchcraft and demonology to the common experience of mankind as represented in the other two plots, from the farce of Cuddy Banks to the tragedy of Frank Thorney. Devils are everywhere, agrees Mother Sawyer, "But is every devil mine?" (V.iii.30). As for her being a witch, "Who is not?"

> Hold not that universal name in scorn, then.
> What are your painted things in princes' courts,
> Upon whose eyelids lust sits, blowing fires
> To burn men's souls in sensual hot desires,
> Upon whose naked paps a lecher's thought
> Acts sin in fouler shapes than can be wrought?
>
> (IV.i.131–137)

As the Dog explains to Cuddy Banks, the source of evil is both without and within the personality, both objective and subjective:

> I'll thus much tell thee: thou never art so distant
> From an evil spirit but that thy oaths,
> Curses, and blasphemies pull him to thine elbow.
> Thou never tell'st a lie but that a devil
> Is within hearing it; thy evil purposes
> Are ever haunted; but, when they come to act—
> As thy tongue slandering, bearing false witness,
> Thy hand stabbing, stealing, cozening, cheating—
> He's then within thee.
>
> (V.i.159–167)

And frequently the humanoids we see are, though imperceptible to our natural sense, devils in human form:

> An hot, luxurious lecher in his twines,
> When he has thought to clip his dalliance,
> There has provided been for his embrace
> A fine, hot, flaming devil in her place.
>
> (V.i.175–178)

In *The Changeling* Middleton and Rowley complete this process of diabolism in characterizing horrifically recognizable human beings: De Flores is the devil for Beatrice's lust (V.iii.53), the serpent that she strokes (V.iii.66). Once their covenant with death has been made, the most significant action in the tragedy takes place in the sealing of it, out of our tantalized view. It is entirely appropriate that the catastrophe occurs off-stage when Alsemero makes them enact one final time their "scene of lust" as a rehearsal for "the black audience" in hell. There, in that infernal playhouse, the characters will eternally exhibit themselves, for the "howls and gnashings" of their own kind, as literal demon lovers.

Jean de Mairet and Poetic Justice: A Definition of Tragicomedy?

PERRY J. GETHNER

O F ALL THE DRAMATIC GENRES cultivated in seventeenth-century France, the tragicomedy is by far the most elusive and the least clearly defined. Although it surpassed all other genres in popularity in the period, roughly, from 1610 to 1640, French treatises on poetic theory showed little success in defining tragicomedy and in distinguishing it from its neighboring genre, tragedy. It is in the writings of Jean de Mairet that we find what is perhaps the most creative solution: the happy ending of tragicomedy is produced by a benign Providence that equitably dispenses rewards and punishments in the final act, whereas the characters of tragedy are subjected to a seemingly irrational power that dispenses death and havoc with little regard to human innocence or guilt. In order to appreciate the value and originality of these ideas, it will be necessary to recall the alternative theories advanced in France during the second quarter of the seventeenth century.

It should first be noted that such theories were not found in abundance. In fact, many playwrights of the period were somewhat unsure of the boundaries separating the dramatic genres. Thus, we find occasional inconsistencies in labeling a play's genre within the same original edition (perhaps the fault of the printer) and embarrassed admissions by certain authors that, although the play is really a tragedy, they are calling it a tragicomedy in order to conform to the taste of the time.[1]

Even those contemporaries of Mairet who took tragicomedy seriously did not succeed in producing clear and useful definitions. For example, Georges de Scudéry, who extolled the genre in the preface to his *Andromire* (1641) as being, if not the most perfect kind of poem, "du moins le plus agreable," and who achieved his greatest public successes with it, disappoints us with the vagueness of the following statement: "Ce beau & diuertissant Poeme, sans pancher trop vers la seuerité de la Tragedie, ni vers le stile railleur de la Comedie, prend les beautez les plus delicates de l'vne & de l'autre: & sans estre ni l'vne ni l'autre, on peut dire qu'il est toutes les deux ensemble, & quelque chose de plus."[2] This hybrid art form, far from being a monster, is a harmonious fusion, and "de l'assemblage de ces diuerses beautez, il resulte quelque chose d'excellent." The only precise element mentioned here is style, but even this is of no help, since Scudéry's tragicomedies, especially those written after 1637, contain no admixture of comic elements and use throughout the elevated style appropriate to the royal personages who appear in them.

Far more significant are the manifestoes of François Ogier and André de Mareschal which attack the unities and contest the whole notion that seventeenth-century French authors should be strictly bound to the practice of the ancient Greeks and Romans.[3] Tragicomedy is seen by them as a recent innovation with no link to antiquity in which the same characters are presented in both weighty and trivial situations. For Ogier such a

1. For example, in the first volume (1624) of Hardy's plays, *Alceste, Ariadne ravie,* and *Procris* are called tragedies in some places and tragicomedies in others. *Le Théatre d'Alexandre Hardy* (Paris, 1624–1626). The same is true of Jean de Rotrou's *Iphygenie* (Paris, 1641) and *La Belissaire* (Paris, 1644). Desmarets de Saint-Sorlin apologizes for calling his *Scipion* (Paris, 1639) a tragicomedy, although it should be labeled a tragedy.

2. Scudéry, *Andromire* (Paris, 1641), unnumbered liminary pages.

3. Ogier's preface accompanied the second version (Paris, 1626) of Jean de Schelandre's *Tyr et Sidon* in the form of a tragicomedy in two *journées.* The work in its original version (Paris, 1608) was a tragedy. Mareschal's manifesto is the preface to the second *journée* of his *La Généreuse Allemande* (Paris, 1630).

mixture is more realistic than the traditional dramas with their strict demarcation between the tragic and comic universes:

Car de dire qu'il est mal seant de faire paroistre en une mesme piece les mesmes personnes traittant tantost d'affaires serieuses, importantes et Tragiques, et incontinent apres de choses communes, vaines, et comiques, c'est ignorer la condition de la vie des hommes, de qui les jours et les heures sont bien souvent entrecoupées de ris et de larmes, de contentement et d'affliction, selon qu'ils sont agitez de la bonne ou de la mauvaise fortune.[4]

Such a theory suggests a type of dramaturgy resembling that of the Elizabethans. While it is quite possible that Jean de Schelandre was influenced by the theater of England, Ogier's preface represents the road not taken by the French.

The way of the future was to deny tragicomedy's existence as an autonomous genre by claiming that it is (or ought to become) merely tragedy with a happy ending. The fact that in practice tragicomedies usually treated the adventures of kings and great lords contributed to this process of assimilation. Jean-François Sarasin, who advocated the elimination of the offending term, went so far as to claim that Scudéry's *L'Amour tyrannique* (1639), which its author labeled a tragicomedy, is not merely a tragedy but a model tragedy, exemplifying Aristotelian doctrine so perfectly that, had the great philosopher lived in the seventeenth century, he would have cited it alongside *Oedipus Rex* as the supreme embodiment of his rules.[5] It was Abbé d'Aubignac's *La Pratique du théâtre* (1657) that signaled the triumph of this view and the doom of the term tragicomedy. The abbé advanced four arguments to support his proscription of the term tragicomedy: (1) since Greek tragedy provides examples of happy endings, there is no reason to deny such plays the name of tragedy; (2) modern tragicomedies contain no comic elements and, hence, have no right to the label "comic"; (3) the term itself, which was coined by Plautus and intended facetiously, has been wrenched out of context by modern writers and made to apply to plays having nothing in common with the

---

4. Schelandre, *Tyr et Sidon* (both versions), ed. Joseph Barker (Paris, 1974), p. 159.

5. Sarasin, "Discours sur la Tragédie" in *Oeuvres,* ed. Paul Festugière (Paris, 1926), II, 3, 32–34.

Amphitruo; (4) the term destroys suspense by revealing the ending of the play before it even begins.[6] By the time Nicolas Boileau-Despréaux published his *Art poétique* (1674), probably the single most influential text in French classical theory, there was no need to speak of the defunct and discredited tragicomedy.

I

What I shall henceforth call Mairet's theory must be pieced together from a group of disjointed remarks found in various prefaces and polemics, supported by his practice in the plays. The first and longest of his theoretical works is the "Préface de la *Silvanire,* en forme de discours poétique" (1631), a highly significant treatise which contributed to the adoption in France of the celebrated three unities. Unfortunately, Mairet is so concerned with citing major authorities that he fails to clarify their relationship to one another or to his own dramatic practice. The most confusing aspect of the preface is the treatment of tragicomedy, despite the fact that *Silvanire* is labeled as a "tragicomédie pastorale." At the start of the fourth chapter, entitled "De la Tragedie, Comedie, & Tragicomedie," Mairet disappoints us by stating, "Le Poeme Dramatique se diuise ordinairement en Tragedie & Comedie." He then paraphrases at some length the definitions and etymologies of those terms as found in the fourth-century grammarians Diomedes and Donatus (who were for men of the Middle Ages and Renaissance the leading authorities on the subject of drama), interjecting only one brief mention of the intermediate genre: "De la definition de la Tragedie & de la Comedie on peut aisément tirer celle de la Tragicomedie, qui n'est rien qu'vne composition de l'vne & de l'autre."[7] Tragedy, Mairet explains, shows the misfortunes of great heroes. Its ending is "tousiours triste" and "pitoyable, comme celle qui fait voir des Roys & des Princes reduits au desespoir"; while its moral purpose is to cause in us "vn dégoust de la vie, à cause des infortunes dont elle est remplie" and to make us realize "la fragilité des choses humaines, d'autant que ces mesmes Roys &

---

6. Aubignac, François Hédelin, Abbé d', *La Pratique du théâtre* (Paris, 1657; rpt. Munich, 1971), pp. 127–135.

7. Jean de Mairet, *Silvanire,* ed. Richard Otto (Bamberg, 1890), p. 14.

ces mesmes Princes qu'on y voit au commencement si glorieux & si triomphans y seruent à la fin de pitoyables preuues des insolences de la fortune."[8]

In the fifth and longest chapter, entitled "Des parties principales de la Comedie," Mairet continues his nonchalant refusal to delineate the genre of his own play. "Mais d'autant que ie veux estre succinct, & que ma Pastorale est tout à faict disposée à la Comique, bien qu'elle soit de genre Tragicomique, il suffira que ie fasse la diuision des parties de la Comedie. . . . "[9] The principal authority utilized in this section of the treatise is Giovanni Battista Guarini, author of the enormously influential *Pastor fido* (1590), also labeled a pastoral tragicomedy, and of various theoretical works, notably the *Compendio della poesia tragicomica* (1601). Guarini, too, had consciously modeled the structure and denouement of his play after the comedies of Terence, thus linking the intermediate genre more closely to comedy than to tragedy.

Curiously, the first indication of Mairet's own theory occurs in a passage where all the critical vocabulary appears to have been taken from the *Compendio*:

Premierement pour ce qui regarde la fable, il est hors de doute qu'elle est tout à faict de genre Dramatique, non pas de constitution double, mais mixte, & de sujet non simple, mais composé. Le meslange est fait de parties Tragiques & Comiques, en telle façon que les vnes & les autres faisant ensemble vn bon accord, ont en fin vne ioyeuse & Comique catastrophe, à la différence du meslange qu'Aristote introduit dans la Tragedie, d'vne telle duplicité, que les bons y rencontrent tousiours vne bonne fin, & les meschants vne meschante. C'est pourquoy ie treuue qu'elle est plus semblable à l'Amphitrion de Plaute, qu'elle n'a de rapport auec le Ciclope d'Euripide. . . .[10]

By using the term "mélange" to refer both to Guarini's totally joyful resolution and the "double constitution" attributed to Aristotle, Mairet seems to be legitimizing both as acceptable denouements for tragicomedy. The contrast between *The Cyclops* and *Amphitruo,* also borrowed from the

8. *Ibid.*
9. *Ibid.*, p. 15.
10. *Ibid.*, pp. 20–21.

Compendio, suggests that both ancient plays were genuine tragicomedies (the assimilation of the Greek satyr play into tragicomedy was by no means a novel idea in 1630), and thus two radically different "catastrophes" were acceptable. In addition, it is obvious that the "Aristotelian" theory of tragic denouement mentioned in the fifth chapter of Mairet's treatise flatly contradicts the theory of Diomedes cited in the preceding chapter. Diomedes had actually said that in tragedy "frequently and indeed almost always, from joyful beginnings proceed sad endings and the recognition to their sorrow of children and of former fortunes." [11] Mairet's more extreme statement of that principle ("la fin en est tousiours triste"), coupled with the mention of Aristotle's "duplicité" (double ending), are reconcilable only if Mairet understands the latter view to pertain to tragicomedy. This would explain the puzzling word "introduit"—Aristotle in the *Poetics* "introduced" into tragedy a denouement which ought to have been reserved for tragicomedy. Since the double ending is a valid "mixture" of tragic and comic elements, we can deduce from this rather disconcerting passage the first premise of Mairet's own position: tragicomedy, unless linked to the pastoral, will combine the rewarding of virtuous characters (the happy ending of comedy) with the downfall of the villains (the unhappy ending of tragedy). This is, to my knowledge, the first time that this explanation of the term "tragicomedy" is given in France.

I shall return later to the specific misinterpretations of Aristotle and of Guarini which make Mairet's theory possible, but first I shall continue the survey of Mairet's statements on poetics. The direction which his thought was taking emerges far more clearly in the "Au Lecteur" to his next tragicomedy, *Virginie* (1635):

Comme ie tiens que le propre du Poëte est de bien inuenter, ie me suis proposé de parestre tel en ce sujet: ce que ie pense auoir fait selon tous les preceptes d'Aristote: i'y fais voir par tout le vray-semblable, & le merueilleux, le vice puny, & la vertu recompensée, & sur tout les innocents y sortent de peril, & de confusion, par les mesmes moyens que les meschants auoient inuentez pour les perdre, de façon que la malice & le crime, y retournent tousiours à leurs

---

11. The translation is that of Harold Lawton in his *A Handbook of French Renaissance Dramatic Theory,* French Classics (Manchester, Eng., 1949), p. 23.

Autheurs: ce qui fait chez Aristote la plus noble & la plus ingenieuse partie de l'inuention. [12]

Here Mairet explicitly combines both elements of the concept known in English as "poetic justice." *Webster's Third International Dictionary* defines it as "an outcome of a fictitious or real situation in which vice is punished and virtue is rewarded, usually in a manner peculiarly or ironically appropriate to the particular situation." (I shall elaborate on the history of this concept in the second section.) On two points, however, the prefaces of *Silvanire* and *Virginie* appear to conflict. Whereas the preface of 1631 intimated that poetic justice could or should be the proper denouement for tragicomedy, the later preface makes no mention of any particular genre. Secondly, Aristotle, who had been mentioned only twice (once in the text and once in a marginal note) in the lengthy *Silvanire* preface, now emerges as the leading authority on dramatic theory, and in fact, the only one mentioned in the brief "Au Lecteur." Mairet, who had earlier referred only in passing to Aristotle's double ending as a solution he had not adopted, openly boasts in 1635 that he has zealously attempted to conform to all the great philosopher's precepts. (The idea that poetic justice was a dogma in the *Poetics* is, of course, completely erroneous, as I shall demonstrate later on.) The reason for Aristotle's new prominence is probably Mairet's role in the quarrel over the unities. Elsewhere in the *Virginie* preface the dramatist notes with pride that "ce n'a pas esté sans peine & sans bon-heur que i'ai pû restraindre tant de matiere en si peu de Vers, sans confusion & sans sortir des regles fondamentales de la Scene." [13] Since Mairet considered himself as the leading exponent of the unities, which supporters and opponents both attributed to Aristotle, he may well have felt compelled to show that his own dramatic practice was in total accord with the doctrines of the *Poetics*. At the same time, though, he knew, for he had officially said so in the *Silvanire* preface, that Aristotle spoke of the double ending in regard to tragedy, not tragicomedy. Because Mairet linked poetic justice with tragicomedy and its absence with tragedy, he presumably thought it prudent to

---

12. Jean de Mairet, *La Virginie* (Paris, 1635), unnumbered liminary pages.
13. *Ibid.*

eliminate specific references to the two genres, thus concealing any differences of opinion between himself and the great Peripatetic.

When the "Querelle du *Cid*" erupted in 1637, Aristotle's name was bandied about by writers on both sides, and it was not uncommon to charge that one's adversaries were using his name improperly. That charge was undoubtedly well founded. One of Mairet's own polemical pieces written during this literary battle suggests either that he had never read the *Poetics* (it is quite possible that he knew it only indirectly, through Guarini), or that, if he had, he did not understand it very well. In the "Responce à l'Amy du *Cid* sur ses inuectiues contre le Sieur Claueret" he declares that "la Tragi-comedie demande au contraire en ses Heros quelque erreur, ou quelque faute; afin que le Ciel ayt sujet de les punir auec Iustice." [14] In fact, it is the hero of tragedy who is supposed to be imperfect and whose fall should be occasioned by an error of judgment. More importantly, Aristotle never claims that divine justice has anything to do with the tragic hero or his fate. [15] Mairet's declaration indicates that he has not abandoned tragicomedy, even though Aristotle does not specifically mention it, and that he still maintains the link between that genre and poetic justice, which he now feels constrained to read (willy nilly, one might say) into the *Poetics*.

The last passage relating to the theory occurs in the dedication of Mairet's last tragedy, *Le Grand et dernier Solyman* (1639): "Vous y remarquerez deux Amants si parfaits & neantmoins si malheureux dans l'innocence de leurs Amours & de leurs vies, qu'ils nous feroient quasi soupçonner le Ciel d'iniustice, si luy mesme ne nous auoit aduertis il y a longtemps par la bouche de ses Oracles, que ses iugemens sont des gouffres & des abismes. . . ." [16] Taken in the light of the earlier passages I have quoted, this declaration completes the theory by officially excluding poetic

14. Jean de Mairet, "Responce à l'Amy du *Cid* sur ses inuectiues contre le Sieur Claueret," published with *Épistre familière du Sr Mayret au Sr Corneille* (Paris, 1637), p. 48 (misnumbered 38).

15. *Poetics* 13. 1453^a.

16. Jean de Mairet, *Le Grand et dernier Solyman* (Paris, 1639), "Epistre," unnumbered liminary pages.

justice from the province of tragedy. What characterizes the most serious
dramatic genre is the fall of great princes— a spectacle so gory and pitiful
that it should move the reader or spectator to beware of fickle fortune and
turn his attention to God and spiritual matters. Thus, while such reading
material as *Solyman* would prove to be unbearably painful for a normal
person who has undergone similar disasters of fortune, it will be eminently
suitable for the heroic and devout Duchesse de Montmorency (the dedi-
catee of the play), by confirming her "dans la sage resolution que vous auez
prise, de ne vous remettre iamais sur vne Mer qui vous a tesmoigné son
infidelité par vn si pitoyable naufrage. . . ." [17]

The dramatic works of Mairet confirm the general theory that we have
distilled from his prefaces and dedications, adding one final element which
has only been hinted at until now: the active role of the gods in guiding the
action toward its happy conclusion and in enforcing poetic justice. For this
reason, belief in the gods and awareness of their providential action are two
of the basic traits of the tragicomic hero, while irreverence for deity,
contempt for moral standards, and an excessive confidence in one's own
powers characterize the villain. Although the gods may intervene directly
in the human action in the form of oracles, dreams, and warning signs, it
is normally the characters who invoke them and who perceive their guiding hand at work. By calling attention to the role of the gods, especially at
the opening or at the conclusion of the play, the virtuous characters
interpret the action as miraculous. Here is a typical example of this process
from *Virginie*:

> Qu'en tous lieux ce miracle eternise vos faits,
> Dieux! de qui la iustice a de si beaux effaits;
> Que la place, & le iour soyent à iamais celebres,
> Où vous auez tiré la clarté des tenebres,
> Et fait voir clairement aux yeux de l'Vniuers,
> Que vos mains tost ou tard punissent les peruers.
>
> (V. 6)

17. *Ibid.*

The very implausibility of the adventures, the frequent use of magic, the extraordinary coincidences—the very elements that will be proscribed by the classical ideal of *vraisemblance*—far from being minimized, are brought to the fore. Mairet presumably feels that no excuse is necessary: miracle is a basic ingredient in the tragicomic world view. His personal endorsement of that view, based on a sincere belief in God and Providence, is confirmed by passages like the dedication of *Sidonie*, his last play (1643), to Mlle de Hautefort: "C'est l'esperance & l'opinion que nous deuons auoir d'vne personne sacree, en faueur de laquelle on ne sçauroit iustement nier, que la main du ciel n'ait operé de tres grands miracles." [18] If tragicomedy presents a fairy-tale world, it is because such an unreal world is required for miracles and poetic justice to flourish.

At the same time, Mairet's aesthetic and religious principles could embrace a radically different view of Providence as shown in his tragedies. As William Bunch has observed, "The absence of any divine dimension stands as one of the most unusual features of Mairet's three tragedies. It is as though Mairet could conceive no tragedy in a world in which providence and the gods exist. Their absence alone defines the tragic atmosphere. The impossibility of help from superhuman powers creates the inevitability leading to the tragic outcome." [19] The tragic heroes, although well intentioned, sincere, and innocent (or at least, believing themselves guiltless), are oppressed by the gods. Yet, while they may lose faith in poetic justice, they manage to retain their belief in the gods' existence and essential, if incomprehensible, righteousness. This attitude is sometimes expressed directly, as in this exchange between Sophonisbe and her confidante:

CORISBE
Mais après tant de maux, possible que les Dieux
Changeront aujourd'hui nos fortunes en mieux.

18. Jean de Mairet, *La Sidonie* (Paris, 1643), unnumbered liminary pages.
19. *Jean Mairet* (Boston, 1975), p. 131.

SOPHONISBE

Ha! Corisbé, le Sort a juré ma ruine,
Et la puissance humaine a choqué la divine;
Les Dieux, que mon bonheur a sans doute lassés,
Ne sont pas satisfaits de mes malheurs passés,
Et je m'ose moi-même à moi-même prédire
Qu'ils me gardent encor quelque chose de pire.

(II.1.441–448)[20]

The denouement of *Solyman* may be seen as a gruesome parody of the happy ending of tragicomedy, for the revelation of past secrets and mistaken identities which could have produced a full reconciliation of the characters arrives but a moment too late. The play ends with a massacre and a mood of unrelieved gloom. However, as the dedication of *Solyman* makes clear, Mairet can accept this pessimistic view of tragedy because of a tradition linking the tragic reversal of fortune to the Christian doctrine of *contemptus mundi*: earthly pomp and grandeur are inherently unstable and should be shunned; only things divine and eternal should occupy the thoughts of a Christian. This view, dating back at least to Boethius, had a fundamental impact on playwrights of the Renaissance but was gradually replaced by a more Aristotelian position in Mairet's lifetime.

Tragedy, then, presents a world where God allows chaos, in the form of evil men and fickle fortune, to reign unchallenged; reward and punishment are reserved for the hereafter. Tragicomedy, on the other hand, portrays a world carefully controlled by Providence, in which rewards and punishments are meticulously dispensed in this life, thus ensuring a happy ending. The direct link between poetic justice and tragicomedy was an innovation in French criticism, and the simultaneous acceptance of that view with the Christian moral interpretation of tragedy is, as far as I can tell, unique in the history of Western drama. The only earlier example I have discovered of Mairet's theory of tragicomedy is the subtitle of George Gascoigne's play, *The Glasse of Gouernement* (1575): "A tragicall Comedie

---

20. *Théâtre du XVIIᵉ siècle*, ed. Jacques Scherer (Paris, 1975), I:684. The play was first published in 1635.

so entituled, because therein are handled aswell the rewardes for Vertues, as also the punishment for Vices."[21] However, this work, essentially a morality play based in large part on the parable of the prodigal son, probably had no influence on French authors. This is not to say that poetic justice was introduced into French drama or into French poetic theory by Mairet. It is to the history of that concept that I now turn.

II

> But in these cases,
> We still have judgement here; that we but teach
> Bloody instructions, which, being taught, return
> To plague th' inventor: this even-handed Justice
> Commends th' ingredients of our poison'd chalice
> To our own lips.
>
> (*Macbeth*, I.vii.7–12)

The history of the doctrine of poetic justice in France is especially hard to trace because the French language does not seem to have a precise equivalent for the term. "Justice distributive" may suggest the meting out of appropriate rewards, but not to the seventeenth century. Bossuet used the term in his "Sermon sur l'aumône" to refer to divine judgment in the hereafter, while the Dictionary of Antoine Furetière, published in 1690, maintains the medieval usage, which contrasts "justice commutative," meaning an "équitté naturelle qui met un prix raisonnable aux choses," with a state "où il faut employer une autorité superieure contre ceux qui ne veulent pas suivre cette équitté naturelle" ("justice distributive"). "Justice immanente," the other approximate French equivalent, is somewhat misleading because it implies an order latent within events themselves, rather than a form of judgment imposed by a transcendent power. In any case, Littré's Dictionary lists no examples of this term earlier than the nineteenth century. Even the English term "poetic justice," although it clearly denotes the phenomenon we are discussing, did not exist in Mairet's day. It was coined in 1677 by the critic and playwight Thomas Rymer, who, to

---

21. Tudor Facsimile Texts (Amersham, 1914).

be precise, called it "poetical justice" and used it as a yardstick by which to measure the moral utility of all dramatic works. Ironically, Rymer derived the essence of his poetic theory, including the principle of rewards and punishments, from the leading French critics of the period who had neglected to find a name for this principle.[22]

Although the name is comparatively recent, poetic justice has an extremely long history. It is found at least as early as the Old Testament, where discussions of reward and punishment are normally limited to happenings in this life. Examples of divine intervention to save good people in distress and of aptly ignominious downfalls for the wicked are too numerous to mention here. The Psalmist describes God as executing judgment for the oppressed, loving the righteous, and turning upside down the path of the wicked (146:7–9). The Book of Proverbs notes the deep psychological satisfaction which such events provide: "When it goeth well with the righteous, the city rejoiceth: and when the wicked perish, there is shouting" (11:10).

Poetic justice enters literary criticism with Plato, who in the *Republic* judged literature exclusively by the criterion of pedagogical utility. Those poets who were allowed to remain in the perfect state, restricted to composing hymns to the gods and eulogies of good men, were forbidden to speak of the misfortunes of the virtuous or of the prosperity of the wicked.[23] Aristotle's *Poetics*, concerned with the aesthetic question of what precisely tragedy is, is in accord with Plato by rejecting as untragic those plots which show the undeserved misery of perfectly virtuous characters or the unjust triumph of villains. But the parallel goes no further. Aristotle proceeds to praise Euripides for giving sad endings to most of his plays and is highly critical of

the construction of Plot which some rank first, one with a double story . . . and an opposite issue for the good and the bad personages. It is ranked as first only through the weakness of the audiences; the poets merely follow their public, writing as its wishes dictate. But the pleasure here is not that of Tragedy.

---

22. The most comprehensive history of this concept that has appeared to date is John D. Ebbs, *The Principle of Poetic Justice Illustrated in Restoration Tragedy* (Salzburg, 1973).

23. Plato, *Republic* III. 392[b].

It belongs rather to Comedy, where the bitterest enemies in the piece (e.g. Orestes and Aegisthus) walk off good friends at the end, with no slaying of any one by any one.[24]

In short, poetic justice is tolerated but not recommended in tragedy. Nevertheless, the philosopher states elsewhere that the best type of plot is one where a person on the verge of slaying a loved one is prevented from doing so by a last-minute recognition.[25] This inconsistency was duly noted by many proponents of tragicomedy. I have not referred to Aristotle's theory of justice, expounded in detail in the fifth book of the *Nicomachean Ethics*, since it is not relevant to the present discussion. Justice is there defined as a human virtue within a social context. Poetic justice, on the other hand, refers to the activity of a divine power acting in human history for the purpose of enforcing moral standards and functions as a didactic instrument in works of literature.

If Aristotle believed that plots with happy endings ought to be ranked second, there was no shortage of critics in the Renaissance who interpreted the *Poetics* as an endorsement for poetic justice.[26] One of the most influential of these theorists, the Italian playwright Giraldi Cinthio, advocated "mixed tragedies" (those with happy endings), while eschewing the term "tragicomedy." He was aware of the advantages of such a denouement: it satisfies popular taste and is morally edifying, as well. "For it gives extraordinary pleasure to the spectator when he sees the astute trapped and deceived at the end of the drama, and the wicked finally overthrown."[27] But while Giraldi Cinthio clearly foreshadows Mairet in this passage, he does not use poetic justice as a principle for distinguishing tragedy from tragicomedy. He prefers to speak of two kinds of tragedy.

24. *Poetics* 1453ᵃ. The translation is by Ingram Bywater, in *Basic Works of Aristotle*, ed. Richard McKeon (New York, 1941).

25. *Ibid.*, 1454ᵃ.

26. For a comprehensive survey of tragicomic theory, with a detailed analysis of Giraldi Cinthio and Guarini, see Marvin Herrick, *Tragicomedy: Its Origin and Development in Italy, France, and England* (Urbana, Ill., 1955).

27. *Discorsi intorno al comporre de i romanzi, delle commedie, e delle tragedie* (1554), trans. Allan H. Gilbert, in *Literary Criticism: Plato to Dryden* (New York, 1940), p. 257.

Guarini, who strongly favored the term "tragicomedy," took an unusual view of poetic justice. In the *Compendio* he cites, in both Greek and Italian, the key passage from the *Poetics* and argues at length that Aristotle considered the double ending appropriate for tragedy, although he ranked it second, and that the philosopher's preference for simple plots was inconsistent with the rest of his theory. However, since Guarini holds that tragicomedy should follow the structure and denouement of Terentian comedy, he uses poetic justice to distinguish between "mixed tragedy" and tragicomedy, but his distinction is precisely the opposite of Mairet's. By "mixed" he understands the presence of both good and bad characters, the former ending in prosperity and the latter in misfortune. In tragicomedy, on the other hand, "just as laughter would not be fitting to the double constitution . . . so the punishment meted out to evildoers in the double [ending] is not suitable to tragicomic poetry, in which, according to the custom of comedy, the bad are not punished."[28] Yet Guarini seems to have been too heavily influenced by didactic theories of drama to allow Corisca, the villainess of his *Pastor fido*, to escape with impunity. He solves the dilemma with a device that would later be linked to melodrama: the villain's totally unexpected conversion in the final scene.

And because it would be repugnant to the tragicomic ending that Corisca should be unhappy, for otherwise [the play] would seem to fall into the double constitution with its good outcome for the good people, and a bad one for the bad, refuted by us earlier. And on the other hand, as it is not suitable, as a thing setting a bad example, that a wicked woman should have a happy fortune, the expedient I adopted was good, namely, that by repenting her fault she might protect herself from scandal, and by receiving pardon from the offended persons, she might remain happy.[29]

Thus, Guarini's attempt to eliminate poetic justice from tragicomedy ended in a compromise. Not only do the repentance and pardon of the thwarted villain constitute an attenuated form of poetic justice, but in fact Corisca is not as "lieta" as the other characters at the end of *Il Pastor fido*.

---

28. Guarini, *Compendio della Poesia Tragicomica* (Venice, 1601), p. 38. My translation.
29. *Ibid.*, pp. 62–63.

Guarini could have ended his play with a triple wedding by uniting Corisca and Coridon, the most persistent and faithful of her swains. Nothing of the kind happens, and Coridon is not even mentioned in the final act. The distinction between tragicomedy and mixed tragedy becomes somewhat blurred here, both in theory and practice.

That Mairet could have misconstrued Guarini's argument to link poetic justice with tragicomedy and with Aristotle is understandable. Sensitive to the didactic usefulness of the "double constitution" and seemingly unaware of the inconsistencies between the authorities he consulted, the French poet forged a theory that was derivative in all its parts, yet innovative as a whole. If, as I suspect, he knew Aristotle's doctrine only through Guarini, then he could not have realized how much his own theory of tragedy, derived from Diomedes and Donatus, flouted the dictum, "A good man must not be seen passing from happiness to misery." Such a situation, for Aristotle, "is not fear-inspiring or piteous, but simply odious to us."[30] Nor did Mairet comprehend that Aristotle would not have endorsed the optimistic vision presented in his tragicomedies.

To what extent did Mairet's ideas affect French poetic theory? Except for his advocacy of the three unities, his influence seems to have been negligible. Poetic justice received unqualified support in the *Poétique* of Jules de La Mesnardière (1640) and in several other critics of the period, but it did not prevail. On this point I differ with the great historian of French classicism, René Bray.[31] The position that was to become representative of classical doctrine, however similar it appears to poetic justice, is not at all identical to it. According to Abbé d'Aubignac, "La principale regle du Poëme Dramatique, est que les vertus y soient toûjours recompensées, *ou pour le moins toûjours loüées, malgré les outrages de la Fortune,* & que les vices y soient toûjours punis, *ou pour le moins toûjours en horreur, quand même ils y triomphent.*"[32] In other words, poetic justice is not required at all; the "principale règle" for d'Aubignac is that the play support, rather than subvert, established moral values. This position is not fundamentally

---

30. *Poetics* 13. 1452^b.
31. *La Formation de la doctrine classique* (Paris, 1926), pp. 79–82.
32. *Pratique du théâtre*, p. 5. Italics mine.

different from that of Corneille, who opposed poetic justice on the grounds that virtue always engages our sympathies, even when it is oppressed, and likewise, that evil is always odious to us, even when it appears to triumph.[33]

If poetic justice did not succeed in establishing itself as a principle of dramaturgy in France, it is largely because of the decline of tragicomedy and because of vastly improved understanding of Aristotle by the new generation of theorists. There was, in addition, a new type of tragedy with a happy ending. Corneille's *Cinna* inaugurated a highly successful denouement in which not the gods' benevolence or the strange coincidences of fortune, but rather the magnanimity of a supremely heroic soul breaks the tragic impasse and effects a reconciliation of conflicting characters and loyalties. With the triumph of Corneille, Mairet's theories of both tragedy and tragicomedy became obsolete, and all his plays (except *Sophonisbe*) were soon forgotten. But his optimistic myth of order and faith emerging victorious in spite of chaos and confusion, though it clashed with the rationalism of Descartes and the classicism of l'Académie française, could not ultimately be silenced.

33. Especially in the dedicatory epistle to his *La Suite du Menteur* (1645)

Racine: Allusion and Adaptation in Iphigénie *and* Athalie

GILLIAN JONDORF

T HE FAMOUS "RULES" of French classical drama, set out by various
sixteenth-century theorists, became the subject of debate toward
1630, and in this debate the principle of *vraisemblance* was at first chiefly
bound up with the question of the unities. It was in the name of *vraisemblance* that the unity of time was both attacked and defended. François
Ogier argued in his preface to Jean de Schelandre's revised *Tyr et Sidon*
(1628) that it was unrealistic to present as happening in a single day events
which would really take far longer. Jean Chapelain, on the contrary,
argued in the *Lettre à Godeau sur la règle des vingt-quatre heures* (1630) that
the illusion of reality would be broken if there was too great a discrepancy
between the supposed duration of the action and the duration of the play in
performance.

Another aspect of the problem of *vraisemblance* is its relation to *bienséance*,
discussed notably by the Abbé d'Aubignac in *La Pratique du théâtre* (1657).
Vraisemblance will be threatened if events or characters in a play diverge
from known history or from an accepted version of myth or legend; but
characters from myth or history might seem so preposterous when judged
by seventeenth-century French standards of behavior, or by the conven-

189

tions of seventeenth-century French fiction, that *vraisemblance* would be lost by too close an adherence to history or legend. Racine justifies his divergence from Euripides' Andromache (who struggled to defend not Hector's son but Molossus, her son by Pyrrhus) partly by appealing to this principle. "J'ai cru en cela me conformer à l'idée que nous avons maintenant de cette princesse," he says in the second preface to *Andromaque,* although in the first preface he had argued in the other direction when he defended the violent character of his Pyrrhus who, as he sarcastically remarked, "n'avait pas lu nos romans." Pyrrhus, although somewhat softened from the model offered by Seneca and Virgil, is not the resigned and polite hero of a sentimental novel.

Corneille discussed the problems of *vraisemblance* and *bienséance* in the *Discours de la tragédie* (1660), with particular reference to historical subjects. A statement in that essay seems to prepare the way for Racine's adaptations of historical fact, literary model, or biblical text. Discussing the degree of license permissible in dealing with matters of fact, Corneille says that inaccuracy is only excusable if the poet "arrive par là au but de son art, auquel il n'aurait pu arriver autrement."

Racine displays in his prefaces an elaborate concern with establishing the historical accuracy of his material or the respectable ancestry of his legends, and vigorously defends liberties he has taken. He rebuts criticisms, and even anticipates those not yet made, as when in the preface to *Britannicus* he defends his extension of the age limits for entry to the Vestal Virgins even though, as he remarks, this is "une difficulté qu'on ne m'a point faite." As Raymond Picard says, "C'est raffiner et aussi se moquer, que d'aller au devant d'une critique qu'on n'a point faite,"[1] and there is certainly mockery or even contempt in the tone of those parts of the first preface to *Britannicus* in which Racine criticizes his critics.

Yet if a certain kind of hair-splitting criticism annoys him, and if he regards certain critics as ill-equipped to judge him ("Il n'y a rien . . . de plus injuste qu'un ignorant"), he also appeals at times to a

---

1. Racine, *Œuvres complètes,* ed. R. Picard (Paris, 1950), p. 1098. Quotations from the plays and their prefaces are from this edition.

cultivated reader or spectator who will appreciate some nuances in the plays by reason of his culture. Racine seems to address himself to this ideal spectator or reader now and then. In the preface to *Britannicus* he mentions that he had considered adding to the published text a selection of those passages from Tacitus which provide the source material for the play. But "le lecteur trouvera bon que je le renvoie à cet auteur, qui aussi bien est entre les mains de tout le monde." Again in the preface to *Mithridate* Racine says he need not cite his sources in detail because "tout le monde reconnaîtra aisément que j'ai suivi l'histoire avec fidélité." In the preface to *Iphigénie* he compliments his audience on the fact that "mes spectateurs ont été émus des mêmes choses qui ont mis autrefois en larmes le plus savant peuple de la Grèce." Racine looks for cultivation, even erudition, in his ideal reader or spectator, and purports not to regard these as rare commodities in the society he is writing for ("entre les mains de tout le monde" . . . "tout le monde reconnaîtra aisément").

There are many instances in Racine's tragedies of his relying on the spectator's or reader's knowledge to enrich the effect of the play. For example Nero's reported last words, "Qualis artifex pereo," are surely intended to come to our minds when we hear Néron describing the impression made on him by the striking scene of Junie's arrival by night at the palace. Néron the artist is captivated by the aesthetic power of the scene, the darkness, the torches, the girl's tears glinting, her vulnerable beauty contrasting with the grimness of the guards. Love at first sight is frequently recounted in Racine, but not with such a wealth of circumstantial detail. Compare the brevity with which we hear of love striking Antiochus for Bérénice and Bérénice for Titus (*Bérénice*, I.iv), Xipharès for Monime (*Mithridate*, I.i), Ériphile for Achille (*Iphigénie*, II.i). Phèdre for Hippolyte (*Phèdre*, I.iii). When Néron gives such a full account of seeing Junie for the first time, we "recognize" him as Néron. Similarly, Néron's known taste for acting comes to mind when he transforms an interview between Junie and Britannicus into a terrible piece of play acting which Junie must carry out while the emperor, a murderous *metteur en scène*, watches and listens from the wings. There is perhaps a hint of Néron the actor again in Act V, scene vii, when Burrhus describes Néron's impassivity at the death of Britannicus:

> Néron l'a vu mourir sans changer de couleur.
> Ses yeux indifférents ont déjà la constance
> D'un tyran dans le crime endurci dès l'enfance.

We know that he was not "dans le crime endurci dès l'enfance," so this wicked calm is an indication of how easily he has slipped into his new role.

Examples of this kind of allusiveness could be multiplied (Oreste's Furies, Phèdre's family history, Alexandre's divine birth), but there are two rather more complex examples that I should like to examine here, where specific facts or notions seem to be alluded to in the plays in such a way that meaning and power of suggestion are enhanced if one catches the allusion, although no ends are left dangling if one does not, and the autonomy of the play is not threatened.

The first example occurs in *Iphigénie*. It is probably true to say that reactions to this play vary principally according to the individual's reading of the character of Agamemnon. In the most favorable light he can be seen as torn between deep love for Iphigénie and a noble ambition to lead the Greeks to Troy. Alternatively he can be seen as weak, vain, self-deceiving, unwilling to take responsibility for his own decisions or face their consequences, visited by rare flashes of lucidity when he briefly sees the implications of his words or actions, intimidated by Calchas and the threat of a mutinous army, and mean in spirit.

Near the end of the play comes a passage that may have some pertinence to the question of how we view Agamemnon. In Act V, scene v, the penultimate scene of the play, Arcas describes to Clytemnestre the scene at the altar, the scene toward which the whole play has been tending:

> N'en doutez point, Madame, un Dieu combat pour vous.
> Achille en ce moment exauce vos prières;
> Il a brisé des Grecs les trop faibles barrières.
> Achille est à l'autel. Calchas est éperdu.
> Le fatal sacrifice est encor suspendu.
> On se menace, on court, l'air gémit, le fer brille.
> Achille fait ranger autour de votre fille
> Tous ses amis, pour lui prêts à se dévouer.
> Le triste Agamemnon, qui n'ose l'avouer,
> Pour détourner ses yeux des meurtres qu'il présage,
> Ou pour cacher ses pleurs, s'est voilé le visage.

What is interesting here is that the image of Agamemnon veiled is not new, and neither is the perception of it as an ambiguous image.

There is in fact a reference to Agamemnon veiling himself in Euripides, or rather in the final portion of *Iphigenia in Aulis,* regarded by modern editors as spurious but accepted by Racine as genuine: in line 1550, Agamemnon is referred to as drawing his robe across his eyes as a mark of grief. At that point in the Greek play it was clear to Agamemnon that Iphigenia was going to be sacrificed. She comes voluntarily to her death (not, as recounted by the chorus in Aeschylus [*Agamemnon,* ll.234–238], borne by Agamemnon's men and gagged), and Achilles has promised not to intervene unless at the last she asks him to try to rescue her. But this may not be Racine's only source for the veiling of Agamemnon, for there was also in antiquity a famous painting which showed Agamemnon veiled at the sacrifice of Iphigenia. It was by Timanthes, a Greek painter who flourished ca. 400 B.C. The painting is lost, and perhaps the nearest idea we can form of it is from the rather crude wall painting by an unknown painter found in the "House of the Tragic Poet" at Pompeii (now in the Museo Nazionale in Naples and reproduced in A. Stenico, *Roman and Etruscan Paintings,* London, 1963, plate 87). This painting shows Iphigenia being carried to the sacrifice in an anatomically rather unlikely attitude suggesting a mermaid, while in the front corner a veiled figure stands with bent head, turned away. This is believed to be imitated from the older painting by Timanthes, which is mentioned by various ancient authors, notably Cicero, Pliny the Elder, Valerius Maximus, and Quintilian. Cicero says this in the *Orator,* XXII.74:

si denique pictor ille vidit, cum immolanda Iphigenia tristis Calchas esset, tristior Ulixes, maereret Menelaus, obvolvendum caput Agamemnonis esse, quoniam summum illum luctum penicillo non posset imitari;

Cicero sees the veiling of Agamemnon as the culmination of the different degrees of grief displayed by the other onlookers, and also remarks that this climactic pitch of grief defeats the painter's skill. Valerius Maximus, in Book VIII, chap. XI, sec. 2, par. 6, of the *Memorabilia,* says:

Quid, ille alter aeque nobilis pictor luctuosum immolatae Iphigeniae sacrificium referens, cum Calchanta tristem, moestum Ulissem, clamantem Aiacem, lamentantem Menelaum circa aram statuisset, caput Agamemnonis involvendo, nonne summi moeroris acerbitatem arte exprimi non posse confessus est? Itaque pictura eius, haruspicis, amicorum, et fratris lacrimis madet: patris fletum spectantis affectui aestimandum reliquit.

Here there is the same notion as in Cicero that the veiling of Agamemnon marks the most intense grief, "summi moeroris acerbitatem," the same idea that the painter admits his inability to portray this state, and the further idea that it is up to the spectator to gauge Agamemnon's sorrow. Pliny the Elder (*Hist. nat.* XXXV.xxxvi.73) mentions Timanthes and the painting in these terms:

Nam Timanthes vel plurimum adfuit ingenii. eius enim est Iphigenia oratorum laudibus celebrata, qua stante ad aras peritura cum maestos pinxisset omnes praecipueque patruum et tristitiae omnem imaginem consumpsisset, patris ipsius voltum velavit, quem digne non poterat ostendere.

This is a somewhat different idea—that there was no way in which the grief of Agamemnon could be suitably portrayed (even had the painter's skill been greater) because all available modes of expression had been used up on the lesser grief of the other characters. (The difference between Pliny's and Valerius's explanation of the veiled Agamemnon is great enough for Lessing to have seen it as almost antithetical, when in Chapter II of his *Laokoön* he discusses the portrayal of grief.)

Quintilian, an author to whom Racine refers in several prefaces including the preface to *Iphigénie,* is closer to Cicero and Valerius Maximus than to Pliny (*Institutio oratoria,* II.xiii.12–13):

Quid? non in oratione operienda sunt quaedam, sive ostendi non debent sive exprimi pro dignitate non possunt? Ut fecit Timanthes, opinor, Cythnius in ea tabula qua Coloten Teium vicit. Nam cum in Iphigeniae immolatione pinxisset tristem Calchantem, tristiorem Ulixen, addidisset Menelao, quem summum poterat ars efficere, maerorem, consumptis adfectibus non reperiens, quo digne modo patris vultum posset exprimere, velavit eius caput et suo cuique animo dedit aestimandum.

This last phrase emphasizes even more, with the words "suo cuique animo," that the individual spectator is allowed, or required, by the artist to guess at Agamemnon's expression, and indeed his feelings, for himself.

This point perhaps brings us back to Racine, with its suggestion that it is left to the imagination of each listener to surmise the sorrow of Agamemnon. The veiled Agamemnon in Racine is not even onstage, therefore no individual actor's interpretation can influence us at this point by posture or gesture; we have only the words of Arcas and our own response to them. If we look back now at Arcas's speech, we see that Racine has transformed the significance of the veiled Agamemnon by his altering of the events and personalities of the play. In the painting, as in Euripides, Iphigenia as far as anyone knows is really going to be killed and so everyone including the *haruspex,* Calchas, is feeling and showing grief. In Racine, the sacrifice is in doubt not because any other solution to the oracle's enigma has yet proposed itself, but because Achille (with the godlike power to "exaucer" Clytemnestre's prayers, and perhaps even representing the god who "combat pour vous") is fighting for her and, unlike Euripides' Achilles, can apparently call on friends to help him defend Iphigénie.

Agamemnon's hiding of his face need not therefore express only grief. We are offered a choice of reasons for the veiling:

> Le triste Agamemnon, qui n'ose l'avouer,
> Pour détourner ses yeux des meurtres qu'il présage,
> Ou pour cacher ses pleurs, s'est voilé le visage.

The use of "triste" recalls the "tristem," "tristiorem," and so on of the Latin authors, although its use here is at the same time faintly ambiguous—is he sad or wretched, "un père triste" or "un triste père"? The two explicit reasons given for the veiling are in the second and third of the lines just quoted. Neither seems entirely convincing. The first implies surprising squeamishness in the commander in chief of the army; the second makes us wonder how, if his daughter's death would so grieve him, he can bear not to join in the movement for her rescue, which has now been started by Achille. Perhaps, however, there is a third reason, insinuated rather than stated in "qui n'ose l'avouer."[2] Here we see Agamemnon as we

---

2. I take the object pronoun in the phrase "n'ose l'avouer" to refer to Achille, and the verb to have the meaning (given by Littré and illustrated by a reference to *Phèdre*, III.i, "Je t'avouerai de tout"): "avouer une personne, approuver ce qu'elle a fait en notre nom." I am grateful to Professor Odette de Mourgues for advice on this point.

have seen him before: unwilling to be frank or bold about his decisions. When he was prepared to obey the oracle he lured Iphigénie and her mother to Aulide by subterfuge; when he decided not to sacrifice her he wanted Clytemnestre to hurry her away secretly. Now when there is both a chance of saving her and a need to decide publicly for or against the sacrifice, Agamemnon retreats from the challenge and hides his face.

Lessing, in the *Laokoön,* was to discuss a work of Greek pictorial art as described by two Roman historians, in order to substantiate a general aesthetic principle about beauty and the depiction of emotion in art.[3] Racine's use of the image also combines elements from different areas and forms of art, for he has taken an image offered by Euripides, his main source for the play, and played over it a refracted light derived from the Roman orators and historians, and indirectly from Greek painting. Taking Euripides' veiled figure, he has placed it in a situation where the same reason for the veiling does not hold good; he echoes the orators in providing two reasons for it, but as a playwright he is able to suggest another, prepared for by the previous presentation of the character. The effect is to sustain the ambiguity of Agamemnon's character and to complicate further the ironies which pervade the play and which center on the altar, where this narrated scene takes place. Imitation has been enriched and transformed to further the meaning of the play, although if this additional coloring is not noticed, the image of the veiled Agamemnon is still powerful, as a simple image of grief and mourning.

A second example of this kind of adaptation of specific detail can be found in *Athalie.* In his preface, Racine explains his choice of timing for the play's action:

> L'histoire ne spécifie point le jour où Joas fut proclamé. Quelques interprètes veulent que ce fût un jour de fête. J'ai choisi celle de la Pentecôte, qui était l'une des trois grandes fêtes des Juifs. On y célébrait la mémoire de la publication de la loi sur le mont de Sinaï, et on y offrait aussi à Dieu les premiers pains de la nouvelle moisson; ce qui faisait qu'on la nommait encore la fête des prémices. J'ai songé que ces circonstances me fourniraient quelque variété pour les chants du chœur.
>
> (Œuvres, p. 874)

---

3. Although Lessing mentions Racine and *Iphigénie* frequently in his critical writings, he does not comment on the veiled Agamemnon in this connexion.

The feast chosen by Racine is Shavuoth, the Festival of Weeks, or Pentecost. This has numerous advantages for him, as well as the one he mentions. As he says, it is one of the "trois grandes fêtes"—that is, the three pilgrim festivals, *shalosh regalim,* on which every male Israelite was enjoined to make the pilgrimage to Jerusalem (the others being Passover and Sukkot, the Festival of Tabernacles). This fact can enlarge our sense of the audience waiting just offstage, to whom Joad refers (Act V, scene vii) when he tells the Levites:

> Appelez tout le peuple, et montrons-lui son roi.

It is also a time when the temple was decorated, in tribute to both aspects of the festival, for the first fruits themselves (*bikkurim*) were beautifully decorated, and the decoration also symbolized Mount Sinai, covered with vegetation in honor of the great event of the Revelation. This decorative element is exploited by Racine, for on the choir's first entry Josabet speaks to them commenting on:

> Ces festons dans vos mains et ces fleurs sur vos têtes.

A well-known alternative name for Shavuoth is "Zeman Matan Toratenu," the season of the giving of our Torah, and this aspect, the revelation of the Law, is stressed by Racine several times, notably in the choral hymn which closes Act I:

> Mais sa loi sainte, sa loi pure,
> Est le plus riche don qu'il ait faite aux humains.
>
> O mont de Sinaï, conserve la mémoire
> De ce jour à jamais auguste et renommé,
> Quand, sur ton sommet enflammé,
> Dans un nuage épais le Seigneur enfermé
> Fit luire aux yeux mortels un rayon de sa gloire.
> . . . .
> Il venait révéler aux enfants des Hébreux
> De ses préceptes saints la lumière immortelle.

(In Ashkenazi rites, the Shavuoth service includes *Akdamut Millim,* an Aramaic acrostic hymn from the eleventh century whose culminating lines run thus in translation:

> We are his choice
> Then let us rejoice
> That he blessed us and gave us the Law.

There are other similarities in theme and tone between the two poems.)

Rejoicing in the gift of Torah does not exhaust the theme of Revelation in *Athalie*, for on this day there is to be a new revelation of the might of God and of the identity, and kingship, of Joas. Also, the Jewish Pentecost must obviously for a Christian audience evoke the Christian Pentecost, and this parallel is suggested on two levels: on Pentecost the Apostles received the gift of tongues which is a form of prophetic utterance, and on this day Joad is inspired to prophesy. Secondly, the Pentecostal gift of the Holy Spirit marks for Christians the fulfilment of the new covenant, as Mosaic Law, celebrated on Shavuoth, embodied the old covenant. Even the fact that Shavuoth is the "fête des prémices" is not insignificant, for Christ is referred to by Paul as the first fruits (I Cor. 15:20, 23).

A further point is that several parts of the Shavuoth liturgy seem to be in harmony with the motifs or moods of Racine's play. For example, the book of Ruth is read on Shavuoth, and while many reasons are given for this by the rabbis, one is that Ruth is David's great grandmother and David, according to tradition, was born and died on Shavuoth (this fits with the many references to David in *Athalie*). Again, one of the appointed prophetic readings is a passage from Habakkuk (3:2) which runs, in part:

O Lord, revive thy work in the midst of the years, in the midst of the years make known; in wrath remember mercy.

And the text goes on to describe the coming of God as a mighty and angry warrior:

Thou didst march through the land in indignation, thou didst thresh the heathen in anger. Thou wentest forth for the salvation of thy people, even for salvation with thine anointed.

A tone very similar to this can be heard at times from Joad (3:12) (e.g., Act I, scene ii). Another prescribed reading, from Ezekiel 1, brings in the theme of revelation again, as the prophet describes how:

the heavens were opened and I saw visions of God.

The choice of Shavuoth, then, seems very apt, and even details of the symbolism and liturgy not explicitly referred to or used by Racine are found to fit the tone and themes of the play, as though Racine had familiarized himself in some detail with the elements of Shavuoth. But there is one passage where he is inaccurate (naturally, the Académie noticed it), and that is in Zacharie's *récit* of the Shavuoth sacrifices in Act II, scene ii:

> Déjà, selon la loi, le grand prêtre, mon père,
> Après avoir au Dieu qui nourrit les humains
> De la moisson nouvelle offert les premiers pains,
> Lui présentait encore entre ses mains sanglantes
> Des victimes de paix les entrailles fumantes.
> Debout à ses côtés le jeune Éliacin
> Comme moi le servait en long habit de lin;
> Et cependant, du sang de la chair immolée,
> Les prêtres arrosaient l'autel et l'assemblée.

Two things are out of place here. One is the presence of the two young boys at the altar; in the various biblical prescriptions (Num. 4:3; Num. 8:24; I Chron. 23:24) as to the age at which the Levites were eligible for service in the temple, the youngest age mentioned (in I Chron. 23:24) is twenty years. In fact, these young boys (although slightly reminiscent of the child Samuel) suggest Catholic altar-servers rather than any participant in temple liturgy. This makes the passage one of those in the play which set up Christian harmonics around the Jewish themes. This parallelism is reinforced by the other inaccuracy in the passage (the one noticed by the Académie).[4] In Racine's account of the Shavuoth sacrifice, the rite is

---

4. The *Sentiments de l'Académie sur Athalie* are quoted from Vol. V of Paul Mesnard's edition of Racine (8 vols. and 2 albums, Paris, 1865–1873). Racine's inaccuracy is referred to by other editors including Athanase Coquerel, *Athalie et Esther de Racine avec un commentaire biblique* (Paris, 1863), Raymond Picard in the Pléiade edition (p. 1166), and Maurice Rat, *Théâtre complet de Racine* (Paris, 1960), pp. 738–739. See also J. Lichtenstein, *Racine poète biblique* (Paris, 1934), pp. 148–149. This critic also points out that the presence of a throne in the sanctuary, and the references to a crown, are inauthentic. I would argue that they are associated with concepts of Christian kingship, and thus like Racine's other "errors" they increase the Christian associations of the play, while the throne is also important as part of the spectacle of the last act.

described accurately to begin with, as the high priest offers the first fruits, then the sacrifice of the peace offering. In Leviticus 3, detailed instructions are given for the sacrifice of peace offering, including precise butchering instructions, and the last prescription before that for the burning of the offering reads:

and the sons of Aaron shall sprinkle the blood thereof on the altar round about.

(Lev. 3:13)

In Racine's rendering, the priests

arrosaient l'autel et l'assemblée.

In the *Sentiments de l'Académie sur Athalie* Racine's "mistake" is commented on in the following terms:

Racine s'est trompé ici sur les rites. . . . L'auteur a confondu avec le rite judaïque ce qu'il avait lu dans le XXIVe chapitre de l'*Exode*, où il est dit que Moïse fit l'aspersion du sang de la victime sur le peuple assemblé; mais il n'y avait pas encore de rite ni de cérémonie légale.

It seems very probable that Racine has derived this aspersion from Exodus, but perhaps it is a deliberate change rather than an error. I surmise that Racine has modified the sacrificial ritual of sprinkling or pouring out the blood of the animal on or near the altar for several reasons. One is that it fits into a pattern of images concerning blood, and forms a sort of sanctified contrast to Athalie's bloody activities in the past, and to the fact that the baby Joas, when found, was wounded and therefore marked with blood. Another reason is that the sprinkling of the congregation with blood by the priests prefigures baptism and also the many New Testament references to purification and redemption by the sprinkling of the blood of Jesus Christ, the Lamb of God (e.g., Heb. 9:12–14; I Pet. 1:2,19; I John 1;7; Rev. 7:14). Furthermore the passage in Exodus 24 has connections with both the "first fruits" and "covenant" aspects of Shavuoth. It comes very shortly after the institution of the pilgrim feasts, including Shavuoth as festival of first fruits (Exod. 23:16–18), and the aspersion carried out by Moses in Chapter 24 is done explicitly as a reminder of the covenant (and thus for the Christian has links with the new covenant):

And Moses took the blood, and sprinkled it on the people, and said, Behold the blood of the covenant, which the Lord hath made with you concerning all these words.

(Exod. 24:8)

It appears then that both Racine's divergencies here from "accuracy" serve to enrich the Christian themes in the play, but both have another function as well. The sprinkling of the blood forms part of one of the most prominent sets of images in the play (blood of kinship, blood shed in war or private murder, the blood of temple sacrifice, the shedding of blood as vile, sanctified, or purifying); the presence of the two young boys, but especially Eliacin, at the Shavuoth sacrifice not only makes that sacrifice like a Christian service with altar-servers but integrates Eliacin into the functions of the temple, and by showing youth active in the holy place underlines Eliacin's messianic quality and recalls to a Christian audience the child who asked in the temple, "Wist ye not that I must be about my Father's business?" (Luke 3:49). Drama becomes liturgy. The figure of Eliacin has many associations including his prefiguration of the child savior. The play contains accounts of liturgy and ceremony but is also itself a sort of rite. Human actions embody the will of God and become signs or symbols of a reality which surpasses them.

"Discovery favors the mind which is prepared," said Pasteur. Recognition of Racine's allusions charges some of his images with greater meaning and symbolic force. By this I do not mean that the play receives another symbolic framework, separate from its ostensible subject, but that the allusiveness increases the potency of the images within the patterns and themes of the play. At the same time, consciousness of Racine's knowledge underlying the text creates enhanced *vraisemblance,* not in the sense of strengthened stage illusion but on a more intellectual level. Corneille said in the *Discours du poème dramatique* (1660), "la qualité de semblables, qu'Aristote demande aux mœurs, regarde particulièrement les personnes que l'histoire ou la fable nous fait connaître, et qu'il faut toujours peindre telles que nous les y trouvons." In Racine, details not revealed in the text, but implicit in it, prove to be verifiable and compatible with what is revealed, although the play is perfectly coherent and intelligible without these additional details. Racine treats the "accuracy" of his legends as respectfully as the accuracy of history or fidelity to biblical narrative.

Where he makes an alteration, as in the account of the Shavuoth ritual, or
in the presentation of Oreste pursued by Furies not because of the murder
of Clytemnestra but because of the deaths of Pyrrhus and Hermione, the
altered detail is appropriate and convincing, and the mere fact that there
has been an alteration makes its own effect and helps the poet to reach "le
but de son art." Very possibly Racine did not mind how much or how
little of the Shavuoth imagery was picked up by his audience, or what
associations the veiled Agamemnon had for them; but he has so contrived
it that recognition of these allusions is satisfying, without being indispensable to understanding or enjoyment.

Notes on Contributors

CATHERINE BELSEY, Lecturer in English at University College, Cardiff, Wales, is author of a number of articles on medieval and Elizabethan drama, and of *Critical Practice* (1980).

HUSTON DIEHL, Assistant Professor of English at the University of Oklahoma, has published essays on Milton, Middleton, Jonson, and Renaissance tragedy. She is presently at work on a book-length study of *Iconography and English Renaissance Tragedy.*

WILSON F. ENGEL, III, Assistant Professor of English and Chairman of the English Department at Allentown College, is the editor of James Shirley's *The Gentleman of Venice* (1976) and founder and editor of *Renaissance and Renascences in Western Literature,* a quarterly newsletter devoted to the influences of the Classics (Greek and Latin) on Western literature.

ANTHONY T. GABLE, Lecturer in French at Queen Mary College, University of London, is working on the plays of Alexandre Hardy and is principally interested in Renaissance and seventeenth-century French and Italian tragedy.

PERRY GETHNER, Assistant Professor in the Department of Romance Languages at the University of Chicago, is working on a history of poetic justice in French theater and the role of staging and spectacle in French drama and opera of the seventeenth century.

GAYLE GREENE, Associate Professor of English at Scripps College, Claremont, California, chaired the Special Session on Feminist Criticism of Shakespeare at the 1979 Modern Language Association Meetings and is co-editor of *"The Woman's Part": Feminist Criticism of Shakespeare* (1980). Her articles on Shakespeare have appeared or will appear in various periodicals, including *Journal of Women's Studies in Literature, Studia Neophilologica,* and *Studies in English Literature.*

GILLIAN JONDORF, Lecturer in French at the University of Cambridge, is interested in poetry and drama of the sixteenth and seventeenth centuries and is working on a study of some aspects of language in tragedy from Jodelle to Racine.

RICHARD A. MARTIN is presently an editor-writer for the federal government and is a consulting editor for a fine-arts museum in San Francisco. His article "Marlowe's *Tamburlaine* and the Language of Romance" appeared in the March 1978 issue of *PMLA.*

J. L. SIMMONS, Professor of English at Tulane University, is the author of *Shakespeare's Pagan World* and has previously contributed to *Renaissance Drama.* His recent work has been on the major revenge tragedies of the period.